Policy Studies Institute

Rational Techniques in Policy Analysis

Policy Studies Institute

Rational Techniques in Policy Analysis

Michael Carley

 Heinemann Educational Books · London

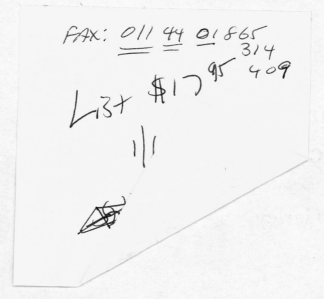

Heinemann Educational Books Ltd
22 Bedford Square, London WC1B 3HH

LONDON   EDINBURGH   MELBOURNE   AUCKLAND
HONG KONG   SINGAPORE   KUALA LUMPUR   NEW DELHI
IBADAN   NAIROBI   JOHANNESBURG
EXETER (NH)   KINGSTON   PORT OF SPAIN

Cased edition ISBN 0 435 83801 6
Paper edition ISBN 0 435 83802 4

Filmset by Northumberland Press Ltd
Gateshead, Tyne and Wear
Printed in Great Britain by Richard Clay (The Chaucer Press) Ltd
Bungay, Suffolk

Contents

List of Figures

Acknowledgements

The author and publishers gratefully acknowledge permission given by the following to reprint or modify copyright material:

The *Public Administration Bulletin* for Figure 3.2; *The Journal of the American Planning Association* for Figure 7.1; Her Majesty's Stationery Office for Figure 7.3; John Wiley and Sons, Limited for Figure 6.2; John Wiley and Sons, Inc. for Figure 7.4; and The Environmental Design Research Association, Inc. for Figure 8.4, from their series *Man-Environment Interactions: Evaluations and Applications*.

Preface

The impetus for this book came from two sources. Firstly, as a planning consultant, I have been involved in a number of projects which sought to apply rational techniques to assist policy making. One such project, which attempted to reorganise the facilities in a criminal justice system, brought home to me how very important it was to relate rational analysis to the political and bureaucratic realities of decision making. Another project, which attempted to predict the future impact of a proposed coal mine and generating station, made clear the importance of mutual understanding among the many diverse analysts from different disciplines who might be involved in the study of one complex problem.

Secondly, and soon after these experiences, I had the opportunity at the London School of Economics, and later the Policy Studies Institute, to have ready access to the incredible diversity of literature from the many disciplines which might fall under the rubric of policy analysis. At this point I had not only a good reason for, but the means of taking, a cross-disciplinary look at the role and value of a number of rational techniques in policy analysis. Such a cross-disciplinary perspective, for all its dangers of generality, upholds I think, one of the first principles of policy analysis and the policy sciences.

This book is directed towards a twofold audience. First, it is aimed at students of the policy making process, in university and government, who would like an overview of the role of rational techniques in that process and an introduction to each category of technique. Secondly, it is directed to analysts and researchers who might find benefit in a further understanding of their relationship to policy making and to other approaches to rational analysis. Part I is an analysis of analysis – it involves the 'disintegration' of rational policy analysis to find out what the pieces are, how they work, how the parts interact and how they relate to the wider policy making environment. Part II considers the types of rational analysis in more detail, and serves not only as a survey of rational techniques but as an introduction to the important literature in each field. References for Chapters 1 to 6 are combined at the end of Part I. References for chapters in Part II are given at the end of each chapter to serve as a convenient bibliography for that particular category of technique.

This book is the result of research time kindly funded in part by the Social Science Research Council (UK) and in part by the Policy Studies Institute in London. At the latter the following staff helped with valuable and constructive advice: Charles Carter, Ellan Derow, Thelma Liesner, John Pinder, and Muriel Nissel. Others who gave a detailed reading to the manuscript and to whom I am indebted include Howard Glennerster of the London School of Economics, Janet Lewis of the Department of Employment, Martin Buxton of the Economic Advisers Office of the Department of Health and Social Security, Vaughn Corbett, a Canadian transport consultant, and Anna Walkey, a social planning consultant, also from Canada. Finally, Susan Johnson and Stephanie Maggin, both at PSI, provided invaluable library and typing services respectively.

Michael Carley
London
December 1979

Definitions of terms

The following are a few working definitions of terms which recur throughout the book. These definitions will be expanded, dissected, and, it is hoped, justified but for the present they will serve the purpose of providing a common vocabulary.

Analytic Rationality — is orderly, systematic problem solving which might also be called rational method

Rational Analysis — is the application of analytic rationality to a particular (policy) problem and involves the disintegration of some complex problem into simpler elements. This process can be called 'modelling'

Rational Techniques — are specific, formal, or mechanical forms of rational analysis, each with distinguishing features

Operationalise — to translate into measurable terms

Policy Maker — is one individual or a group of individuals who make explicit or implicit single decisions or groups of decisions which may set out directives for guiding future decisions, initiate or retard action, or guide implementation of previous decisions

The last definition is by no means comprehensive. It implicitly defines policy and as Jenkins (1978) and others have pointed out, competing definitions of policy are numerous and varied. It does serve to emphasise that the policy maker may, in fact, be a body of individuals, i.e. a cabinet, a committee, heads of one department, etc. This fact, and others like the relationship of implementation to the policy process, or questions of the dynamics of the political system, will be considered later. A simple definition of the emerging supradiscipline 'policy analysis' is not given here because half the book considers why simplistic definitions have failed. Chapter 2 defines policy analysis in some depth.

PART I

1 Introduction

In modern mixed-market economies in developed and developing countries there has been increasing intervention by government in the workings of what is often termed 'the free market' over the last three decades. In the simplest terms this intervention, involving the allocation and distribution of public resources, is meant to provide goods and services which are not supplied by the market or to attempt to alleviate inefficiencies or inequalities which are caused by the workings of the market. This intervention has resulted in a large increase in the number of public sector operations, and a continued growth in the size and range of functions performed by government. It will not be argued here whether these market failures and insufficiencies are simply a deviation from some ideal working of a free economy or whether they are extensive and endemic to economic systems (Pearce, 1978b). Rather our concern is with the fact that *any* attempt to allocate public resources, or make policy, must necessitate at least some reference to the differential returns which might be secured from alternative allocations of those resources.

This need to get 'a good deal for the money' in the already large range of public sector activities is coupled with a growing demand for accountability regarding the results of government programmes and for a careful consideration of future government expenditures. In turn this demand has led to a steady increase in the use of analytic and often quantitative techniques to assist in resource allocation and the policy making process. These techniques are based on a kind of 'analytic rationality' which stems for the most part from the tenets of welfare economics and systems analysis.

The available number of these techniques has expanded greatly in the last ten years and, although their applicability is controversial, many are in widespread use in the public sector. Cost-benefit analysis, for example, is one of the oldest of these techniques and in constant use. First developed in the United States of America to assess the implications of alternative water resource schemes, its application rapidly expanded to a variety of public sector activities in all parts of the world. Cost-benefit is commonly used in transportation planning and resource development. Less well known perhaps is its application in such diverse fields as the location of new industry, the assessment of medical and other social services, new town development, and the worth of improvements in education.

Also commonly used in transport, resource, and industrial planning are environmental impact assessments (EIA). Required in the USA by legislation for many potential government development expenditures, EIA has been termed, sometimes cynically, a 'growth industry' there. In spite of any excessess, the application of EIA to potential projects is spreading throughout the world. For example, the Organisation for Economic Co-operation and Development (OECD) has recently recommended to its member states that a system of EIA be used to assess all major new developments. A spin-off from EIA is a group of techniques now coming to be called social impact assessment (SIA). These attempt to make up for what is seen as an overemphasis on the biophysical in EIA to the detriment of the study of social effects. Although mostly confined to date to resource and energy development projects in North America and Europe, recent United Nations Environmental Programme (1979) guidelines called for social impact assessments of new industrial sites in all parts of the world.

Another field which is of world wide interest is the use of social indicators to complement economic data, for example, by the United Nations Organisation (UN), the OECD, and many national and local governments. Related to the forward looking aspects of social indication are various techniques associated with futures research and forecasting which are themselves an extension of a mode of analysis called technology assessment. Finally a last grouping of rational techniques is based on the desire to gauge the success of past and existing government programmes. This is evaluation research which tries to assess the worth of a programme to the client, consumer, or community or to improve the design and internal operations of organisations. Often this is done by setting up a controlled experiment or a quasi-experiment such as in education research in the UK or negative income tax research in the USA. A facet of evaluation research is performance, or productivity, measurement which is concerned with the conversion of organisational inputs to measurable output, especially in local government. These and other techniques are examined in detail in later chapters.

Controversy Abounds

The widespread promotion and use of rational techniques is accompanied by a voluminous literature espousing and exploring various aspects of their application to policy making and resource allocation. Alongside this, however, there is also a substantial body of literature warning of dangers inherent in such analysis, dissenting from the overly enthusiastic expectations of some for rationality, and decrying the application of rationality to what are seen as political decisions. It is worth reviewing briefly the ebb and flow of these comments to get a feel for the nature of the issues.

In 1965 Prest and Turvey (p. 728) pointed out that cost-benefit analysis could be viewed 'as anything from an infallible means of reaching a new Utopia to a waste of resources attempting to measure the unmeasurable'. Soon after Wildavsky (1966) explored what he saw as the serious limitations of economic rationality and argued for the overriding importance of the political aspects of decision making. In 1970 the report of the Roskill inquiry in the UK into a third London airport location occasioned Self to describe the use of cost-benefit analysis as 'nonsense on stilts', because of the 'disparate items' in, and 'important items' excluded from, the analysis. This was followed by a rejoinder from other commentators who argued that Self's criticisms were mistaken or exaggerated or both and that his prescription of a planning alternative was 'a recipe for obscurantist intuitionism' (Williams, 1972). This, in turn, was followed by a lengthy and reasoned critique by Self (1975) of the role of cost-benefit analysis in planning.

Recently Ackoff (1976) has suggested that rationality which tried to maximise some expected relative value could be irrational if it ignored the alternative means to whatever end was sought. Strauch (1976) warns against what he calls extreme 'quantificationism' which holds that a quantitative solution to a policy problem is *a priori* better than a qualitative one. In the same vein Churchman (1975) suggests that the process of assigning numbers to social changes, and then allowing the numbers themselves to carry the conviction of their accuracy suggests how facile the work of some social accountants and economists has become. Other authors fault rational techniques for presuming a neutral value stance, hiding implicit political bias, and for ignoring political reality. Some suggest that what passes for rationality lacks the rigour of theory and yet others condemn its mystifying mathematics.[1]

If this were not enough there is a related problem with these tech-

[1] See for example, Brooks, 1976; Wynne, 1975; Edwards, 1975; Carley, 1979; and Clifford, 1978.

niques which is the vast amount of printed output which may be associated with their application. Recently London's *Guardian* headlined an article 'Reports Mountain Grows' which dealt with the problem one Area Health Authority had in coping with the amount of printed evaluation material administrators were expected to digest before arriving at a decision (Stuart, 1979). In the USA the environmental impact statement alone on a major project the size of the Alaskan Slope pipeline can easily result in a stack of reports three times the height of the average decision maker. It is only recently that agencies which commission or produce such voluminous publications are beginning to realise that potential users may lack the requisite time, confidence, or understanding to use the reports properly and this problem of 'information transfer' might be seen as an important aspect of the more general resource allocation problem.

Does this long list of contentious issues associated with the rational approach to policy making suggest that the best stance is to abandon or ignore these techniques altogether? The answer is 'no, but' and that qualification is that a proper understanding of the role of this kind of analysis in policy making, what can be termed a 'balanced perspective', demands that a grasp of the mechanics of the techniques be complemented by a realistic understanding of the theoretical and practical problems associated with their use.

A Balanced Perspective

There is nothing particularly evil or odious about rational problem-solving in general. Indeed it is a common human process which we all indulge in daily in such activities as making consumer purchases or deciding how to make the journey to work. This rational method is of great value as an orderly, logical process which assists in decision making, and it is as a problem solving *process* that its value to policy making lies. Unfortunately, rational techniques have too often been touted as optimisation methods, i.e. providing one solution, and much of the criticism levelled against the rational model revolves around a confusion and a misunderstanding of the value *and* limitations of the techniques.

Some advocates of rational techniques for example, deservedly bring down the wrath of all and sundry on their heads by their naive ignorance of the importance of the political, or value judgement, element in policy making. One could easily argue that most public sector decision making is in the end the result of a political bargaining process. This being the case rational analysis carried on in ignorance of political reality may well end up so divorced from social reality as to be of little use to anyone. By the same token, however, vague and unsystematic 'political' research loaded with implicit causality and value judgements, and not subject to exposure or dissection, is of no great value to policy making either. A balanced perspective helps policy makers and researchers select criteria for judging the relevance of analysis to a particular policy problem. It does this by encouraging examination of the divergence between the problem as defined by the policy maker and as defined by the analysts, and by arguing that no analysis is understood until it is clear what, and whose, value judgements are part of the analysis – value judgements which must be considered an integral part of every analysis. The perspective is based on the argument that in the policy making process analytic rationality has a limited, but valuable, role that can only be played out in the light of the overriding political and bureaucratic aspects of policy making. An exploration of policy making, policy analysis and this balanced perspective is the first task of this volume.

The second task is to take this balanced perspective and to use it to examine the plethora of rational techniques available to assist policy making. This is especially important in that the mechanics of such techniques, and the issues surrounding their application, tend to be enclosed within particular disciplines or groups of practitioners, with the techniques themselves often offered as 'black boxes' for solving policy problems. This results in confusion over the basic concepts of each technique, lack of agreement on definitions, little consensus on what the scope of the various techniques is or should be, and often a misunderstanding as to the relative advantages and disadvantages of different techniques.

For the party that commissions the research, and the analysts, this often makes it difficult to select the most appropriate techniques or combination of techniques, and to evaluate the relevance of their conclusions. For the policy maker this means not only attempting to gauge the relevance of one set of conclusions but trying to understand why it is that different analysts come up with different answers or advocate opposing policies. Here I attempt to shed some light on these difficulties by examining the similarities and differences among techniques and by relating them to a common problem-solving orientation. This raises a final point. Because the proponents of these various techniques come from different disciplines and write in different publications, and because a balanced perspective on the techniques tends to be clouded by the complicated jargon associated with them, it is sometimes difficult to grasp one basic fact: all the techniques are variations of the *same* rational approach to problem solving.

An examination of this common approach will, it is hoped, have two useful by-products. Firstly, it might facilitate the necessarily difficult integration of different types of analysis relevant to a problem, rather than the current practice of presenting an array of specific studies, seemingly unconnected with one another. This is especially important with large projects in a world which is increasingly complex and inter-related, and yet at the same time experiences increasing demands for many second-order impacts to be considered in the decision making process. Secondly, and perhaps more importantly, the grasp of a common approach with some common definitions might help to develop a common language among policy makers, bureaucrats, analysts and researchers, and the interested public. This attempt at aiding communication is to run counter to the trend where the results of analysis appear sophisticated and yet simultaneously unintelligible to policy makers, where those who commission research are unsure of what to do with the mountain of stuff they get, where researchers in one field never talk to those in another, and where the public often perceives of the purpose of analysis as obfuscation.

This Book
This book is an analysis of analysis – it involves the 'disintegration' of policy analysis to find out what the pieces are, how they work, how the parts interact, and how they relate to their environment. Chapter 2 defines analytic rationality and examines some common objections to this approach – especially the issue of the possibility of a social welfare function. Chapter 3 begins by examining the major components of the policy making process and goes on to look at policy analysis: some definitions, the scope, and the relationship between the political and the rational aspects. The role of value judgements and the question of scale are considered and the benefits of attempting rational analysis are enumerated. Chapter 3 concludes with a consideration of the role of the policy analyst.

Chapter 4 discusses the process of rational analysis beginning with common roots in economics and systems analysis. The past or future time dimension of analysis is examined and suggestions are made for avoiding confusion in terminology. Then the problem-solving process common to most rational techniques is proposed which, it is argued, encourages understanding of those techniques, promotes communication and integration, and facilitates development of methodology.

Chapter 5 aids understanding of the growing number of rational techniques by proposing categories reflecting distinctions drawn in the literature and in practice. Chapter 6 explores the important issues surrounding the use of rational techniques including further problems of rationality and value judgements, and problems associated with measurement, valuation, distributional effects, aggregation and integration, and the relationship between rational analysis and public participation in planning. Chapters 1 to 6 comprise Part I of the book and readers whose main interest is the role of rational techniques in general will, it is hoped, find their curiosity satisfied. The bibliography for Part I is at the end of Chapter 6.

The chapters of Part II consider each category of rational technique in more detail including the main issues associated with specific techniques, their relationship to other techniques, problems of methodology, and references to practice. Part II is a survey of rational techniques and an introduction to the important literature in each category. It is not, however, a handbook for engaging in rational analysis but rather seeks to help to lay out the issues and cite numerous references which might be followed up by the interested reader. Each chapter of Part II concludes with the bibliography for that chapter, and therefore, a bibliography for that category of rational technique.

2 Analytic Rationality

In later chapters of this book many issues are raised surrounding the application of specific rational techniques in the policy making process. To get to that point, however, it is important to understand the general role of rationality in this process since all these techniques are grounded at a larger level in a common rational approach to policy problems, as opposed say, to a moral, aesthetic, or political approach. It is therefore worthwhile to start with a brief examination of the concept of rationality itself.

Rationality: A First Look

The Oxford English Dictionary defines the word rational as 'exercising one's reason in a proper manner; having sound judgement; sensible, sane'. Unfortunately the use of the word related to public policy formulation is not as clear and there are a variety of definitions. Levine et al. (1975, p. 89) point out that for some people rationality:

> 'means achievement of goals, some associate it with individuals maximising satisfaction, others conceive of it as a decision making process without regard to how successful a person is in achieving goals, and still others consider rationality to be broadly synonymous with intelligent and purposeful behaviour.'

In spite of this multiplicity of perspectives on rationality in general there is, in fact, much in common among authors concerned with rationality when one considers the working definitions in use. All relate to two very similar ideal types of the 'rational man'. First, in economic thought, to be rational is to select from a group of alternative courses of action that course which maximises output for a given input, or minimises input for a given output. Secondly, in systems analysis, decision theory, or game theory, to be rational is to select a course of action, from a group of possible courses of action, which has a given set of predicted consequences in terms of some welfare function which, in turn, ranks each set of consequences in order of preference. This second application of rationality can also be applied to the concept of 'planning' in so far as planning 'is that activity that concerns itself with proposals for the future, with the evaluation of alternative proposals, and with the methods by which those proposals may be achieved' (Simon, 1958, p. 423) and is considered 'a process for rationally determining the framework of future decisions' (Smith, 1976, p. 24). In all of these definitions rationality refers to consistent, value-maximising choice given certain constraints. This analytic rationality is embodied in rational analysis and generally undertaken by what we have termed rational technique.

In almost every case working definitions of rationality can be expressed by five sequential activities undertaken by the idealised 'rational man':

(1) A problem which requires action is identified and goals, values, and objectives related to the problem are classified and organised.

(2) All important possible ways of solving the problem or achieving goals and objectives are listed – these are alternative strategies, courses of action, or policies.

(3) The important consequences which would follow from each alternative strategy are predicted and the probability of those consequences occurring is estimated.

(4) The consequences of each strategy are then compared to the goals and objectives identified above.

(5) Finally, a policy or strategy is selected in which consequences most closely match goals and objectives, or the problem is most nearly solved, or most benefit is got from equal cost, or equal benefit at least cost.

There appears to be widespread agreement that these five steps constitute the basic activities of the idealised model which underpins all the techniques discussed here. We will run into them time and again in different guises and we can safely assume that when authors talk about rationality they are talking about some variation of these activities. Later, this underlying rational model will be used to compare and contrast a range of rational techniques. For now it is worth stressing for the first of many times that these steps constitute an ideal, or a model, which is well defined as 'an abstraction from reality that is intended to order and simplify our view of that reality while still capturing its essential characteristics' (Forcese and Richer, 1973, p. 38). A model, therefore, is not reality. In so far as this rational model diverges from reality in its attempts at simplification it is bound to be open to criticism, and there is indeed a considerable body of critical literature. Later it will be argued that the rational model is a valuable but *partial* perspective on policy problems and in Chapter 6 we will examine a number of critical issues related to the techniques themselves.

The Policy Process and Analytic Rationality

For a simple model of the policy process we might assume that there is a problem to be dealt with which will eventually require a decision by one or more policy makers. Like the stone falling to earth which moves the furthest planets, this problem and the subsequent decision involves complex inter-relationships and extensive effects which ripple throughout the system. The first task for anyone must be to define the problem in a manageable form – no person can grasp the entire complexity of the system and so one must draw a line around the influences and effects considered relevant. These effects are contained in what we might call the decision space.

Isolating, or defining, a decision space involves the first of the value judgements which permeate the policy process. One possible way of isolating these effects is to consider the personal implications for the policy makers. For the politician this means looking to the future decisions of voters: a decision space might be defined in terms of those effects which will cause people to vote for the policy makers. For the civil servant the decision space may involve factors influencing the distribution of administrative power, or career promotion. This is rational thinking for the persons involved, that is personal rationality, but it is not analytic rationality which is born of a distrust of allocating resources by means of personal rationality. The rational analyst therefore proposes what might be a quite different decision space based on those factors which are amenable to consideration in the form of the five step model given above. But distrust of the politically defined decision space is no guarantee that some other definition, like the rational analytic one, is necessarily any better. Both might well ignore important factors which would be relevant if the decision were put in a broader form.

A study of the literature of the various conceptions or definitions of policy making reveals a marked tendency to emphasise either the rational analytic aspect, or the political, but seldom both. At the one extreme we find the 'policy making is systems analysis' approach, in other words, equating policy making with rational analysis. At the other extreme there are those who find 'the power and survival ability of the rational system model surprising' and who suggest it is 'a dignified myth' which helps 'the researcher towards a comfortable life' (Gordon et al., 1977, p. 29). In fact one finds in the literature of the last fifteen years something in the order of a cyclical pattern where overemphasis on the rational aspects breeds a reaction against rationality and for a 'political' perspective. This is obviously with the best intentions and reflects a number of real problems with the rational approach. Unfortunately, however, it leaves researchers and policy analysts alike with a rather vague and unworkable analysis process – so the pendulum swings back once again towards the rational model. In fact, most good policy analysis consists of some varying mix of the political, the administrative or bureaucratic, and the rational elements in the definition of the decision space.

To attempt to restrict policy analysis to one element, or to disregard one element for one reason or another, results in a less than complete approach to policy making and leads to the rational versus political conflict apparent in the literature and, indeed, in public debate. A review of the articles surrounding the use of cost-benefit analysis in the selection process of a site for the third London airport for example, reveals only too well how individuals can line up on one side or the other of the rational-political border when the decision space is ill-defined. The key to the problem is that the decision spaces reflecting different perspectives must overlap – otherwise tension will exist between each partial perspective, or model, of reality.

To go back to a simple model of policy making: if the decision is not to be taken solely on personal grounds then we might assume that the policy makers will require information which will help clarify policy problems, outline practical alternatives and their consequences, and generally assist in decision making. For this information, the policy makers most often turn to assistants or to some internal research unit within the agency which will either undertake the necessary analysis or commission an outside institution or firm to undertake it. The internal research unit or outside institution will usually undertake a systematic analysis and may specify one or more rational techniques which might shed light on the problem. The definition of the decision space will be done partially in terms of a perceived political issue by the policy maker and refined or sometimes changed by the group undertaking the analysis. The results of the analysis will be passed back 'up the line' to the policy maker either more or less intact, or 'interpreted' by those immediately under the policy maker who, in turn, can either accept or reject the analysis, all or in part.

This admittedly simple model is a variation of what is sometimes called the 'market model' of policy analysis, where the analysis is a product commissioned or 'bought' by the policy makers. It does not mirror a reality far more complex nor is it intended to be a complete model of the policy analysis process. Elsewhere it is the subject of constructive criticism. For example, Lineberry (1978) points out that the indirect effects of the diffusion of the results of a policy analysis can have more impact than the directly transmitted results. Weiss (1977) calls this the 'enlightenment' function of research. Meltsner (1979) makes the similar point that researchers tend to ignore the organisational context in which their analysis is presented by assuming a single policy maker client. Later, a number of such limitations on the market model of policy analysis are considered. For now, however, it remains useful as a starting point because it approximates more to reality than other models while still retaining the virtue of simplicity.

In this model then the analysis may be rejected for reasons unrelated to its content: the policy maker wished only to be seen 'doing something' or wished to buy time, or perhaps perceived a large shift in the political situation since the analysis was commissioned. The policy maker may also find the analysis dangerous in so far as it explicitly includes in its decision space factors which engender conflicts among various parties, or which are potentially 'embarrassing' to the politicians concerned in terms of performance considerations which reflect on them. These cases, although of great interest to students of policy making, are beyond our scope here. On the other hand, the analysis may also be accepted or rejected based on its content and its relevance to the problem at hand. This is the concern of this book. In judging the relevance of a particular piece of rational analysis, i.e., its usefulness, the policy maker makes an implicit judgement as to the usefulness of rational analysis in general. As for most areas of human endeavour informed judgements tend to be better judgements. And for a judgement to be made as to the relevance of a particular piece of rational analysis informed judgement demands some understanding of the role and limitations of rational analysis in policy making – what we have termed a balanced perspective.

General Problems with the Rational Model

Before moving on in Chapter 3 to consider rational policy analysis it is worth considering briefly a few common and general criticisms of the rational model. Gershuny (1978) identifies two main threads in these criticisms. The first stems from the assumption that to be rational one also has to be comprehensive. At its extreme this view assumes that rational analysis must involve the collection of all data relevant to a problem and the ordering of all human goals and subsequent objectives to facilitate proper comparison of the consequences of alternative strategies. The need for comprehensiveness therefore makes it impossible to define a decision space. Lindblom (1968, p. 10) uses this impossibility as the basis for arguing that the rational model (as proposed by Simon) is too divergent from reality and that 'a concept of rationality appropriate for judging a complex political system cannot be defined'. Lindblom proposes instead incrementalism or the 'science of muddling through', which emphasises only marginal changes in policy thus drastically reducing the number and complexity of policy alternatives, but also severely limiting the decision space.

It is obvious, however, that nobody is arguing for full-grown comprehensive rationality and that what is described is a limited or partial rationality – only *some* alternatives and *some* consequences are related to *some* objectives. This limiting is done by (i) the decision makers ignoring consequences which are of no interest (ii) decision makers 'learning' from past decisions and thus adjusting the scope of their concern accordingly; and (iii) 'satisficing', which means the decision makers pursue sufficient, satisfactory goals rather than some 'one best' goal (Simon, 1957). Such satisficing is rational because it follows rational procedures (the five steps), but it is a limited rationality. Many authors accept the notion of limited rationality under a variety of terms. Rawls (1971, p. 418) calls it 'deliberative rationality' which is:

'an activity like any other, and the extent to which one should engage in it is subject to rational decision. The formal rule is that we should deliberate up to the point where the likely benefits from improving our plan are just worth the time and effort of reflection. Once we take the costs of deliberation into account, it is unreasonable to worry about finding the best plan, the one we would choose had we complete information. It is perfectly rational to follow a satisfactory plan when the prospective returns from further calculation and additional knowledge outweigh the trouble.'

This process of taking a rational decision to be deliberatively rational is what Dror (1968) terms 'meta-policy making' or policy making about policy making and we will return to it in the next chapter. Deliberative rationality is, of course, as applicable to the day-to-day decisions of individuals as it is to the policy making process.

Other authors more or less concur with Rawls. Self (1974, p. 193), often critical of techniques like cost-benefit analysis, nevertheless admits that 'planning can be described as rational, in some not infrequent circumstances'. Etzioni (1967) and later Gershuny (1978) propose variations of 'mixed scanning models' which, while taking into account the criticisms of the incrementalists, view rationality not as an achievable ideal but as one worth approaching. Allison (1971) argues that limited rationality is a common and satisfactory assumption. In summary, the criticism that rational behaviour is impossible because complete comprehensiveness is impossible is generally resolved by the concept of limited rationality, given that this basic limitation to rationality is made clear.

The second common criticism of the rational model is of the assumption that it is possible to develop a social welfare function (SWF), which can be defined as a preference ranking by society on some set of alternative strategies. In other words, if steps (4) and (5) of the rational man's tasks are to be applied by some group of people then this 'society' must prefer one strategy or policy over another based on the greater good (or social welfare) which accrues from choosing that alternative. If any two alternatives result in equal social welfare the society is 'indifferent' to the choice. A theoretical problem arises in that, while it is accepted that an individual (or rational man) can order a preference ranking, it may not be the case that a number of those rankings can be added up to some overall societal ranking. The best known form of this argument is that advanced by Arrow (1954) who demonstrates in the 'majority voting' paradox that aggregating individual preferences through democratic means always poses the possibility that no clear preference will emerge. A recent issue of *The Economist* (1978) gave a good example of this paradox in which a society consisting of three individuals attempted to rank three mutually exclusive policy alternatives: (a) environmentalism (b) efficiency and (c) goodheartedness. This was done in the hope that some social welfare function would evolve upon which policy decisions could be based. The ranking went like this:

	1st choice	2nd choice	3rd choice
Prof Econut	(a)	(b)	(c)
Mr Tycoon	(b)	(c)	(a)
Rev. Goodchappe	(c)	(a)	(b)

The result is a 2 to 1 vote that environmentalism is preferred to efficiency, a 2 to 1 vote that efficiency is preferred to goodheartedness, but also a 2 to 1 vote that goodheartedness is preferred to environmentalism. In other words, (a) is preferred to (b), (b) is preferred to (c), but (c) is preferred to (a). No rational policy decision based on a social welfare function is possible in this hypothetical situation.

A second difficulty with the social welfare function is that there are situations where the results of actions taken by a group of rational individuals may lead to a non-rational outcome. For example, if all dairy farmers restrict their output of butter the price will go up and they will benefit. But each will assume that his output cannot affect the total price of butter so he will opt for full production. If each dairy farmer follows the same reasoning then full production occurs, the price drops, and they all fare badly.[1]

Do these logical dilemmas preclude a role for rationality in the policy analysis process? Possibly in simple theory, but not in practice for a variety of reasons, which are discussed at length in Brown and Jackson (1978). First, the voting paradox assumes an individual self interest, direct voting model, but it may be that some public interest model or a representative government model more closely approximates the complex reality of the political process. To this we return shortly. Even, however if one accepts the self interest, direct voting model there is still at least two reasons why the voting paradox does not hold in many cases. The first reason is that it is quite likely that the number of voters will be considerably more than three, in which case the probability of a unique majority outcome rises rapidly to over ninety per cent as the number of voters increases (De Meyer and Plott, 1970). Secondly, wherever there is a degree of consensus in a voting group the probability of a majority outcome also increases.

More importantly, however, is the fact that the political process is not the simple democracy put forward in the voting paradox but a representational system in which such elements as power wielding, vote-getting, argument, and party or bureaucratic maintenance are as important as simple choice. The role of government, which is in a sense determined by this process, also ensures that the simple 'free market' assumption of our dairy farmer example need not hold true in a mixed economy with government intervention. In such a system self interested voters will often have some means of expressing the intensity of their preferences, if not in the vote itself, then in the amount of resources they may put at the disposal of groups or parties espousing one alternative over another. Also quite common is what Brown and Jackson (1978, p. 77) call 'log-rolling', that is, a voluntary exchange of votes to the mutual benefit of different partisan groups. In other words, 'I'll vote for you on this issue, if you'll vote for me on that'. Such vote trading is quite in keeping with the economist's self interest model and adds to the unlikelihood of a voting paradox. Tullock (1967) for example, argues that in the real world the probability of

---

[1] A similar example is found in Luce and Raiffa (1957).

the voting paradox occurring is too small to make any practical difference.

Another possibility is that social welfare functions emerge, not as a result of aggregating individual self interests, but from some wider public interest which is the result of a process of political conflict which tries to produce agreement, establish consensus, and minimise instability. In this model political decisions are not reached simply by adding up preferences, but by a dynamic process which involves changing preferences towards a sufficient coalescence of opinion for action to take place. If a social welfare function does emerge it is a result of this dynamic process. Brent (1979) for example, argues that economists can construct social welfare functions based, not on individual preferences, but on values revealed in the political system related to particular social objectives. These values are ascertained by imputing motives to past government decisions and examining explicit policy statements. In fact, the public interest and the self interest models of preference determination need not be mutually exclusive, and later in the book we will see that where it is necessary to put weights to values it is best done by combining self interest and public interest approaches. Both are valuable partial models of the reality of the policy making process, which serve their disciplines of economics and political science for theory formation and which could profitably be integrated by policy scientists.

What about the social welfare function? Is it possible to formulate one, and is it a necessary precondition for rational analysis? The answer to the first question, I would argue, is that it is not possible or necessary to formulate a unique, immutable social welfare function to the exclusion of all others on a particular issue, but that governments must continually have a series of 'working' social welfare functions upon which to base policy. As Cutt (1975, p. 226) argues:

'We do not imply that there is a uniquely defined social preference function, but simply that for elected government there must be ascertainable, if there is to be meaningful policy analysis, a set of objectives and weights, in a continuing process of adjustment in response to changing government interpretation of public preference, and that the objective of public policy is the optimisation of that objective function. Alternative functions are the stuff of political opposition.'

These functions are formulated in an iterative manner, and are subject to continuing reappraisal and modification as their impacts become apparent. At a general level in democratic societies where higher order goals and objectives are 'preference-ranked' by society the political process itself is certainly the mechanism by which individual value judgements are gradually translated into policy decisions. This is most often through representational politics, but also through such activities as lobbying, forming pressure groups, or 'log-rolling'. Here the guiding, if changing, SWF may well be implicit rather than stated. As policy problems become more specific it may become possible to formulate an explicit objective function based on operationalised programme objectives, as a guide to social improvement through programme achievement. In the next chapter we will discuss the relationship between problem scale and the applicability of rational techniques to policy problems.

A second view is that the issue is not very critical because rational analysis has a valuable role to play in policy making whether or not an explicit social welfare function is identified. Gershuny (1978), for example, argues that even in the absence of a welfare function, rationality serves a valuable purpose in 'vindicating' the selection of particular policies over others to those 'losers' whose value judgements were not necessarily represented in the selected alternative. At one level, vindication constitutes the demonstration that the policy choice is a necessary consequence of the 'winners' value judgements and that there was no other alternative which might better serve the losers' value judgements without damaging the winners' interests. Vindication by rationality at this level promotes consensus in the sense that people accept policy decisions even though they may not agree with them. For example, Labour party members in the UK do not become revolutionaries when the Tories are in power because a rational view suggests that the best available alternative is not revolution, but rather waiting for a future Tory defeat. Rationality can also vindicate in the more specific sense of convincing a group of individuals to pursue some course of action. For example, trade unionists may accept an incomes policy in so far as rational analysis demonstrates to them that they should forego short term wage gain for longer term benefit in the form of less inflation. In addition, rationality may also vindicate in so far as it demonstrates to individuals the greater good of forsaking their particular interests for some larger interest of society. Any willingness on the part of the better-off to see their income redistributed through tax may be a case in point.

Conclusion

Finally, this book will argue that in many cases the role of policy analysis in policy making is not to identify the one single, optimal alternative which requires a unique, explicit social welfare function for its identification. Rather the role of policy analysis is to enlighten the policy process from its *particular* perspective, which is not expected to be completely comprehensive. Such enlightenment may take the form of espousing one explicit welfare function over another, based on its particular merits, or it may simply, but importantly, involve exposing new facts and details which fuel political debate. In either case, the possibility of the derivation of a unique social welfare function is not a critical issue for the policy analyst, and a role for rationality in policy analysis is not precluded. The next chapter looks at the relationship of policy analysis to policy making and argues a valid role for analytic rationality in that relationship.

3 Exploring Policy Analysis

The application of rational techniques to policy problems is part and parcel of the activity which has come to be known as policy analysis. To get a balanced perspective on the former requires an understanding of the nature and the context of the latter. This chapter undertakes to do that in two ways. First, policy analysis is examined from the 'outside-in' – that is, defined in terms of its loci in the wider world of policy making. This outside-in look suggests the importance of value judgements in this process and in turn in rational techniques. The second way of looking at policy analysis is from the 'inside-out', that is, in terms of its scope: the range of problems it addresses and the responses that tend to be forthcoming. This inside-out perspective points up the importance of an understanding of the scale of policy problems to an understanding of the role of rational techniques. Finally, a case is put for the positive, if limited, value of rational techniques in policy analysis.

Policy Making and Policy Analysis

First of all policy making is about politics. And although no lengthy definition of politics is needed, it would be remiss not at least to skirt around a definition to give some flavour to our analysis. Some might say that all human interaction is politics, Bismark said that it was the art of the possible, and the *Oxford Dictionary* calls it the science and art of government. Politics is certainly partisanship meaning political parties, pressure groups, lobbying, public opinion and the power struggle for preferment, dominance, control, influence, and position (Dimock and Dimock, 1953). Politics is also deciding the content of policy, the promotion of values, and choosing among alternatives in an attempt to solve problems and improve human life. This latter aspect corresponds most directly to our concern: politics as policy making.

The process of policy making is represented in a schematic extension of the simple model of Chapter 2 in Figure 3.1 where we find policy

Figure 3.1   Activities and elements in policy making

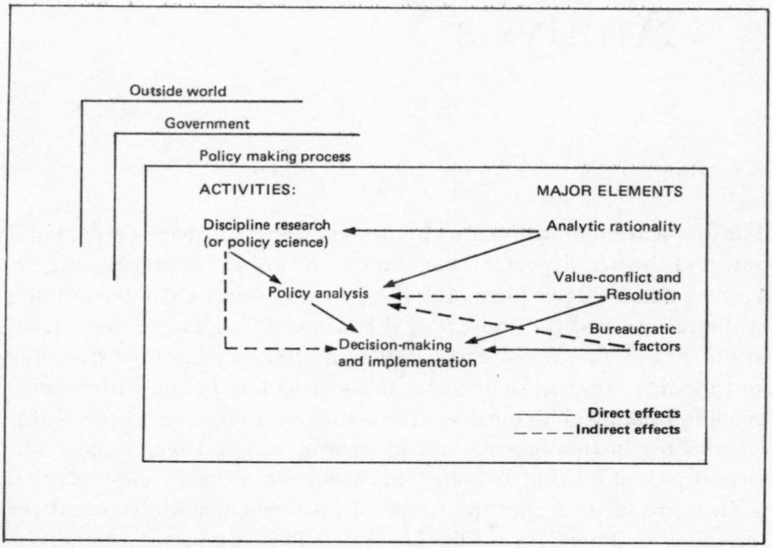

making in turn a subsystem of higher level systems. This process is seen to consist of three elements: value-conflict and resolution, bureaucratic maintenance, and analytic rationality; and four activities: policy science, policy analysis, decision making and implementation. A look at each in turn throws light on the nature of policy analysis.

The Elements of Policy Making

The value-conflictive element in policy making involves the promotion of values related to a multiplicity of goals and objectives. This value promotion is the natural human result of a diversity of value judgements in society on the means to and the ends of, 'a better life'. The tools of this process are activities like negotiation, bargaining, and mutual adjustment, and it is manifested in many ways such as debates in Parliament, pronouncements by politicians, in-fighting in cabinet, public hearings, and a host of other activities which are the tangible aspects of politics to many people. This societal process has as its goal the allocation of resources according to some form of resolution of conflict between value-holding groups in society. The resolution may take the form of satisfactorily completed bargaining, or power wielding perhaps with a vindication of the resultant policy.

The topics of the conflicts themselves are usually more concerned with matters of distributional equity rather than allocative efficiency, that is deciding 'who gets what' rather than how to provide most efficiently the 'what'. This value conflict is a dominant element in policy making and we will return to it shortly.

The second important element of policy making is the administrative or bureaucratic. This includes routinised activities, which are those employed for the purpose of simplifying the decision environment, and avoiding conflict in the policy process, by means of a series of standardised procedures and criteria for dealing with policy questions (Fry and Tompkins, 1978). This process is not necessarily purposive in nature – actions and small decisions may accumulate to result in resource allocation by the workings of the bureaucratic process. It is also within the bounds of this component that the implementation of decisions takes place. And because government at any level is multi-functional the resultant policy may devote part of the resources available to functional tasks like co-ordination of organisational sub-units, maintenance or acquisition of new resources or power, career promotion, or adaption in some way to the external environment (Goldstein et al., 1978).

The third distinctive element of policy making is the application of analytic rationality to resource allocation decisions. This is reflected in the rise of this field of policy analysis and in the use of numerous rational techniques as aids to decision making. This element involves, of course, the five steps in our rational man model and probably arose in reaction to government which was perceived as overly dependent on the other two elements in the face of increasingly complex policy problems.

The rational element is purposive in nature and its origins are two-fold. Firstly, there is a general level of analysis which is concerned with problem solving and is based on the precepts of systems analysis and its mathematical offshoot – operations research. Secondly, there are a variety of techniques which draw heavily on the discipline of economics for its strong rational orientation, its theoretical base, and its apparent logical consistency. Because these two groups of rational methods have been in the past concerned with allocative efficiency rather than equity they first tended towards optimisation, that is, they treated resource allocations as problems with a single solution. For some, this stance proved impossible to maintain and Simon (1957) suggested instead what he called 'satisficing', that is, attempting to identify an acceptable, sub-optimal solution. In other words, not looking for the best but simply a good solution to a resource allocation problem. Most recently, techniques are evolving which are more concerned with problem-clarification than either optimising or satis-ficing. To an extent these have arisen in true dialectic fashion as a reaction against over-emphasis on allocative efficiency at the expense of distributional equity, and are embodied in such fields as social impact assessment.

Most policy decisions then are made up of some mix of these three elements of the policy making process and the mix varies according to the nature and scope of the policy problem at hand. In the next section we look at some of the activities associated with policy making and the links between elements and activities in our simple model.

The Nature of Policy Analysis

Definitions of policy analysis abound. More than a decade ago Dror (1968) put forward one of the first in terms of some criteria for defining the boundaries of the concept. These included:

(1) Attention paid to the political aspects of decision making.
(2) A broad conception of decision making.
(3) A main emphasis on creativity and search for new policy alternatives.
(4) Extensive reliance on qualitative methods.
(5) Emphasis on futuristic thinking.
(6) A systematic approach which would recognise the complexity of means-end interdependence, the multiplicity of relevant criteria of decision, and the partial and tentative nature of every analysis.

It is especially worth noting the emphasis on the broad conception, the political aspects, and the qualitative method. Wildavsky (1969) broadened this even more by arguing that policy analysis was equivalent to strategic planning, that is the process of deciding on the objectives of an organisation, on changes in these objectives, and on the resources used to attain these objectives. Policy analysis in this vein was to be concerned with big and important plans with major consequences.

In the 1970s attempts to define policy analysis became simpler. For Dror (1971a) policy analysis now becomes an approach and method-ology for design and identification of preferable alternatives in respect to complex policy issues. It provides heuristic aid to better policy making, without any presumptions to provide optimisation al-gorithms, and is based on systems analysis and behavioural sciences. For Ukeles (1977), more simply, policy analysis is defined as the systematic investigation of alternative policy options and the gathering and display of evidence for and against each option. This means a problem-solving approach, the collection and interpretation of information, and some attempt to predict the consequences of alternative courses of action. Most other recent definitions are in a similar vein, and it is no doubt the case that the wide-ranging early definitions of policy analysis were bound to give way to those which approximate to analytic rationality to a greater or less degree. Recently there has been concern with this emphasis on rationality and calls for a policy analysis which recognises the importance of the non-analytic elements in the policy making process.

Policy analysis is also defined by distinguishing it from policy science, and meta-policy making. Basically policy science is discipline research: an academic endeavour pursued by an independent investigator who is free to choose the set of values which will be applicable in the research and who is usually divorced from the decision making process (Reynolds, 1975). The policy scientist is often concerned with academic excellence and the pursuit of knowledge. In addition, within the broad policy field there is a valuable role for a general philosophical perspective on policy, akin to what Dror (1971a) terms meta-policy making, or policy dealing with the characteristics of the policy making system. Neither, however, are policy analysis which usually involves working directly or indirectly for government or private institutions interested in influencing decision making. The policy analyst, unlike perhaps the policy scientist, must be very careful and explicit about what values and whose values are injected into the analytic process.

Other important distinguishing characteristics are to be found in Coleman's (1972) perceptive article on policy analysis in which:

(1) The audience is a set of political actors, ranging from a single client to a whole populace, and the research is designed as a guide to the action.

(2) Partial information available at the time an action must be taken is better than complete information after that time.

(3) The criteria of parsimony and elegance that apply in discipline research are not important; the correctness of the predictions or results is important.

(4) The ultimate produce is not a 'contribution to existing knowledge' in the literature, but a social policy modified by the research results.

(5) It is necessary to treat differently policy variables which are

subject to policy manipulation, and situational variables which are not.

These 'action oriented' principles clearly distinguish policy analysis from its academically-oriented kin, which as noted in Figure 3.1 usually has only indirect, or enlightening, effects on decision making. Policy analysis, on the other hand, may directly affect decision making, and it is the channel through which the element of analytic rationality is conveyed into policy decisions. But the elements of value conflict and bureaucratic maintenance have equally direct effects on decision making and cannot be ignored. Now it is in the nature of policy analysis to tend towards the orderly and the systematic, especially when faced with an exceedingly complex modern reality, and it is not surprising that the definitions emphasise the rational. But policy analysis which oversubscribes to the rational model or undervalues the value-conflictive and bureaucratic elements in policy making will be poor policy analysis because its model will be overly divergent from social reality. The development of a healthy supradiscipline of policy analysis depends to a large extent on the recognition of the linkage between the rational and the value-bureaucratic elements of policy making. The advantage of a rational approach will go unrealised or be properly resisted if this linkage is ignored.

Finally, like any model which seeks to simplify reality, the one illustrated in Figure 3.1 runs some risks. For example, although the relationship of the activity of policy implementation to analysis has been ignored for the sake of simplifying the argument, it is not to be underestimated. On the contrary, it is not unusual to see top level political initiative coupled with the most rational of forward plans ground to a dead halt by failure to come to terms with the bureaucratic aspects of a particular policy. Study of this administrative aspect of policy making, especially implementation research, is a vital subject in its own right and we will return to it again in Chapter 6. Also the arrows in Figure 3.1 could have signified effects in two directions, as a simple way of representing the complex process of learning and iteration in policy making. Lastly, it is worth remembering that activities of policy making are equally activities on the other subsystems or models, for example, policy science in the world of academia, or decision making in a model of party political activity. Each policy problem, therefore, exists in a complex social reality of which the rational aspects represent only one element in a larger system. These rational aspects gain relevance if they are integrated with the other elements of the policy problem. The better the integration the closer towards (but never attaining) social reality the policy analysis model moves, and its value to decision makers rises accordingly.

Essential Value Judgements

Churchman (1975, p. 28) argues that 'every social policy needs not only a cost-benefit number but requires that the basic social theory used for assigning such a number should be revealed and assessed for its moral implications'. In other words, the output of rational analysis has no special meaning in and of itself – it only becomes relevant to a policy problem when value judgements are applied to that output. Human value judgements, of course, reflect an enormous diversity of political, moral, philosophical and aesthetic orientations towards some notion of what contributes to quality of life. This diversity makes it inevitable that policy making means debate and not agreement, and ensures that there is seldom one optimal solution to a policy problem but rather a coalescence of value judgements towards a policy decision. Once this is conceded, it becomes easier to accept a valuable but limited role for rational analysis. Such analysis can help provide much needed information, fire necessary debate, help towards coalescence of value judgements, and 'vindicate', or help reconcile decisions to those whose values have not won the day.

In some cases, the policy analyst may be most concerned with the rational analytic aspects of a policy problem, say in an environmental impact assessment, and will leave it to the policy maker to filter this information through a value screen. At other times the analyst may be required to develop a value weighting scheme of one sort or another, as in some cost-benefit analyses. In either case the integration of the two aspects of the problem must take place if a realistic decision is to be arrived at. Difficulties arise when this integration does not occur or is somehow misguided. The argument here is not that the analyst takes over some portion of the decision maker's 'political' role. It is rather that the value of rational techniques is only realised when the techniques are constructed and administered with regard to the limitations which stem from their less than holistic perspective on policy problems. One of those limitations is that the results of analysis can only 'come alive' through the application of value judgements.

The Scope of Policy Analysis

The scope of policy analysis can be defined, firstly, by an examination of the classes of policy problems to which it is applied, and secondly, by looking at the range of activities which are termed policy analysis. One classification of policy problems suggests four categories of analysis based on the type of analytic activity necessary for problem resolution. There are: specific issue analysis, programme analysis, multi-programme analysis and strategic analysis. These classes are distinguished by (i) increasingly complex policy questions; (ii) increasingly imprecise policy making environment; (iii) a wider range of possible alternatives; (iv) increasingly broad criteria; and (v) increasing lead time to do policy analysis (Ukeles, 1977). This is shown in Figure 3.2.

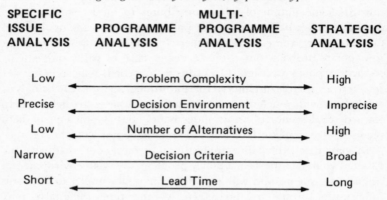

Figure 3.2   Policy analysis, by problem type

SPECIFIC ISSUE ANALYSIS	PROGRAMME ANALYSIS	MULTI-PROGRAMME ANALYSIS	STRATEGIC ANALYSIS
Low	Problem Complexity		High
Precise	Decision Environment		Imprecise
Low	Number of Alternatives		High
Narrow	Decision Criteria		Broad
Short	Lead Time		Long

Issue analysis is specific short-term decision making such as the type characterised by day to day management. For example, choosing between schemes for street cleansing would require issue analysis. Programme analysis is concerned with design or evaluation of a programme in a single subject area, for example, a programme to provide health clinics across the country. Multi-programme analysis is resource allocation between competing programme areas, for example, deciding whether to allocate limited funds to detached health clinics or to expand hospital out-patient services. Finally, strategic analysis deals with large-scale policy decisions and broad resource allocations, for example, between competing project areas like housing and health.

A second mode of dissecting policy analysis is by distinguishing between analysis done for the purpose of enlightening or influencing policies and analysis of existing policy content or its constructive process. This distinction was first put by Dror (1971b) who argued that the term policy analysis as a process which was an aid to identification of preferable policy alternatives had to be kept strictly apart from the use of the same term in the behavioural study of policy making. This distinction is expanded by Gordon et al. (1977) who devised the continuum outlined in Figure 3.3 which describes a range of activity within the dichotomy of 'analysis for' to 'analysis of' policy. The five types of policy analysis include (i) policy advocacy which is research that terminates in the direct advocacy of some policy identified as serving some end valued by the researchers; (ii) information for policy which provides policy makers with information and

Figure 3.3   Policy analysis, by activity

	Analysis *for* policy		**Analysis *of* Policy**	
Policy Advocacy	Information for Policy	Policy Monitoring and Evaluation	Analysis of Policy Determination	Analysis of Policy Content

(from Gordon, Lewis and Young, 1977, p. 27)

perhaps advice; (iii) policy monitoring and evaluation which is *post hoc* analysis of policies and programmes; (iv) analysis of policy determination which is the study of the inputs and transformational processes operating on the construction of public policy; (v) analysis of policy content which is the study of the intentions and operation of specific policies. This continuum serves to describe the great majority of activities falling under the rubric 'policy analysis' and helps us to grasp the somewhat elusive nature of the beast.

Problem Scale is sometimes a Problem
Just as misunderstanding the importance of value judgements in analysis engenders misperception of rational techniques, so does a misunderstanding of the effect of the scale or magnitude of the policy problem. In terms of the continuum of policy analysis activities from specific issues to strategic analysis, the general applicability of rational techniques tends to change as the scale of the policy problem increases

and the importance of the value-conflictive element increases more or less proportionately to scale.

In specific issue and programme analysis concentration is often on allocative efficiency and the effect of value judgements on a decision may be low. Here rational techniques, such as productivity measurement, may be of considerable value to the decision maker. In multiprogramme analysis trade-offs are being made between programme types – concentration moves towards distributional equity and value judgements as the value aspects become of increasing importance. Rational analysis here cannot be expected to come close enough to social reality to indicate anything like *an* answer and the most valuable rational techniques here are those which explicitly endeavour to link the rational and the political. Finally in strategic analysis one is dealing with, as Wildavsky put it, 'big plans with major consequences'. The variables involved are complex and inter-related, the time horizon may be long, the amount of uncertainty is high, and there are large numbers of intangible considerations. The political aspect is paramount and rational techniques can only make a partial contribution to the overall questions of 'whose values are to prevail?'. In this case, policy analysts will concentrate effort on outlining broad alternatives and elucidating the value choices and the value sets of participants relevant to the problem.

Now it is no doubt true that some aspects of both specific issue analysis and strategic planning require the same research in terms of evaluation of consequences, the measurement of output, and the estimation of production relationships and real cost and benefits. It is also true that the application of rational techniques to any policy problem has value, especially in so far as knowledge fuels debate which leads to healthy policy making. This situation often leads to some confusion as policy making problems are perceived as either amenable to rational analysis or not, depending on one's predisposition to the type of analysis and without regard for scale. Proponents of rational analysis assume that because a technique works well in programme analysis it will work equally well in strategic analysis. Anti-rationalists, on the other hand, argue that because it fails to produce solutions at the strategic level, rational analysis is obviously suspect in every case.

In the case of the third London airport site for example, proponents of the cost-benefit exercise did not seem to grasp that the problem was strategic, i.e., 'Do we need and want another airport?' rather than programmatic 'Where do we best put this airport we agree is needed?'. The cost-benefit was bound to fail to provide any reasonable answer to this policy problem because it was incorrectly defined, not necessarily insoluble. To give another example, a socio-environmental impact study would be essential to any discussion of the impacts of locating a surface coal mine in a prime agricultural district but the prior question 'What are our likely energy consumption patterns in future which require this coal to be mined?' would have to be answered in the political market place.

In summary, a balanced perspective on the role of rational techniques in policy analysis requires an understanding of the importance of integrating this rational approach with the overriding value judgemental aspects of any policy problem – overriding because the results of rational analysis only take meaning when weighted values are ascribed to those results. This perspective also requires that due regard be given to the scale of the policy problem because the ability of these rational techniques to approximate or model social reality tends to decrease as problem scale increases.

The Value of Rational Analysis

A number of limitations in rational techniques have been described and there are numerous critiques of their use in policy analysis. Rittel and Webber (1973) suggest that the limitations of rational analysis are due to the fact that policy problems are 'wicked' problems, which cannot be clearly defined and which exist in pluralistic societies which lack objective definitions of equity. For Strauch (1975) the difficulty with policy problems is that they are 'squishy' meaning that they are less amenable to analytic technique than some analysts would like us to believe. The implications of 'wickedness' and 'squishyness' are of considerable importance in assessing the value of rational techniques and might be itemised under the following headings: problems of political realism; questions of a proper theoretical base; problems revolving around measurement, valuation, and aggregation; the question of the relationship between 'hard' objective data and 'soft' subjective data; or similarly the question of the relationship between analysis and public participation in policy making. Chapter 6 considers each of these problem areas in detail.

Given, however, that we accept the limitations to these techniques, they do offer advantages as a partial perspective on policy problems that preclude their being ignored or dismissed from a role in policy analysis, and that role is to *assist* choice. It is not, however, as Williams (1972, p. 201) points out, 'to *make* choice, nor to *justify* past choice, nor to *delay* matters so that some previously chosen course of action has a greater chance of adaptation'. In assisting choice the following advantages are suggested:

(1) Rational analysis promotes a systematic, orderly approach to the study of policy problems. This is important because of the contentiousness of policy issues, the vast amount of data which may be involved, and the need for a rigorous form of analysis to simplify complex reality for decision makers. Kramer (1975, p. 511) suggests that in spite of the limitations of rational analysis '... most administrators feel more comfortable with order rather than chaos. Analysis ... of social programs gives us a feeling of orderliness and rationality that is valued'. The alternative to this systematic approach is often a loose unstructured collection of information that mixes up conceptual levels, hides bias in its presentation, lacks any readibly graspable perspective on the problem, and so confuses decision makers if they do not ignore the information altogether.

(2) Rational analysis assists in problem definition, or locating a decision space, which is the first and often the most important step in policy analysis. Political issues seldom emerge cut and dried and ready for debate. Rather they come to the fore clouded in half-fact, fancy, and value-predilection. A systematic approach helps to define, and equally importantly, to redefine the decision space as more facets of the problem become apparent.

(3) Rational analysis assists in satisfying the information needs of all the parties to a policy decision (insofar, of course, as the policy making process itself allows a free flow of information among interested parties). Wildavsky (1969, p. 189), no great fan of such techniques as cost-benefit analysis, nevertheless notes that 'In some organisations there are no ways at all of determining the effectiveness of existing programs; organisational survival must be the sole criterion of merit. It is often not possible to determine if the simplest objectives have been met. If there is a demand for information the cry goes out that what the organisation does cannot be measured. Should anyone attempt to tie the organisation down to any measure of productivity, the claim is made that there is no truth in numbers. ... Their activities are literally priceless; vulgar notions of cost and benefit do not apply to them.' Good decisions are based on adequate information and some information is always better than none, and although rational analysis is only partial analysis, it is a useful source of information for decision makers.

(4) It is only through rational analysis that efficiency can be measured. Policy problems always involve trade-offs between

various benefit and cost mixes given limited resources, and rational techniques, if coupled with a clear manner of presentation, can help force consideration of these costs and benefits which otherwise might have lain hidden in rhetoric. Rational analysis can also help articulate and clarify the range of practical choice and the consequences of various potential choices.

(5) Rational techniques, coupled with an aggressive public participation model of policy making, can help to extend and deepen the involvement of various interested parties in the policy process. And by imposing patterns on problem settings and data it may help to promote coalitions among interested parties to a decision, in government and out, by permitting a common perspective to evolve among individuals and groups with differing interests in the same problem. This can promote action on a problem, for example, as individuals distributed throughout a government bureaucracy transfer various ways of looking at a policy problem into forces which help determine the actions of the system (Rein and White, 1977).

(6) Finally, rational analysis promotes explicitness in presentation of data basic to a problem and in causal linkages and transformations postulated in the analysis. This reduces the incidence of hidden value judgements, the effect of fashion in problem resolution, and the incidence of implicit causality in the form of tenuous causal relationships which may pervade less rigorous forms of analysis. It is within the confines of the rational model that cause and effect can be rigorously tested – this may not be critical for policy analysis specifically but is certainly of great importance to the development of the policy sciences generally. This type of exercise also helps to separate the effects of a particular programme from the impact of ongoing social processes which would have occurred in the absence of the programme under consideration.

Perhaps the best perspective on rational analysis is to view it as just that: a perspective. One of the problems with the application of rational techniques is that they tend to be viewed as models to be used as *surrogates* for the problem at hand (Strauch, 1976). When this happens the analyst adopts, in effect, the problem as defined by the model rather than the problem in reality. The model adopted, however, will seldom have a high degree of 'fit' with complex reality because it cannot take into account all aspects of the problem but only those readily included. In other words, the rational element is more easily set into a model than the political and bureaucratic elements and thus the model as a surrogate for reality fails to live up to what is expected of it because it is a partial and incomplete surrogate.

The model should instead be viewed as a perspective on the problem – one way of viewing the policy problem but not necessarily a comprehensive or uniquely valid way. This 'analysis as perspective' allows a reasonable stance towards rational analysis: as a partial view of reality which is often best coupled with other views which help round out the policy analysis. If this is accepted then it is right to be suspicious of techniques that promise optimal solutions at the same time as advantage is taken of the benefits of rational technique. If, as argued earlier, the results of a rational analysis have to be filtered through value judgements to 'come alive' and as all policy is about political choice (to a greater or lesser extent depending on scale) rational analysis can never offer up a solution based solely on a formula or a quantitative model. But it can, depending on the problem, at best approach a solution and at least offer a valid, if incomplete, perspective to assist decision making. The acceptance of rational analysis *and* its limitations frees us from unreasonable expectations and allows us to reap its benefits.

Finally, it is not unusual for the situation to arise when different rational analyses suggest different policy options or even the same technique manipulated in differing ways suggesting different options. Similarly, various parties to a decision may use the results of an analysis to support different, or even radically opposed, courses of action. This can be the case, for example, when traffic engineers on the one hand, and road building objectors on the other, come to interpret projected traffic flows and their implications. This is when, as Rein and White (1977, p. 133) suggest, 'science seems to speak out of both sides of its mouth about the course that policy should take'. This paradox is not inconsistent with our view of rational analysis as a valid but incomplete perspective on policy decisions and the important thing in this situation is to grasp why perspectives differ: what criteria, assumptions, values, and valuations are included in each analysis which causes them to differ? A thorough discussion of these questions cannot help but shed new light on the policy problem at issue, and it is likely that in the end the policy maker will have to select that option which reflects most closely his own criteria and values. A way out of this paradox can never be based wholly on analytic rationality and this only serves to reinforce our contention that political choice can be enlightened, but never resolved, by analytic rationality alone.

4 A Process Approach to Analysis

There is nothing short of an overwhelming array of rational techniques which might be brought to bear on any policy analysis problem and more are evident in the literature every day. They range in name from the traditional cost-benefit analysis and its variations like goals-achievement matrix analysis, through the somewhat more recent environmental impact assessment, to exotica like judgement analysis or stochastic multicriteria analysis and a host of others. As suggested earlier what is sometimes lost in the gaps between disciplines and in technical jargon is one basic fact: all the techniques are variations of the rational approach to problem solving. They can be better understood and related to one another by a more detailed look at this basic approach.

The 'Roots' of Analytic Rationality

Although its philosophical antecedents no doubt go back to the origins of the scientific method, in the twentieth century analytic rationality is linked with the development firstly, of welfare economics, and later, of systems analysis. During the early development of welfare economics in the 1920s, the British economist, A. C. Pigou (1924) argued in *The Economics of Welfare* that neoclassical economics could no longer ignore the concept of social costs which might cause public welfare to differ from private welfare. This difference reflected an imperfect working of the market economy and a role for state intervention in the workings of that economy.

Pigou went on to point out that public welfare could be lessened by these social costs, or disservices, which exceed the private costs of production, and he gave examples: the lessening of the amenity of residential neighbourhoods by factory construction, or the cost of police services related to liquor sales, neither of which would be the concern of factory owners or distillers in their corporate balance sheets. He argued that these types of social costs had to be quantified to determine their impact on the net social product.

Pigou's work was integrated in the 1950s into another basic thread in welfare economics which developed in the 30s. This is the question of what criteria should be used to judge the desirability of proposed alternatives in the allocation of resources. The earliest well-known social welfare criterion is that of Pareto: any change in the social state is desirable if at least one person judges himself to be better off because of the change while no one else is worse off. Because of limitations in Pareto's formula, the later developments of Kaldor-Hicks and Little expanded and refined the social welfare criterion and they were incorporated into cost-benefit analysis. The main purpose of these efforts was to expand the set of situations and policies about which statements may be made as to whether economic welfare was increased, decreased or left unchanged. The objective was to define the net effects of resource-using public expenditure and to establish criterion for choosing between alternative policies. The use of cost-benefit analysis and related techniques has expanded to encompass many areas of government decision making ranging from energy policy and industrial project evaluation to assessment of alternatives in the health and social services. Chapter 7 considers these in detail.

The second approach to problem solving to which most rational techniques can be related is the development of systems analysis and its early predecessor, operations research. Operations research evolved during World War II and after and is basically the application of mathematical technique to operational problems. Beginning with some objective, operations research seeks to optimise pursuit of that objective in terms of some straightforward, quantifiable criteria like cost, time, or distance. This relatively narrow mathematical format broadened into systems analysis which most simply is systematic analysis, and generally is problem solving which tries to define a highly comprehensive and relevant decision space.

For one author 'systems analysis is nothing more than quantitative or enlightened commonsense aided by modern analytical methods' (Enthoven, 1970, p. 277). Probably the most quoted and the best definition is by Quade (1968, p. 2):

> 'Systems analysis . . . can be characterised as a systematic approach to helping a decision maker choose a course of action by investigating his full problem, searching out objectives and alternatives, and comparing them in light of their consequences, using an appropriate framework – insofar as possible analytic – to bring expert judgement and intuition to bear on the problem.'

The important elements in this definition are that it is a problem solving strategy rather than a particular activity; that it is policy oriented in that its principal role is to aid decision makers; and that while emphasis is on rigorous methodology, judgement and intuition are important (Boucher, 1977). This definition of systems analysis, of course, is very similar to some definitions of policy analysis we examined earlier. Other authors define systems analysis as virtually identical to cost-benefit analysis in that it is designed to maximise the value of objectives achieved by an organisation minus the value of the resources it uses (Fisher, 1977). This is too limiting, however, and Quade's definition is preferable. Further references to systems theory include Laszlo (1972a, 1972b) Lilienfeld (1978) and Jeffers (1978).

Virtually all the rational techniques used or proposed for assisting policy analysis are related to one or the other or both of these two approaches: cost-benefit analysis and systems analysis, and some researchers now speak of CBA as one method of systems analysis, which on certain assumptions is true. In the next chapter a number of these techniques are categorised under the headings (i) cost-utility analysis (ii) impact assessment (iii) futures research (iv) evaluation techniques and (v) social indicator research, and are described in greater detail in the light of the process common to the techniques. Before describing this process, however, it is useful to look briefly at the time dimension in analysis.

The Past and the Future in Analysis

There is some confusion in terminology over analysis with an outlook to the future and that with an outlook to the past. *Ex ante* analysis is concerned with the future and involves the prediction of the consequences of various proposed courses of action on the basis of some model of the processes involved. This means visualising alternative states of the world and then comparing these alternative futures in terms of established criteria (Freeman and Bernstein, 1975). *Ex ante* analysis is sometimes termed anticipatory research (Hy, 1976) or future oriented policy analysis (Wolf, 1974) in that it provides information to decision makers before particular actions take place. *Ex post* analysis, on the other hand, is a check on what did happen – examination and measurement of the actual consequences of some programme or policy. *Ex post* analysis provides evidence on which to base decisions about maintaining, institutionalising, or expanding successful programmes or modifying or abandoning unsuccessful ones, but not about predicting future effects (Weiss, 1972).

Ex post analysis is most commonly called evaluation or evaluation research. Unfortunately there are a number of *ex ante* techniques which are also termed evaluation or plan evaluation thus leading to confusion in the literature and in practice. For O. F. Poland (1974), evaluation clearly involves a 'retrospective examination'. Pederson (1977) goes as far as to distinguish evaluation from policy analysis – the latter confined to *ex ante* analysis. For Wolf evaluation research gauges the effectiveness of public programmes already in operation. Lichfield et al. (1975), on the other hand, use the term evaluation for studies which attempt to predict the impact of planning options. Smyth (1976) follows in this vein by describing evaluation as an assessment of the impact of a proposal on the physical and social environment.

It is probably best if the term 'evaluation' be confined to *ex post* analysis as this conforms to the majority of its applications. Terms like plan evaluation and others which mean in effect *ex ante* analysis can conveniently be termed appraisals in line with the current *ex ante* use of the term project appraisal. Unlike Pederson, however, there is no point in suggesting that evaluation is not policy analysis. Rather it is useful to refer to Gordon et al.'s (1977) typology of policy analysis which distinguishes policy advocacy and information for policy, which are *ex ante* analyses, from policy monitoring and evaluation which they identify clearly as *ex post* analysis.

For many techniques it is difficult to maintain a clear time dimension distinction, nor is it always necessary. For example, the results of evaluation are often a basis for future action so being overly rigorous might be self-defeating. Techniques like cost-benefit analysis or impact assessment are almost always *ex ante* but not necessarily so. Social indicator research is firmly entrenched in both camps. Figure 4.1 outlines this situation. In the grey area which divides the *ex post* from *ex ante* rigorous distinctions may fail but a valuable formal interaction may take place where the *ex post* analysis can be used as a check on the validity of *ex ante* techniques. In this sense, they are complementary techniques, both valuable in policy analysis.

The Common Process in Analysis
Related to their common heritage in welfare economics and systems analysis, the rational techniques under consideration share an underlying common process, or conceptual framework, which is simply described as the rational approach to problem solving. This process begins with problem formulation and ends with the presentation of the results of the analysis to the decision maker (meaning most likely

Figure 4.1   The time dimension in analysis

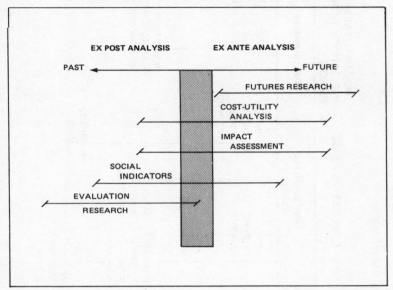

the decision making body) who may or may not make a judgement
to implement some project, programme or body of policy. The process
can be described in a series of phases of activity which include the
definition of the decision space, projection of alternative courses of
action, development of models, and comparisons of the results obtained in the model to some judgemental criteria. An examination
of this process or approach, which is shown in Figure 4.2, aids our
understanding of the advantages and disadvantages of each category
of these techniques and provides a means for comparing and contrast-
ing the various techniques.

The first, conceptual, phase in this process is where the problem
arises, perhaps quickly and clearly, perhaps over a long period of time,
at first vague and then gradually coming into focus. At some point,
if the problem is to be delved into by rational technique, a decision
space must be formulated which allows the problem to be systematically disintegrated into its constituent parts. Those objectives relevant
to the problem must be identified which can later be operationalised,
or translated into measurable terms. This conceptualisation of the
policy problem will be undertaken by any number of parties to the
problem – the analyst's conception may be very similar to most or
quite different. The main actors in the rational analysis in this phase

Figure 4.2   The steps of rational analysis

CONCEPTUAL PHASE		RESEARCH PHASE		EVALUATIVE PHASE		JUDGEMENTAL and IMPLEMENTATION PHASES
Problem Formulation		Search and Identification	Projection and Prediction	Aggregation and Weighting		Interpretation

setting out terms of reference, study parameters and/or objectives

data base development

delineating potential options

indicator development, operational-isation

formulation of cause and effect model

testing of model

projection of trends

prediction of change related to alternative options

non-weighted aggregation

transformation to common scale

attempts to clarify actors' value sets

selection of judgement criteria

value-weighted aggregation

integration of two or more analytic exercises

sensitivity analysis

presentation, dissemination, or "shelving"

possible public participation thread . . . .

will be the analyst and/or the policy maker, or more profitably both. During this phase preset terms of reference, or study parameters, may be passed along to the analyst. Otherwise the analyst may be left to formulate his own terms of references relative to the problem, that is, define his own decision space.

The second phase in this process is the research phase in which the main actor is the analyst – with the decision making body in a consultative role. Various facets of the problem, and inter-relationships between the problem area and the wider world, are exposed and these indicate the likely scope necessary for the data base which describes 'what is' and serves as the baseline or zero point from which the dimensions and positive or negative directions of change are examined. A variety of alternative options relative to the problem are then put forward for consideration. The range of the options considered is confined by the decision space and what usually happens is that an initial list of options defined by the policy maker is refined by the analyst. In some cases, however, the task of identifying plausible options may be left to the analyst. Then various aspects of those options are singled out as worthy of examination as to their potential effects on change. These aspects are operationalised by a selected series of indices which it is hoped will forecast the dimension and direction of change resulting from the activity, or lack of it, implicit in each option. These forecasts are in turn based on some explicit, or often implicit causal model, which will be an abstraction from reality. During this phase a series of important value judgements are made which are endogenous to the research and to which we will return in Chapter 6. With some rational techniques, like impact assessment, the results of the activity in this phase, that is baseline data, indices, possibly the model, and the projected changes related to each option are usually transmitted to the decision maker or to a more generalist adviser, usually in report form. With other groups of techniques, like cost-utility analysis, no report is usually made until the following phase.

It is in the third, evaluative, phase that value judgements are applied to the results of the research phase and this enables these results to take on 'meaning'. The actors in this phase will be the analyst in some cases, a second more generalist analyst in others, the decision maker acting alone, or most profitably the analyst and decision maker in conjunction. In this phase the first activity may be the setting out of some criteria by which the results of the analysis will be judged. These may be fairly general or quite specific. If specific, developing judgement criteria may involve establishing what Bunn (1978) terms decision criteria or dominance criteria. The former involves a decision model, as a surrogate for the problem, which attempts to rank the options based on some knowledge of the policy maker's preferences. The latter does not seek to rank options but rather to eliminate them, one by one, as being dominated by another. In either case, indices of change projected in the research phase are aggregated and may be transformed to a common scale – often money. Then these results might be value weighted so as to express the differential contribution of each index to the overall value of the option. This may be followed by the integration of two or more analytic exercises into a further coherent statement on the overall value and impact of each option under study. This activity may be explicit as when, for example, a researcher is asked to integrate a number of studies into a cost-benefit type framework. It is not uncommon, however, for it to be implicit, as when a decision maker takes two or three analytic reports on a possible option, digests them, and assigns interval value weights to each to help arrive at a decision. The important thing is that this phase always occurs, be it explicit or implicit.

A number of contentious issues arise around the question of who is doing the value weighting and with what value judgements and these issues are also discussed in Chapter 6. The value weighting itself will generally take three forms. Firstly, if some decision maker assigns his own values, the weighting is based on the original choice of indices and the judgement of the decision maker. Explicit value weighting on the other hand, is usually based on estimation of weightings related to either secondly, citizen preference studies or thirdly, expert or professional opinion. The results of this activity is usually transmitted in report form to the decision maker.

If the research phase does not conclude the rational analysis then the evaluative one does, although here of course rationality is tempered and given meaning by the application of value judgements. This phase is usually followed by a judgemental phase during which a decision is actually taken or not as the case may be, and then comes implementation, monitoring and feedback through the system. This idealised continuum of activity is common to the variety of rational techniques we are considering and there are important advantages to relating these techniques back to this framework.

First, however, there are a few caveats to such a perspective. One is that it must be reiterated that this is an analysis of analysis – we are pulling things apart to see how they work and interact. So at the risk of repeating: the argument is not that political decision making is or should necessarily be rational – this is a description of the rational element and an attempt to put it in a reasonable perspective. Secondly, the fact that this process is described as linear is because it is an idealised conception. It is, of course, nothing of the sort but rather an iterative process which might be visualised as a series of circular loops leading towards a decision. For example, the research phase will assist in a better redefinition of the problem, or perhaps value judgements made in the evaluative phase may result in rethinking of the options to be researched in the second phase, and so on. The essential elements of the process, however, remain embodied in each phase. The third caveat is that in describing the actors involved in this process we have limited ourselves to the decision makers and the analysts. This is for simplicity's sake. In Chapter 6 we will discuss the important role other parties have in the process.

The Advantages of the Perceiving Process

If these caveats are kept in mind, there are a number of advantages to be gained from examining rational techniques in the light of this process. Firstly, an understanding of the rational method generally and the various techniques specifically is encouraged by adopting this simple perspective. The common vocabulary proposed can help to de-mystify the techniques and promote communication among researchers, decision makers, and the public. This question of improved communication is an important one for proponents of rational techniques in that a lot of hostility to analysis on the part of decision makers and others can be laid at the feet of poor communication. Techniques which hope to be of practical value to policy making lose much of their policy impact if their terminology is unintelligible to those who must take decisions. This is not to undervalue the importance of complex terminology to methodological development – indeed it is essential that researchers have meaning-packed words which replace tedious and lengthy explanations at simplistic levels. Nevertheless, it is important to differentiate between rigorously defined sophisticated analysis and the need to communicate useful advice to policy makers. Giving such advice is not precluded by sophisticated analysis but greater attention does need to be paid to means of communicating with some ease.

Secondly, this common approach promotes concentration on the *process* orientation of problem solving rather than a technocratic 'output of solutions' one. This accords with Dror's (1968) admonition that policy analysis had to be without any presumption to provide optimisation algorithms, or black boxes where data is fed in one side and solutions slide out the other. In other words, expectations of optimality are reduced and a more realistic stance towards rational techniques is fostered.

Thirdly, this perspective facilitates the integration of two or more analytic studies related to some proposed course of action. The necessity for such integration often arises in large scale projects where a variety of techniques are brought to bear on the same problem. For example, a proposal to build a large electrical generating station may result in the commissioning of social and environmental impact assessments, a cost-benefit analysis and numerous engineers' reports, all of which must be integrated before any recommendation can be made to policy makers. A process perspective assists in this by demonstrating which techniques are applicable at each phase and by allowing comparison to be made between different techniques at the appropriate phase. Similarities and differences between methodologies are more apparent and models and assumptions inherent in similar activities in different studies are made clear, for example, in weighted aggregation in the evaluative phase. Much more attention will have to be given to this question of how to go about integrating a number of increasingly complex and lengthy studies of various dimensions of the same problem, especially given the difficulties of information overload. The process will aid in the evolution of such integrative approaches.

Fourthly, and more specifically to the technique themselves, the development of the methodology associated with the techniques is enhanced because methodological problems can be perceived as inherent in each phase of the process rather than as necessarily unique to a technique or a discipline. This common conceptual framework is often unrecognised because the various techniques arise from different disciplines, and because the highly practical nature of policy analysis often precludes the opportunity or inclination for an overview. This results in a low level of methodological cross-fertilisation among research efforts and across disciplines and a lack of productive interaction between the practical and theoretical (or academic) orientations in what are seen as different disciplines. An understanding of this process, common to many techniques, can foster learning which takes place by examining the literature and comparing international notes related to a methodological problem area rather than a specific technique. For example, a continuing difficulty in impact assessment is how to operationalise indicators which will begin to measure potential project impacts. In this case a great deal may be learnt by studying the literature of social indicator research and interacting with researchers in this field who are grappling with similar problems. This type of 'back and forth' interaction among policy analysts and between the academic and policy worlds is facilitated by a common viewpoint and can only benefit policy analysis.

The Role of the (Rational) Policy Analyst

Given that rational analysis does have a substantial role in policy making and that the results of analysis depend on value judgements for meaning, what then is the role of the analyst? Does the simple market model hold in that the policy analyst 'produces' research for later consumption and he is divorced from political constraints? Or is something more involved?

At one extreme we have the school exemplified by the economist Mishan who argues that the cost-benefit analyst, for example, must derive the parameters of analysis wholly from rational economic criterion and without regard for any politically determined values. These political values include regard for democratic participation, the effect of a proposal on distribution of incomes, and intangibles which are unmeasurable. Mishan goes on to argue that it is the analyst's responsibility to make clear to the public the exclusions and to claim no more for the cost-benefit exercise than what it is – an analysis of potential Pareto improvement in which the calculations of gains and losses is made on a purely economic principle. Thus, 'if the government calls upon an economist to undertake a cost-benefit study, it presumably expects him to apply economic principles and only economic principles' (Mishan, 1974, p. 91). Mishan concludes his argument by stressing that a cost-benefit analysis, based wholly on rational criterion, is just one useful technique in the service of social decision and not by itself socially decisive or a substitute for policy.

Others take a wider view, for example, Williams (1972) who argues that rational analysts may well have to accept political restrictions and constraints on alternatives under consideration if the analysis is to be politically practicable. He warns, however, against the situation where the cost-benefit analyst becomes the policy analyst and argues for 'specialist' and 'generalist' analysts – the specialist more rational in approach while the generalist is able to consider the rational and political aspects of the problem, and interpret them to policy makers, without necessarily being adept at rational techniques. The specialist presumably would be directly involved in the research phase of analysis while the generalist would be more concerned with the conceptual and evaluative phases. Lichfield (1975), Smyth (1976), and others attempt to extend the range of techniques such as CBA to encompass all necessary data for a decision – stopping short of the final value weighting but certainly taking into account political constraints on the choice of alternatives.

The range of approaches to analysis is in fact very wide. Some analysts engaged in such techniques as environmental impact assessment see themselves as simply providing raw data for decision making and excluding all political value weighting (Waters, 1976). At the other extreme, some technically esoteric rational techniques go so far as to attempt to quantify political value judgements by a series of explicit social welfare functions, attach some uncertainty factor, and sum up and arrive at a composite figure (Local Government Operational Research Unit, 1976). Others also try to link the rational aspects of policy making with the political value judgement aspects but only in a fairly subjective fashion (Lonsdale, 1978).

Clearly, neither actual practice nor the literature is any real guide to the analysts' role unless 'anything goes'. In fact, although highly aggregated value weighting may be far-fetched, most other activities may be required of the analyst at one time or another depending on the policy problem at hand. The issue is not really to define a role for the analyst but rather to stress that what is important is that the dimensions of the analyst's role should be clear and explicit to all concerned. Specifically, rational policy analysts might be involved in three different but related activities:

(1) They might engage in rational analysis generally by conforming to the rational method and specifically by carrying out one or more rational techniques; this might be called an informative role.

(2) They might engage in activities which help to highlight and to overcome some of the inherent limitations in rational techniques so as to assist in making the policy analysis more holistic in perspective; this is a methodological role.

(3) They might assist in uncovering and making explicit the political value judgements of various interested and perhaps disinterested parties to a decision, and further they may attempt to marry these value judgements with the results of analysis so as to give it social meaning. This might be called a value enlightening role.

These three activities encompass most of the tasks and prescriptions for rational analysis and are each, separately or together, reasonable activities which operationally define the role of the policy analyst. From the first to the third, the activities slide up conceptual levels from the specific towards the general. The first may be taken as tending

towards a more technical role and the third more towards a consultative advisory one, or in Williams' words, specialist and generalist roles
respectively. And while one may perceive these activities as lying
along a continuum, the end of which is a policy decision, it must be
kept in mind that they are indeed separate activities although they
may well be carried out at the same time. The important thing is
that the first role must not be confused with the third. Such a confusion
is far from uncommon and it is when the first activity is put forward
as, is perceived as, or implicitly encompasses, the third that confusion
reigns and rational technique comes rightly under fire for ignoring
the political facets of life. And although a continuum of activity is
described, it is in fact iterative: engaging in the second or the third
activity often means a revision in the results of the first. The process
can again be envisaged as a series of loops moving towards a policy
decision.

Within the first and second role one important task for analysts
may be to carry out and encourage the use of *sensitivity analysis* where
there is a large amount of uncertainty inherent in the projections and
predictions in the analysis, and the subsequent outcomes. Here the
analyst may present alternative best and worst, or upper, lower, and
middle boundaries for projections. Alternative values for uncertain
variables can be examined for their sensitivity to variations in the
assumptions and parameters of the analysis (Brown and Jackson, 1978,
p. 172). Where outcomes are ranked, an extension of the sensitivity
analysis is to develop a 'robustness measure' which indicates how much
change in variables must occur before there is a reversal in the ranking
among outcomes. The range of these figures indicates the flexibility
of a policy option in meeting the types of uncertainty considered.

Finally, problem scale plays an important part here. At the specific
issue level carrying out one or more rational techniques might provide
a 'model perspective' close enough to reality for the decision maker
to take it more or less at face value – given that it will be 'screened'
by his value judgement in any event. But as we move up the scale
towards strategic analysis the third level of activity, exploring value
judgements, assumes increasing importance. Here the analyst will find
that concentration on the value enlightening role will ensure a valid
contribution to the overall policy analysis. If assigned an informative
role, the analyst will further the case for rational technique by pointing
out its limited applicability (the second role) and stressing the importance of value enlightenment. The point is that some form of the third
role will go on implicitly no matter what, but that the more explicit
the results of this activity the better the policy analysis. Although a

few areas where rational analysts are incompetent to tread will later be suggested, the emphasis here is not on what the analyst's role should or should not be but rather on the importance of making explicit which type of activity is being undertaken and the relationship of that activity to policy analysis.

5 Categories For Rational Techniques

This chapter examines briefly a variety of rational techniques and classifies them under seven headings. Although not strictly mutually exclusive these categories do distinguish among most rational techniques and generally reflect the distinctions drawn in the literature, in practice, and as the result of activity in different and unrelating disciplines. Four of the categories, namely impact assessment, futures research, evaluation studies, and social indicator research are common enough, although the links between them are often ignored. Here, there is much to be gained from understanding the nature of techniques within a category and from examining the similarities and differences between categories. The other three categories are related, as all are concerned with the relationship between cost and utility in a project. I take the opportunity to distinguish among a group of techniques which previously have been more or less lumped together, to the detriment of attempts to examine their relative advantages and disadvantages over one another. The techniques themselves within each category are described briefly – readers interested in a more thorough examination of the practice, issues and literature of the techniques are referred to Part II. Finally, for simplicity's sake, this categorisation ignores the strictly mathematical techniques of operations research, like linear programming, which seek to optimise a well-defined quantitative function and are more relevant to specific operational, rather than policy, problems.

Cost-Utility Analysis

A variety of techniques can be classified under the term cost-utility analysis. All cost-utility techniques are related to the most common one, cost-benefit analysis, and are generally designed to assist rationally some decision maker in choosing among alternative policies or projects. This choice may be based on the fixed utility approach, that is gaining a pre-specified level of utility at lowest cost in choice of alternative, or a fixed budget approach, that is, choosing the alternative, which produces the highest activity level for some pre-specified budget level (Fisher, 1977). In other words, the same output for less input or greater output for the same input.

Cost-utility techniques have the following steps in common: (i) identification of some feasible alternative; (ii) predictions of the outcomes of each alternative; (iii) valuation of the outcomes in commensurate units, almost always money; and (iv) choice of alternative based on some decision criterion (Luft, 1976). As such cost-utility analysis usually spans the conceptual, research and evaluation phases of the rational process with the main focus in the literature and in practice on the evaluative phase or steps (iii) and (iv).

Cost-benefit analysis (CBA), the oldest and most common of these techniques, is a method for assessing the desirability of prospective projects and involves the enumeration and valuation in money terms of all relevant costs and benefits, no matter when they occur or to whom they accrue. Costs are determined by:

(1) Enumerating all adverse consequences arising from implementation of an option in monetary terms.
(2) Estimating the probability of occurrence.
(3) Estimating the cost to society should it occur.
(4) Calculating the expected loss related to each consequence by multiplying (2) by (3).
(5) Discounting from year of occurrence back to present to give a net present value.
(6) Computing expected cost for each option by summing expected losses (Fischoff, 1977).

A similar procedure determines expected benefits.

Cost-benefit is most commonly used, firstly, to assess whether a project offers a net economic return to society at large or not and secondly, to evaluate alternative means of achieving a specific objective, for example, the choice of a mode of transport or the location of a particular transport route, given that the decision has been made to provide transport. There are a number of decision rules in CBA and the choice of which is applicable is a matter of long-standing contention (Brown and Jackson, 1978). One rule is the present value method where a particular discount or interest rate is chosen, for example, an adjusted market rate of interest, and the present value of net benefits is calculated. The project with the largest positive present value is chosen. Another common decision rule compares the ratios of benefits to costs and selects that project with the highest positive ratio. Closely related to CBA is cost-effectiveness analysis (CEA) which ascertains the least cost means of achieving a specified objective, often within a budget ceiling or restriction. This is the fixed utility approach and is concerned with the unit cost of output for a proposed programme or service, allowing comparisons on the basis of cost.

Criticisms of cost-benefit analysis abound and will be discussed in further detail in Chapters 6 and 7. The main criticisms relate firstly, to difficulties in attaching values to quantified costs and benefits and the problem of intangibles, or unquantifiable costs and benefits. Problems in this area gave rise to the development of various impact assessment techniques. The second major problem area is the question of the distribution of benefits and costs, and income and employment effects, across various sub-populations of society – an issue on which there are numerous points of view within the field. A third problem area is related to the practical and theoretical difficulties associated with aggregation, which is the value weighting and summing of several measures in an analysis to give an overall composite figure. These three problem areas gave rise to a variety of reformist off-shoots of CBA and CEA which attempt to alleviate one or more of these difficulties while retaining the CBA framework. These techniques can be further broken down into two groups. The first are those that generally avoid value weighting and aggregation, i.e. they confine the rational analyst's role more or less to the research phase of the process. These are termed non-aggregating techniques. The second group consists of those techniques which actively promote the analyst's involvement in value weighting and the evaluation phase – these are aggregating techniques.

This distinction permeates the literature and practice of rational analysis. The non-aggregating techniques are a reaction to criticism which argued that aggregation, as in cost-benefit analysis, over-emphasised the quantifiable aspects of problems and merged a host of information into a few ratios or indices thus ignoring or hiding in their aggregations a great amount of information vital to decision making. Soon after, however, the non-aggregating techniques came to be criticised for overloading the decision making process with a mountain of descriptive information which was virtually incomprehensible to the decision maker because no aggregation had taken place. This then is one of the classic dilemmas of rational analysis – to what extent and on what basis does one aggregate data relevant to a decision?

Non-Aggregating Cost-Utility Techniques
The first of these related techniques was the Planning Balance Sheet

Analysis (PBSA) developed by Lichfield (1971) in an attempt to overcome the distributive difficulty in CBA. The PBSA approach breaks down the incidence of costs and benefits and ascribes them to 'producers' and 'consumers' who in turn can be further broken down into specific groups of people. 'Instrumental objectives' for each group can be described and used to develop criteria by which to assess the relative impact of cost and benefits. PBSA also deals with the problem of intangibles (or unmeasurables) by providing an accounting format for displaying non-monetary data. This avoids problems of aggregation by leaving that task to the decision maker who ascribes implicit value weights to various measures and who select the groups in society which will reap new benefit or suffer from increased cost as the result of the selection of some alternative.

A very similar technique, 'multivariate cost-benefit analysis' is proposed by Stern (1976) who argues that conventional CBA 'can make any proposition, no matter how simple, impenetrably complex and incomprehensible by misguided quantificationism and faulty aggregation which attempts to add together disparate factors in a problem like noise, pollution, journey time capital cost, etc.'. Instead, Stern proposes what is essentially a tableau listing all the main items relevant to a decision, in a variety of units, which allows the decision maker to supply the weighting factors and carry through with the evaluation phase. At this point, of course, Stern and others who advocate non-aggregating techniques leave themselves open to the criticism of those who argue that unwieldly mountains of information are of no help to decision makers and that some aggregation must take place.

Aggregating Cost-Utility Techniques
The aggregating techniques are generally dedicated to overcoming difficulties associated with aggregation so as better to assist decision making. One of the most well-known of these techniques is Hill's Goals-Achievement Matrix (GAM), developed as an alternative to Lichfield's planning balance sheet analysis. Hill argued that Lichfield's approach and others which listed the effects of a proposal according to the sub-group of the population affected ignored the fact that various enumerated costs and benefits had to be seen in terms of well defined planning objectives to take on meaning. In his example, the retention of an ancient building had to be viewed in light of its historic, economic, and space value, all of which related to different objectives. Hill went on to argue that this lack of objectives not only failed to give meaning to the presented data but provided no

criteria for judging whether a particular cost or benefit was relevant to the problem at hand. Instead he proposes a matrix approach in which objectives and alternative courses of action are listed and the various factors of each scheme are measured as to their extent of goal acheivement. A weighting is then introduced which reflects the community's valuation of each objective and the costs and benefits associated with that objective. This value weighting is meant to reflect the community's desired distribution of benefits related to objectives, in other words, 'equity'. Hill (1968, p. 27) suggests that the weighting (aggregation) could be left to the decision maker but that the key to the best use of a GAM was 'the weighting of objectives, activities, locations, groups . . .'. Hill also argues that improving the ability to determine value weights was the first priority for successful application of the GAM technique as it was 'not very useful if weights cannot be objectively determined or assumed'. A highly logical extension of GAM, the Plan Evaluation and Robustness Programme (PERP) is discussed in Chapter 7.

Another group of aggregating techniques stem from decision analysis, also described by the terms multi-attribute or multi-criteria analysis. These seek to deal with the multi-dimensionality of complex policy decisions by expanding the ability of matrix methods to deal either with complex objectives, or complex alternative options, or both. One such proposal describes the logic behind it as 'the decomposition of an alternative into its constituent attributes, the determination of the utility of each attribute, and the mechanical combining via some mathematical function of the utilities into a composite or total utility' (Einhorn and McCouch, 1977, p. 270). These utilities are sometimes based on the features of individual preference structures or the nature of attitudes towards risk. The important aspects of these techniques are:

(1) Consideration of quantitative and qualitative or monetary and non-monetary information.
(2) Risk assessment and value weighting based either on a unitary decision maker, expert opinion, scaling individual preferences gathered by public opinion sampling, or some combination of these.
(3) Use of cardinal scales to rank alternatives as to total utility.
(4) Emphasis on systematic mathematical methods of aggregation.

All cost-utility techniques are discussed in more detail in Chapter 6.

Impact Assessment

The various types of impact analysis or assessment (environmental, social, socio-economic) are generally non-aggregating techniques, and again arose as a reaction to the deficiencies of cost-benefit analysis, especially the problems of intangibles and the distribution of costs and benefits (or impacts) across various sectors of society. Environmental impact assessment (EIA) came to the fore in the United States in the late 1960s in response to pressure from the so-called 'ecology movement'. This resulted in the passing of the National Environmental Policy Act in 1970. The primary motive of the act was to make explicit and to mitigate deterioration of the bio-physical environment caused by an over-emphasis on economic criteria in judging project worthiness (Sondheim, 1978). No particular methodologies were specified for studying environmental impact and early efforts were perfunctory. In an attempt to provide a comprehensive perspective the emphasis on the biophysical aspects of development was expanded to include the socio-economic aspects as well. However, the resultant environmental impact statements, while becoming increasingly sophisticated in biophysical analysis, usually gave a token and simplistic nod to the social aspects of development.

This gave rise in turn to social impact assessment (SIA) in which the emphasis is on separating the demographic, social and economic aspects from the biophysical so as to give them proper attention. This resulted in the issuance of social impact statements – generally analyses of varying comprehensiveness and without any consistent methodology. As might be expected the definitions of such a new and broad activity are vague and all-embracing. Wolf (1974), for example, in putting forward SIA as a newly emerging field of interdisciplinary social science knowledge and application, argues that the 'analytic problem of SIA is nothing less than that of estimating and appraising the condition of a society organised and changed by large scale application of high technology'. While this may sound grandiose, it is not in a sense unexpected, because SIA is defined by what most other techniques do not cover. It is the 'grab-bag' technique which has to consider all those important but often intangible impacts left untouched by other types of analysis.

The processes of EIA and SIA are similar and usually involve these steps:

(1) Establishment of a data base which describes the existing situation.

(2) Development of the means of describing change related to the project.

(3) Forecasting changes in the base situation with and without the given project, including qualitative and quantitative aspects.

These steps correspond to the research phase of the rational analysis process. In this research phase SIA is especially concerned with isolating the distributional properties of potential change – who benefits and who suffers which impacts. SIA may additionally include an evaluation phase although there is considerable controversy about whether this is a proper role for social impact analysts. Some authors suggest that SIA must be confined to the research phase – it simply presents data and information which are evaluated elsewhere (Waters, 1976). Others argue that the analyst should assist in exploring the political value judgements which enter into any weighting scheme, that is, take a strong value exploring role (Carley and Walkey, 1978). Few argue for any type of complex quantitative aggregation scheme in SIA. EIA, too, is almost always confined to the research phase with evaluation left to more general analysts or the decision maker. Chapter 8 explores the methodology of these techniques in more detail.

Although both techniques share a common heritage and involve much the same tasks they are increasingly seen as quite different activities. This reflects the differing subject matter, the biophysical on the one hand and the socio-economic on the other, and the different disciplines involved in the study of each – natural and social scientists. Both techniques, however, are often used to study the same proposal and impacts may well be closely related. In the study of a possible road alignment for example, increased noise and pollution (environmental) may lead to psychological stress and relocation decisions (social) and reduced property values (economic). At some point, the results of various studies must be integrated as trade-offs are made among project benefits and social and environmental costs. This integration is again the role of the more general analyst or the decision maker. Finally, both these techniques differ from others, for example, futures research, in that they are almost exclusively project oriented and concerned with projection in the short and medium term.

Forecasting and Futures Research

The most general approach to the study of the future is variously called social forecasting or futures research. At its broadest 'the primary purpose of futures research is to assist the formulation of policy: as such, futures research is an instrument of policy analysis'

(Lonsdale, 1978, p. 213). Overall futures research is very similar to the approach of systems analysis but what is said to set it apart is its special emphasis on making explicit the models of reality that are shared by particular groups in society and underlie the future choices they might make (Boucher, 1977). The futures researcher attempts to be useful to the policy process by inter-relating forecasted social-psychological data (people's vision of the future) with other kinds of forecast information (demographic or economic) for the purpose of atttempting some reasonably comprehensive picture of what the world, or some aspect of it, might be like in the future given certain hypothesised parameters as to the nature of the change.

Some researchers use the term social forecasting and futures research interchangeably. Others define them at ends of a continuum. McHale et al. (1976) argues that forecasting tends to assume a set of causal relationships between events which may enable one to predict their future state with some degree of probability. The emphasis here is on prediction and is similar to a rigorous sociological approach to extrapolating the past in a model so as to develop testable propositions which can be used for prediction. Futures studies, on the other hand, may be said to extend to questions regarding the structural premises and assumptions about the world which underlie the basis for forecasting. Forecasting, in this definition, tries to set out what will be, given certain assumptions, while futures research is about alternatives – what could be. This involves setting forth possible futures and assessing the likelihood of their coming into existence – concentration on broader aspects of the future rather than prediction of certain events. This concentration on alternative futures and invention of broad alternative policies is seen as a major contribution to policy making. Futures researchers, in this definition, might make use of various forecasting techniques but would not be limited to those techniques.

Forecasting and futures techniques have their roots in postwar technological and economic forecasting efforts. These have been divided into the (i) exploratory – extrapolating or analysing trends and presenting alternatives to show what might happen and the (ii) normative – defining the future to show what should happen (Holroyd, 1978, p. 213). This distinction is the same as that between 'policy advocacy' and 'information for policy' noted in Chapter 3. Most research is now exploratory given some early, and serious, criticism of futures researchers who would try to be 'prophets' (Cazes, 1971). In any case, futures researchers have to work from explicitly stated assumptions – implicit and possible inconsistent assumptions underlying 'invented' futures are of little use to policy makers.

A second way of distinguishing between approaches to futures research is between those techniques which are based on the assumption of continuous situations and those on discontinuous situations (Holroyd, 1978). The former is concerned with extrapolating trends and cycles which might range in scale from forecasts of national gas depletion rates to 1990 to world population models to the year 2020. The underlying premise of continuous situation forecasting is that the conditions which produced the trend in the past will continue to do so in the future. That this view ignores contextual events that might upset trends gave rise to non-continuous situation forecasting techniques in which the emphasis is on the role of change and discontinuity. One way this is done is by studying the process whereby important groups in society gradually or suddenly restructure some basic tenets and beliefs which affect the nature of society. Holroyd gives an example of one of these 'paradigm shifts', or restructuring of beliefs and methods, as the increasing tendency in the western world for ethnic groupings to desire autonomy, for example, the Basques in Spain or the Quebecous in Canada. Another topical example of a technologically led discontinuous future is those effects in society which might be occasioned by the widespread introduction of micro-processing technology – a number of studies foresee the necessity for a great change in ideas about labour and leisure to accommodate these changes (Barron and Curnow, 1979).

There are, of course, a variety of pitfalls in attempting futures research. Duncan (1969) points out that:

(1) Social forecasters are inclined to be biased in their projections by their own personal, untested convictions about how the future might develop.

(2) Forecasters do not always resist demands to make forecasts which they know cannot be reliably made.

(3) Forecasters become enamoured with their own predictions, and tend to forget the uncertainties and ignorance on which these forecasts rest.

(4) Forecasters may be inclined to be biased towards conservatism by their desire to appear scientific or responsible; this can discourage unconventional thinking.

(5) Forecasters exhibit a tendency not to question assumptions that have proved useful in earlier projections.

(6) Forecasters may overfocus on the elegance of the techniques they are using – especially if they invented those techniques.

In spite of these and other limitations, the need to try and get some picture of the future for planning purposes is essential to modern life and it is likely that futures research will grow in vitality if not necessarily reliability. The fact that attention is now more directed towards 'what might be' in the form of alternative futures rather than 'what will be' means that futures research can provide valuable and necessary fuel for political debates – as, for example, is occurring around micro-processing technology. A range of such techniques are explored further in Chapter 9.

Evaluation Research

The past decade has seen a proliferation of social programmes and an increasing concern for assessing their effectiveness or efficiency. This has resulted in a steadily increasing interest in various types of evaluation research, and there is already a very large literature and a number of definitions. Weiss (1972, p. 4) terms it research whose aim 'is to measure the effects of a program against the goals it set out to accomplish as a means of contributing to subsequent decision making about the program and improving future programming'. Gordon et al. (1977, p. 28) suggest that 'monitoring and evaluation can be aimed at providing direct results to policy makers about the impact and effectiveness of specific policies. But it can do more than this. *Post hoc* review of policy impact may be used for feasibility analysis in future policy design, via the sepcification of a feasible set of actions'. Wilner (1974), in a review of 25 publications on evaluation, found that evaluation research concentrated on firstly, the assessment of benefit or cost to the client, consumer or community, and secondly, improving the design and internal operations of programmes and organisations.

Three main aims in evaluation can be identified. The first is the use of controlled experiments and *ex post* studies undertaken in the context of the research design of the social scientist (Poland, 1974). These are experiments with research design as rigorous as practicable, consisting ideally of experiments which allocate individuals at random between control and experimental groups, measure each group before and after the experiment, and make statistical comparisons. Examples of efforts along these lines include the negative income tax experiment in the US (Haveman and Watts, 1976), similar research in Canada (Canadian News Facts, 1978) and educational research in the UK (Barnes, 1975). More commonly researchers make do with some form of an *ex post*, quasi-experimental research approach when controlled experimentation is not possible. The difficulties associated with such experimentation are examined in Chapter 10.

A second theme in evaluation is simply the *ad hoc* research effort without a theoretical framework. These consist largely of analysis of data, review of the inputs and/or outputs of programmes, and various statistical manipulation of this type of information. The need for an *ad hoc* approach often arises when a particular question about a particular programme must be answered in a short time. The *ad hoc* approach can be inexpensive and is widely used, especially at a local level. It relies heavily on the skill and ingenuity of the researcher and is most suitable for problems without undue complexity where it can be a valuable aid to policy making. The main dangers of the *ad hoc* approach include oversimplification and wrongly imputed or ignored cause and effect relationships.

A third theme is evaluation in the context of a cost-benefit or cost-effectiveness approach with concern for programme objectives. Here programme evaluations are structured in terms of efficiency and effectiveness so that the basic questions asked are those of whether and to what extent did the programme achieve its objectives and at what cost. The emphasis in this approach is on: (i) the efficiency of the programme – measures of output per unit input; (ii) effectiveness – the extent to which the programme achieves objectives; and (iii) appropriateness – whether a programme needs to be done (Poland, 1974). During the past decade there have been various manifestations of this approach – in the late 1960s there was great interest in linking comprehensive evaluation to budgeting and this resulted in Planning Programme Budgeting Systems (PPBS) and Zero-Based Budgeting. PPBS was soundly criticised for its overly rational approach and poor implementation procedures and the debate on its worth raged extensively (Glennerster, 1975; Merewitz and Sosnick, 1971). These techniques and the arguments surrounding them are discussed in more detail in Chapter 10. A portion of this approach is termed productivity or performance measurement and considerable interest in it is now apparent in the UK and the US. Productivity measurement is concerned specifically with the relationship of inputs to outcomes, especially in the provision of local government services.

These approaches, from PPBS to productivity measurement, all face four similar difficulties:

(1) Attainment of programme goals and objectives must be demonstrated but programmes often have multiple goals which are

not easy to specify and measure. These goals may change over time.

(2) The causal relationship between programme inputs, activities and outcomes must be known. It cannot be assumed or left implicit.

(3) The relationship between programme implementation and outcome must also be demonstrated. It is not enough to relate input to output. The most rational appearing programme may get nowhere because it does not work administratively – this is as important as any efficiency measure.

(4) Programmes with the same objectives and priorities must be available for comparison purposes – an isolated productivity measure, for example, is meaningless.

(5) Evaluation may well be resisted by any party whose interest is best served by doing so.

These various evaluation techniques are examined in more detail in Chapter 9. Although the 'fit' of these *ex post* techniques to the process described in Figure 4.1 is not as close as for most of the *ex ante* techniques, it is not a matter of different components of the process. Rather, it is essentially the same conceptual, research, evaluative phases turned to past judgements and implementation as a guide to further judgements. Attention is not on prediction *per se* but on 'evaluation for prediction'.

Social Indicator Research

A decade-old development which relates in one way or another to all the rational analysis techniques is the advent of what has been called the 'social indicator movement'. There is considerable variety in definitions of social indicators. One of the most straightforward is that of Zapf (1975) who describes systems of social indicators as all attempts to operationalise and measure the components of multi-dimensional conception of welfare. Now it could be argued that all the other rational techniques considered in this book require social indicators in so far as all are attempting to gauge the strength and direction of social change and therefore social indicator research does not constitute a category in itself as much as a component of other techniques. Many researchers, for example, attempt to integrate social indicator knowledge into a variety of other techniques, such as cost-benefit analysis (Seidler et al., 1975), impact assessment (Olsen and Merwin, 1977), or futures research (Johnston, 1978). It is worthwhile to consider it as a separate category, however, because in addition to relating to other techniques, it is evolving as a theoretical and practical effort in itself with a constituency of researchers and administrators and its own literature. There is, in a sense, far too much and valuable social indicator research to subsume it under other headings. In addition, much *ex ante* social indicator research conforms to our process perspective on analysis – operationalising, model building, forecasting, and weighted or non-weighted aggregation are all important aspects of indicator research. This brings up a related point – social indicator research can have *ex post* or *ex ante* dimensions in so far as it involves studying time series data which is descriptive of the past and may be used to predict certain relationships between phenomena in the future. In addition, research using subjective social indicators may involve asking people about their feelings in the past or potential reactions to postulated future events.

This suggests that a second dimension of social indicators is that they are commonly called objective or subjective. Objective indicators are the occurrences of given phenomena, such as environmental stimuli and behavioural responses, which are measurable on an interval or ratio scale. Subjective indicators are those based on reports from individuals on the 'meaning' aspects of reality and as such represent psychological variables which are usually presented on a ordinal scale. For example, time series criminal arrest statistics or money income levels are objective social indicators while feelings and perceptions about street safety or relative deprivation are subjective social indicators. The specific study of well-being as defined by subjective social indicators is often called rather vaguely 'quality of life' research.

A third important dimension one can use to examine the various efforts at social indicator research is one of scale – national, regional, or local. For example, social accounts as published by the United Nations Organisation are at a national level, regional indicators are used by the European Economic Community (EEC) to determine the eligibility of regions for assistance, and local projects, such as housing improvement areas, are defined by local indicators. A fourth dimension is that any social indicator effort may be descriptive or evaluative-predictive. Descriptive research is solely a collection of apparent fact – it is not based on any explicit causal model, means-end relationship, or prospective theory about the allocation of resources (Davies, 1977). Evaluation-predictive research, on the other hand, is usually based on a model and either draws a conclusion on the relationship of two or more factors in the past (evaluation) or attempts to predict the relationship between two or more factors in the future. Evaluative-predictive research may also be called normative (Gordon, 1978), analytic (Clark, 1973), or diagnostic (Hakim, 1978). For example, in the UK the Small Area Statistics based on census data are descriptive – no conclusions are drawn and the studies serve only to classify similar residential areas. On the other hand, the use in the UK of a complex indicator called the Rate Support Grant to allocate funds from central government to local authorities is evaluative in that it is based on a preconceived model and is used to make resource allocation decisions.

Finally, like cost-utility techniques, groups, sets, or systems of social indicators can be described as aggregated or non-aggregated. An aggregated indicator is a composite of several indicators formed into a summary figure. The argument is that this summary figure is more useful than a host of individual indicators because it combines data into a more meaningful whole. This composite indicator requires that unlike measures be transformed into a common scale so they can be added together and this procedure is sometimes accompanied by the value weighting of indicators in an attempt to express differences in the relative importance of the individual phenomena indicated within a composite indicator. A non-aggregated indicator system, on the other hand, is simply a grouping of separate indicators. As in the other rational techniques over-emphasis on aggregation with all its pitfalls leads to some rather dubious social indicator exercises, where, for example, the quality of life in a city is summed up by a single composite indicator.

Almost all efforts at social indicator research can then be described in terms of these five dimensions. For example, the Small Area Analysis mentioned previously can be succinctly described as a local, *ex post*, descriptive study using aggregated objective social indicators. A study which explored people's feelings and expectations regarding a proposed motorway might be a regional, *ex ante*, evaluative study using non-aggregated subjective indicators. By considering social indicator research in light of these five dimensions it becomes somewhat easier to sort through the wide variety of research efforts making use of social indicators in one way or another. Chapter 11 describes a number of examples of social indicator research and the specific problems associated with their development. In the next chapter we examine a variety of problem areas common to all the categories of rational analysis.

6 Problem Areas in Analysis

In Chapters 3 and 4 it was argued that a variety of rational techniques, often arising out of different disciplines and perceived of as diverse, in fact shared a common, simple, rational approach to policy problems. Given this, it is not surprising that these techniques also have in common a number of problem areas related to definition, to the reality of the policy making milieu, to values, and to quantification. In turn, as the problems are held in common, so are many of the solutions which do not really solve, so much as mitigate, the distortions inherent in any technique based on a rational model and caused by the inevitable divergence of this simplifying model from reality. A number of these problems are examined in this chapter.

Efficiency and Effectiveness

There are at least three important dimensions to be considered in most policy making and implementation. The first is equity — the distribution of benefits, costs and opportunities among society, the second is bureaucratic maintenance, and the third is programme achievement. The question of equity consideration is taken up later in this chapter and the role of analysis in assisting the coalescence of values necessary for bureaucratic stability has been discussed. The remaining dimension, programme achievement, is almost always described in terms of measures of effectiveness or efficiency. These terms, unfortunately, are bandied about with a wide variety of meaning in the literature and in practice. This makes it difficult to generalise (i.e. to learn) across a variety of studies, and hinders communication, for example, between economists and policy analysts from other disciplines. Figure 6.1 attempts to impose some definitional order in this area by delineating three different measures of programme achievement.

First there is a measure of efficiency which concerns the relationship of inputs to the direct programme, or intermediate, outputs. Put another way, this is about the capacity of the individual, organisa-

Figure 6.1   Efficiency and effectiveness

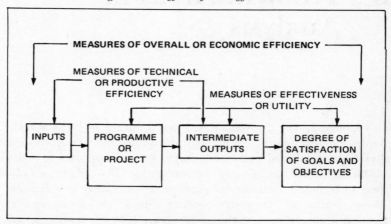

tional unit, facility, operation or activity to produce measurable results in proportion to the resources extended. This is termed *productive* (Sen, 1975) or *technical* (Maynard, 1979) efficiency and it can and should be distinguished from a more comprehensive overall measure of economic efficiency. Productive efficiency is concerned with maximising output for a given set of inputs or with producing a given level of programme outputs at least cost.

Productive efficiency is a fairly simple concept but measuring it is not without problems. The measurement of input is not usually difficult. Labour requirements can readily be quantified, for example, in a hospital the numbers of doctors, nurses, laboratory technicians, administrators, bed spaces, special equipment, drugs and other items is readily counted up. Output is more difficult – the measurement of productive efficiency requires a recognised input-output relationship, or production function, which identifies the particular input or mix of inputs that yields less or more of the desired output. In the hospital example, assigning extra doctors to a programme may mean ancillary and administrative staff, and perhaps more equipment. Would more nurses at lower salaries have had the same effect? And does an increase or a decrease in caseload constitute efficiency? These can be difficult questions. In addition the measurement of productive efficiency is complicated by the potential effects of exogenous environmental effects on programmes. For example, changes in public attitudes or demographic changes may affect health programmes as much as increased input and it is often difficult to separate these effects.

A second type of programme achievement measure looks at programme objectives and tries to gauge the degree to which they have been attained as a result of the programme activity. This is the measure of *effectiveness* which may in turn be concerned with direct project outputs or more general final outputs. In the former case, quantitative project objectives are assessed as to their degree of attainment. In the health field, for example, this is often done by randomised controlled trials (formal experiments) which measure the effect of a particular medical action in altering the incidence of a particular disease for the better (Cochrane, 1972). More general effectiveness studies may be concerned with maximisation of consumer satisfaction or utility, that is, trying to gauge the relationship between programme activity, intermediate output, and final output (Maynard, 1979). In the above example, a consumer utility study would need to consider whether the programme activity resulted not only in reduced incidence of disease, but in improvement in the health status of the individuals under test. That this might not be the case could be due, for example, to side effects of the treatment which would lessen overall health status.

Effectiveness studies are essential for gauging the worth of programmes and many are undertaken, usually within a context of evaluation research. Such studies do require that objectives be specified and be generally anenable to quantification, and this may be difficult, and increasingly so as the evaluation moves from looking at intermediate output to whatever measures of final output are available. Moreover, as Brand (1975) has warned, it may be illogical to believe that quantifiable information is any more relevant to decision making than unquantifiable information. Even when objectives are amenable to quantification the choice of the measures of success, or indicators, may be a value-laden process. For example, the objectives of a health programme may well be to 'improve health status' which is laudatory. For any measure of effectiveness to take place however, it must be decided what mix of reduced morbidity constitutes a healthy life and how degrees of impairment can be reduced to a common measurement scale. Other issues in such studies are considered in Chapter 10.

In spite of these difficulties, studies of effectiveness are a necessary component of efficiency evaluations at both levels. First, because increasing productive efficiency may not necessarily promote the most effective means of attaining objectives. For example, if a health service objective is to reduce the incidence of lung cancer then a vigorous 'no-smoking' campaign may be far more effective than the most productive medical research programme. On the other hand, because effectiveness studies ignore input costs, they are not sufficient in themselves for indicating the best use of scarce resources. Although it makes sense to eliminate ineffective programmes as they are likely to be inefficient, it is more often necessary to choose between mutually exclusive *effective* treatments (Williams and Anderson, 1974). In that case the most effective treatment may not be the best choice given scarce resources, and a less effective (but less costly) programme may be the better choice.

These limitations to measures of productive efficiency, and effectiveness, indicate that both are necessary, but not sufficient, for measuring a higher level of efficiency or *economic* efficiency, as it has been termed (Sen, 1975). Some of the unfortunate confusion over the use of this term probably has been generated by those non-economists who mistake 'economic' efficiency for 'money' efficiency and so assume it ignores relevant but non-monetary aspects of policy decisions. This is not the case, and the meaning of the term economic efficiency is that a good or service is provided at least cost in terms of the use of society's scarce resources, and that the goods and services so provided are those most highly valued by consumers who are seeking to maximise their satisfaction or utility (Maynard, 1979). Measures of economic efficiency are made up of a sum of measures of productive efficiency and effectiveness, and as such the level of difficulty in so measuring rises accordingly. Nevertheless, the concept should serve as an ideal of sorts for policy analysts, even as the needs of vote-getting and bureaucratic maintenance may weigh against it.

The difficulty of assessing economic efficiency rises as problem or programme scale moves from issue to strategic analysis. This reinforces the need to understand the difference between the research and evaluative phases of analysis (Figure 4.2) and to consider problem scale in the application of any particular rational technique. As scale increases the contribution of the analyst may be to assist in problem definition and value clarification which in turn helps to define programme objectives, rather than to attempt definitive statements on economic efficiency. Conversely, as problem scale decreases it becomes easier readily to specify sub-objectives to which efficiency analysis can be applied. For example, if the issue is whether to allocate health resources to kidney patients, cancer research, or to influenza prevention programmes, the rational analyst can provide important information which will help make the allocation but may find it difficult to try to develop some welfare function which would indicate an absolute choice. If the issue moved down in scale, say to the choice between home versus hospital treatment for a particular disease, then evaluative techniques such as cost-benefit and cost-effectiveness analysis can, and often do, assist decision makers (Buxton and West, 1975). In any event this situation reflects our general inability to measure economic efficiency for many government programmes, but does not diminish the usefulness, and even necessity, of attempting to do so.

The related problems of specifying input-output relationships for productive efficiency analysis, determining the effects of exogenous variables on output, and learning to measure consumer utility, must be addressed by rigorous model building which formally relates the variables under consideration. As all decision making contains at least implicit assumptions of input-output relationships and utility, policy analysis can only be improved by making the assumptions explicit and subjecting them to testing. This explicit specification of causal relationships can also help to expose value judgements which all parties to a decision bring to that decision, a point that will be discussed shortly. This model building and testing is more properly part of the policy sciences (or the academic milieu) than policy analysis *per se*, but the use of rational techniques which promote specification of objectives and explicit statement of important problem dimensions greatly facilitates this process. This is a case where the policy sciences and policy analysis serve each other in the interests of better decision making.

Pluralism and Implementation in Decision Making

Our definition of the policy maker included a group of individuals and, in fact, it is often the case that policy is not decided by a single actor or even a readily identifiable small group. Longbottom (1977, p. 20) suggests that:

> 'It is with regard to this issue that the limitations of orthodox management techniques for liaison-making in public services manifest themselves. Regardless of the fact that it may be desirable to justify the use of resource allocation techniques by assuming a unitary organisation, the facts of organisational life in the public services indicate that pluralism lives and thrives.'

It is also the case that the success of policy decisions is related to the implementation of those decisions – policy making is not a linear process resulting in *a* decision but an iterative process. Recently there has been increased concern to assess the importance of implementation in policy analysis and its effect on the viability of rational analysis. For a few authors the deviations of the rational method from reality are seen as sufficient grounds for abandoning the rational approach (Gordon et al., 1977). Instead, they argue that an implementation perspective should be cultivated which concentrates in behaviour and observable action, i.e., how things get done. There is no doubt that this is another important, limited, and valid perspective on the policy process. As a necessary adjunct to rational analysis an implementation approach brings policy making models that much closer to the complex reality it is. However, the dangers of oversubscribing to this perspective at the expense of others are firstly, that 'what is' may be confused with 'what might be or should be', and secondly, that the resultant model will be so vague and/or complex as to provide little aid to the simplification of complex reality often necessary for policy making. The value of implementation research is indisputable as are the limitations of rational analysis but the dismissal of rationality is an over-reaction.

Given our argument that the value of analysis is limited but real it is necessary to take account of the problems pluralism and implementation pose for the analytic perspective. This is done by promoting an awareness of this gap between the rational model and reality, and by working actively to narrow the gap during the policy analysis process. Two means must be pursued by those interested in undertaking rational analyses. Firstly, the role of the analyst should not be limited to that of technician, but to that of an interested party involved in other aspects of the decision making process so as to become as sensitive as possible to the nature of that process. Meltsner (1976, p. 269), for example, argues that:

> 'Analysts should be encouraged to consider implementation concerns when defining the problem and presenting their recommendations. It is not enough to determine . . . . what to do, analysts should also get into the business of how to do it. I realise that our current dearth of knowledge about implementation makes this rather empty advice, but at least it pushes us in an appropriate direction.'

In this vein it is important that the analyst attend crucial meetings related to the proposed policy change, make recommendations at a hierarchical level appropriate to the level at which implementation will take place, and foster co-operation among the various interested administrators.

In addition to taking part in the development of implementation strategies the analyst must involve as many as possible of the pluralist actors in the policy process in the analysis and must make every effort to establish a dialogue with administrators and others who will interpret the analyst's findings. Capps (1977), for example, in discussing the use of performance measurement techniques in UK local government, argues that it is important for local government officials to participate in the development of the methodology to ensure that all parties are fully aware of the strengths and weaknesses of that methodology. Also analysts must make the analysis process as open as possible as part of the second role suggested for rational analysts in Chapter 4 – that they should readily engage in activities which highlight the advantages and disadvantages of such analysis. This will include such activities as making clear the partial nature of analysis, and pointing out how the application of different techniques to a particular policy problem may shift the emphasis to different aspects of the problem. Within the framework of a single technique the analyst should demonstrate in simple fashion how sensitive to change or error particular parameters, variables, or predictions are and how this may alter the results of analysis. There is a good case for integrating such sensitivity analyses into most attempts at policy analysis.

Finally, the analyst deals with problems of pluralism and implementation by paying attention to values. Role three of the analyst's possible roles is to assist in uncovering and making explicit the political value judgements of various interested and perhaps uninterested parties to a decision, including the analysts themselves. If policy analysis means to help improve decision making it is important to ask: improved by whose standards? The next section looks at this important relationship between analysis and values.

Value Judgements within Analysis

A value, as defined by Rokeach (1973, p. 25) is 'a standard that guides and determines action, attitudes towards objects and situations, ideology, presentations of self to others, evaluations, judgements, justifications, comparisons of self with others, and attempts to influence others'. All humans possess a good number of values, or a value set, arranged in a hierarchical manner with the more abstract lying at the top of the value hierarchy. This value set is considerably less complicated than the world and this is a great virtue: a few standards apply in a multiplicity of situations (Fowles, 1977, p. 305). In this sense, the value set is like a model which attempts to simplify reality. A value set has at least one important function: it provides a basis for orientation in, and interpretation of, a complex world and for formulation of the appropriate responses to that world. The application of these value sets, or standards, to a situation is a value judgement and there are two general types of value judgements important in national analysis. The first are the value judgements within, or integral to, any rational analysis and the second are those specifically fed in to some rational technique. They might be called endogenous and exogenous value judgements. The former are considered here, the latter a few sections hence.

One of the most common and telling criticisms of rational analysis is that it postures 'under the guise of neutrality' when in fact the value sets and assumptions of the researchers tacitly guide both policy definition and analysis (Clifford, 1978, p. 155). This is often the result of the dichotomisation of the means and ends of decision making, and the resultant separation of the role of decision maker from that of technician-analyst. At the extreme, this results in the case where the analyst is given the objectives determined by the decision maker together with the 'facts' and expected to deliver the one best 'means' which will accomplish the objectives – black box optimality. Even in less extreme cases the value laden aspects of the concepts and procedures of rational techniques are concealed and this fosters the myth of value neutrality. This has caused some people to suggest that the notion of neutrality 'serves primarily as a cover-up to protect the social scientist from moral self-scrutiny and moral question by others' (Ladd, 1975, p. 180). Our argument is not that the roles of analyst and decision maker become confused, but that there is a clearer understanding of the limited parameters that govern each role, and the relationships between them.

The choice of policy problem and the subsequent definition of that problem are also areas where exogenous value judgements play a commanding role. In the former case it is almost always politicians or vocal or influential interests whose values prevail but in the latter, which is part of the conceptual phase of analysis, the analyst often takes part. For example, in the case of 'urban deprivation' those who define the problem as sub-standard facilities have quite different value sets from those who define it as one of inequality (Edwards, 1975). Here it is the case that politicians and analysts who share similar value sets, or what might be termed ideologies, will generally gravitate towards similar types of solutions, which are consistent with the requirements of their values.

Finally, the very choice of one particular rational technique over another is also value laden, often implicitly. This is for one or more of a number of reasons. First, in the research phase, the delineation of the particular options to be considered reflects the combined value sets of politician and analyst, as in the example of urban deprivation. Secondly, the selection of the particular indicators which serve to give dimension to the problem reflect some value choice, usually the analyst's, as to which dimensions are important and which are not. In the urban deprivation example some researchers may therefore emphasise indicators of sub-standardness in housing, health service provision, etc. while others would emphasise indicators of income inequality. Finally, in the evaluative phase, the selection of criteria for judging the acceptability of alternative options is also value laden. Nash et al. (1975a, p. 84) argue that in the case of cost-benefit analysis 'any project selection criteria must reflect some value set ... which determines what things are to count as benefits and costs and how they are traded off against each other' and 'the net social worth of a project depends on the project selection criteria used'. In addition to different value determined methodological options within one technique (like the choice of a discount rate in CBA), different analysts will opt for different rational techniques given their predisposed value sets. Economists will argue that CBA is essential for project appraisal while sociologists will criticise the values underlying CBA and may put forward socio-environmental impact assessment as the most suitable form of policy analysis.

Value judgement or ideology within rational techniques is inevitable and value neutrality impossible. This does not negate the value of rational analysis but it does mean that it is essential that value judgements be expected and made as explicit as possible in the analysis. The pretence (or myth) of value neutral objectivity must be actively discarded and the people best able to do this are the analysts themselves. This is done firstly, by promoting communication between analyst and decision maker to break down as much as possible the means-ends role dichotomy and encourage understanding of the values and limitations of the techniques. Secondly, a kind of intellectual pluralism needs to be institutionalised alongside any analytic operation (Kramer, 1975). This entails formalised debate among different analysts and between analyst and those with other, differing, limited perspectives on the problem at hand. This debate would be fruitful in promoting synthesis among actors to a decision. Thirdly, institutional or 'task-responsibility' must be complemented by a moral responsibility on the part of the analysts (and those who would make use of their services) to make explicit the value judgements within the research (Ladd, 1975). This moral responsibility cannot be abrogated by someone else's responsibility: one cannot say 'it is the politicians' job to point out the value judgements, not mine'.

In addition to this array of endogenous value judgements rational analysts often try to bring their models closer to reality by making use of value judgements exogenous to the analysis itself. These are elicited directly or indirectly from politicians, administrators, experts and the public. These value judgements, which are fed in to the analysis, are often used in the evaluative phase of analysis to 'value-weight' the indicators selected in the research phase. This value-weighting process is the second important role of value judgements in analysis. First, however, the more general use of quantification itself is considered.

Quantification and Qualification

In rational analysis the tendency is to operationalise by way of quantification and many people equate analysis with quantification. The issues and problems associated with quantification are contentious. Some commentators suggest that the advocates of increasing use of quantitative methodology are more concerned about the technical competence of their methodology than about the fit of the postulated rational model to the policy problem at hand (Strauch, 1975). This 'quantificationism' occurs in spite of the obvious illogicality of allowing 'hard' quantitative data to drive out 'soft' qualitative data. The simple cause of these events is that the measurement of quantities and changes in quantities is easy compared with measurement of qualities and changes in qualities and this difficulty is common to most of the rational techniques (Wingo and Evans, 1978). For example in cost-benefit analysis it is the problem of evaluating and pricing extra-market factors which are likely to be subordinated to those factors to which some market value can be ascribed. In environmental impact assessment it is the problem of the non-measurable value of amenities. In social indicators research it gives rise to the distinction between objective and subjective social indicators, and so on.

Even with those factors amenable to quantification there are numerous difficulties. Firstly, many indicators of change are based on tenuous cause and effect relationships which reflect a general lack of theoretical development related to policy analysis. For example, Clark et al. (1978, p. 20) note the claim that 'the assessment of likely impacts included in many EIS's (Environmental Impact Statements) does not stand critical scientific examination' and 'are unsupported by scientific data'. Carley (1979) notes a similar problem in social indicator research. A second problem area is that the aggregating techniques require that diverse indicators be normalised, or related to some common denominator, so they might be compared and contrasted. One common method of doing this is to use monetary values, as in cost-benefit analysis, but of course there are many important factors which cannot be expressed in monetary terms, or even if they could, the choice of a proper figure would be exceedingly difficult. The problems of normalisation and aggregation are explored further in the next section. Finally, if the quantitative information is left unaggregated in its generic form, for example, noise in an environmental impact statement, then it is difficult to assess the meaning of a particular change in the indicator for the people involved. How does one trade-off two decibels of increased noise for x units of increased transport accessibility, especially when these impacts may accrue to different individuals?

One of the main responses to the general problem of quantification and assessing the meaning of change has been the attempt to integrate subjective preference rankings into the rational techniques by using some form of indifference analysis. This approach argues that individuals can differentiate between combinations of alternatives that yield greater or less satisfaction to them, and that it is unnecessary that they be able to measure this exact difference. If alternatives offer the same level of satisfaction the person is 'indifferent'. In this way ordinal rankings can substitute for interval data where that is impossible to obtain. These rankings are usually based on the preferences of politicians, experts, or some sample of the public at large and, although they cannot be aggregated with other data, they do illuminate aspects of the policy problem which might otherwise go unexamined and offer some guidance as to the nature of the trade-offs that might be made. The next section looks at preference rankings in more detail.

A second way of dealing with qualitative impacts is to use sensitivity analysis to establish possible upper and lower, or best and worst, estimates for those impacts and then to demonstrate the effect of the various cases on the different policy choices. This has the advantage of bringing the qualitative impacts into the analytic framework. Related to sensitivity analysis is the development of what Mishan (1976) calls a contingency calculation. This involves rearranging the quantitative analysis so that a potential threshold value for an unknown quantity indicates a possible choice as either obvious in terms of net benefits or absurd in terms of net costs. For example, if net money benefits of mining in a national park equals £250,000 per annum then, rather than try to quantify the value of undisturbed parkland as a whole, this question can be asked: is the value of an undisturbed park more or less than the above amount?

If 1.4 million visitors use the park each year, then a payment of less than 18p each would more than offset the benefit, and it is likely that their visits could be valued at obviously more than that. In some cases such a calculation will show that the unknown quantity is obviously large enough to more than offset any financial gain due to a project. In other, less obvious, cases the contingency calculation may result in political debate which fruitfully addresses itself to the issue.

Fourthly, and more generally, the problem of tenuous cause and effect relationships will be attacked by an increased emphasis on a theoretical approach to the policy sciences with causal relationships explicitly formulated in a model. These models have operationalised concepts and causal relationships expressed in propositions which are empirically tested to establish whether linkages exist between indicators and other unobservable variables. Even in many policy analyses when no hypothesis testing is intended, thinking casually about a problem will facilitate clearer, more rigorous statements and may generate additional insights into policy problems. In addition, there is a trend towards the introduction of indirectly measured qualitative (or subjective) variables into causal models. Blalock (1976), for example, argues that although this introduces additional unknowns into a causal system, those unknowns have always been implicitly present in any event. He suggests that a careful conceptualisation of the causal relationships in a model before data collection commences is a necessary step in incorporating these subjective aspects.

Finally, the problems of quantification are lessened by explicitness in analysis, as were the problems of implementation and value judgements. Although explicitness is hardly a universal panacea, it is in fact a necessary prerequisite for the balanced perspective advocated here. This is crucial because in cases where unmeasurable data is of paramount importance it will mean the analyst will have to be content with weak inferences and suggestions rather than any determinant solutions. In other words, when the amount of uncertainty which unmeasurable aspects introduce into the analytic model mean that no clear statement about a policy problem can be made from a rational perspective it is the analyst's responsibility to state this explicitly.

Aggregation and Value Weighting

Following the necessary quantification of indicators in the research phase of analysis is the choice in the evaluative phase of whether to aggregate (or sum) the resultant data into some simpler composite indicator or to leave it in an unaggregated form. The aggregation usually requires that unlike measures be transformed into a common scale so they can be added together, for example, in studies of housing quality which sum measures of dilapidation and overcrowding into common indicator. This is sometimes followed by a value weighting which attempts to express the differential contribution of each indicator to some person's or group's general quality of life or more specific decision criteria as measured by the composite indicator.

For those who do not support aggregation, the main argument is that it hides or loses information important to the decision process and may serve to obscure the strengths and weaknesses of alternative options (Bisset, 1978). Further, they argue that the value weighting all too often reflects the values of the analysts and not those of the persons who are most affected by the decisions. Rather, the value weighting is best done, they often argue, by elected politicians who when presented with the variety of data important to a decision, make mental trade-offs among alternatives which reflect some sum of the value judgements of the constituents. Those who support aggregative techniques argue, on the other hand, that a completely disaggregated analysis usually results in a mountain of indigestible documentation, and that since aggregation and value weighting are at least implicit in every analysis, there is value in making the process explicit and thus exposing it to scrutiny and debate (Einhorn and McCouch, 1977).

There is in fact no cut and dried answer to the dilemma of aggregation and it is worthwhile to explore the issue further. Nash et al. (1975a) identify some important dimensions of aggregation, especially the questions of 'whose preferences count?' and 'how should they be aggregated?'. Regarding the latter it might be argued that aggregation without value weighting, that is simply adding up the quantified measures converted to some common scale (money, utils, units, etc.) without regard to value judgements solves some problems. For example, we have seen that one school of analysis argues that benefits and costs must be measured in a straightforward fashion in monetary terms without regard for any value judgements on the part of politicians or others (Mishan, 1974). This approach, however, is criticised for implicitly measuring impact significance on the basis of the system of values reflected in the market price mechanism (Lee and Wood, 1978a). Further, this type of approach may simply transfer the value weighting to the choice of indicators and so the choice becomes all important because the scheme presupposes a model of social behaviour which says its components are additive. That might be the case in the housing quality example above, but not the case for example, for measures of health status and social mobility which if combined might give a meaningless indicator. Nor would it necessarily be the case for many combinations of social effects and so, except in a very few cases, some form of value weighting must accompany the aggregation. The key question in the value weighting is of course 'whose?' and three answers are generally put forward: the politician's, the expert's or the public's.

Value weighting based on politicians' preferences takes two forms. The first is to study past government decisions and, if consistent, to use the implicit preferences in those decisions to impute value weights. This has recently been done, for example, in a study by Brent (1979) of the closure of branch railroads lines by British Rail. The revealed preference approach argues that the appropriate source of the expression of such values for weighting is within the political system and that such studies avoid the problems of trying to get potiticians to express preferences directly. It is seen as a useful means for the politician to come to grips with the weightings implicit in past decisions, to use them in all or part if thought satisfactory, or to change them in duration or magnitude in the future if they were wrong. The proponents of the revealed preference approach are quite ready to point out its main limitation: that it is a sufficient, but not necessary, explanation of past behaviour in that it assumes rationality and full information for decision makers – a situation which, as has been belaboured here, does not exist and causes models based on revealed preferences to diverge from reality. However, all models diverge from reality and the approach is a valid if partial perspective on policy problems, especially if similar situations are to occur in the future and the preferences revealed demonstrate a consistent pattern in decision making. British Rail, for example, may embark on more branch line closures in the 1980s and Brent's study may well help to reveal underlying and more specific criteria for decisions than is normally available for public consumption.

The second way of dealing with the politicians' preferences is, of course, to ask them, and then to operate on the assumption that their preferences reflect some democratic mix of their constituents' values. For example, one recent proposal suggested that various combinations of programme outputs could be ranked by asking politicians to put their selected units of output in rank order (Schmid, 1975). The methodology of 'asking' is much the same for politicians as it is for experts and involves either more or less rigorous straightforward interviews or the establishment of some panel which assigns value weights.

For example, one proposal for assessing environmental impact suggested the formation of a weighting panel which would include representatives of government, industry, public interest groups, community organisations and other parties potentially affected by the outcome of the assessment (Sondheim, 1978).

Sometimes weights are developed by way of the Delphi technique which is basically iterative polling with feedback. This involves a group of anonymous experts who are interviewed in two or more rounds, and in each round are presented with the cumulative results of the previous rounds and asked if they would alter their projections accordingly. The end result is the presentation of seemingly concurring expert opinion. Studies of the usefulness and validity of Delphi-generated weights are conflicting: some suggest that Delphi does produce reasonable weightings which stand up to de post facto analysis, others decry its lack of a theoretical base or criticise it on political grounds. Bisset (1978, p. 53), for example, says 'that averaging the implicit weightings of a group of experts is not satisfactory unless it can be demonstrated that such value judgements meet with popular approval'. Delphi is explored further in Chapter 9.

The second means of ascertaining politicians' value preferences, by rigorously designed questionnaires, is another valid if partial approach given that the fairly developed methodology associated with questionnaires can be assumed to sort out the problems connected with their use. As for so-called 'expert' opinion it would be easy and probably fashionable to dismiss it as undemocratic. Nevertheless, there are issues in which value weightings based on estimation by professionals, administrators and others with experience in a given area are useful. These are indirectly related to problem scale and involve those fairly specific problems in which value judgements, attitudes, and social relations play a minimal role. The detailed and fairly routine planning problems pursuant to more general policies can often be weighted, if necessary, by professional opinion, without any great danger to democratic principle. This is not true of more strategic level policy problems where value judgements often constitute the main basis for choice.

Finally, value weighting can be undertaken based on the preferences of some sample of the public. This approach finds favour with numerous authors in a variety of disciplines concerned with policy analysis (Stanley, 1977; Gordon and Niedercorn, 1978). The dissenting voices tend to be those who are critical of any weighting scheme and who feel that disaggregation is the only honest approach to rational analysis. This issue of public participation in the policy process is explored in a later section. First, however, it is worthwhile to look briefly at one way of value weighting, by equity consideration, which often makes use of either revealed preferences or politicians' judgements.

Distributional Equity

One of the most contentious issues in rational analysis is the role of distributional equity – whether 'who gets what?' should explicitly influence the analysts' recommendations as to which option is preferable from a rational perspective. The issue, like many, first arose in relation to cost-benefit analysis (CBA) and the arguments there are generally mirrored in the other techniques.

The mainstream of analysts generally fall into three schools on the issue. The first argues that cost-benefit analysis should remain silent with regard to the distribution of wealth in society as it is only competent to consider questions of efficiency and overall additions to or subtractions from social welfare. The argument is not that questions of distributional equity are unimportant but that equity is best reached through other types of government action like taxes and subsidies, and need not be considered in assessing new programmes. All distributional value weighting should therefore be done *post* analysis by politicians. And since value weighting requires interpersonal comparisons of utility which can only be highly inaccurate, to engage in such an activity is to confuse clients of policy advice or to lend spurious scientific authority to personal prejudices. Other perceived dangers of explicit value weighting are (i) the risk that numerical value weights are determined by non-representative bodies, for example, bureaucrats masquerading as responsible policy makers; and (ii) that such value weights can and would vary not only from country to country but from time to time according to changing power structure and political fashion (Mishan, 1974). Given this line of argument CBA would have nothing to say on programmes like social security specifically designed to redistribute income or wealth and would ignore the redistributive aspects of other programmes like special education for deprived students or motorway construction.

An increasing number of economists, however, now argue that redistributive effects are an important policy consideration. Little and Mirrlees (1974, p. 53), for example, say:

> 'The argument that the project evaluator, if he be a civil servant, should take the existing distribution of income or wealth as ideal (implying that he need not 'weight' the consumption of different

income groups differently), on the grounds that the government has the power to make it what it likes through other measures, principally taxation, does not hold water.'

Analysts of this school recognise that the weighting of costs and benefits according to some judgement about justice or equity is implicit or explicit in any project selection approach. In other words, that some value judgements are exogenous to analysis – our point earlier – and that value judgements on the general scheme of distributional equity are among these. In this case, the economist does not promote any particular income distribution weighting scheme but should certainly consider the implications of any number of schemes put forward by politicians. Meade (1955), for example, argues that the economist's job is to advise various political factions about the implications for economic welfare of their particular set of distribution weights. These weights cannot be objectively tested but 'they are not altogether unnatural. Indeed, they are part of the normal stock in trade of politics' (p. 70). In this view the analyst has an important, neutral, technical role in advising on the social welfare and efficiency implications of any number of redistributive schemes.

Some analysts of this school seek to supplement CBA insofar as it does not sufficiently explore the distributional issues. Within this group are the practitioners of those techniques like the planning balance sheet, which seeks to expand CBA to include sector by sector distributional effects; distributional weighting schemes which are inferred from political behaviour or reflect a decision maker's judgement; and social impact assessments which examines projected impacts on various groups in the community, often by means of surveys. Other techniques (e.g. environmental impact assessments) it should be cautioned, may reject CBA for other reasons (e.g. failure to consider externalities) but may themselves be criticised for ignoring questions of distributional equity.

Finally, a small school takes an overtly value laden stance to distributional equity. Among these are analysts who accept the existing distribution of income and the concept that the market alone can determine value through prices. Others reject this possibility in its entirety in that their value judgements on distributional equity are quite different, for example those who have a Marxist perspective on economics (Edwards, 1977).

Attempts to analyse distributional equity, however laudatory, do face problems. Firstly, redistribution itself may involve administrative and informational costs which have to be considered in the project appraisal. Secondly, identifying exactly who benefits and who bears the costs can be difficult, especially for the latter. And it is quite possible for any one person to benefit and bear costs from the same project, for example, a person who flies a lot and lives near a noisy airport. Thirdly, inter-personal comparisons are fraught with difficulty – a new motorway can be a benefit to a commuter and a cost to his home-working next door neighbour. Fourthly, what economists term the marginal level of utility may vary according to income level, i.e., a pound to a poor man is worth more than a pound to a rich man. Filthy, substantial externalities may make it difficult to identify distributional effects. Lastly, any incorporation of distributional weights by analysts might be viewed as an attempt to usurp decision makers' power.

In conclusion, it can be suggested that equity considerations – who gets the benefits and who pays the costs – are vitally important in most policy issues today and it is no longer sufficient merely to calculate the aggregate costs and benefits of the impacts of a policy. A considerable amount of work on the methodology of assessing distributional impacts remains to be done, however, and at present equity is probably best considered without recourse to a single highly quantified weighting scheme which may mask what are, essentially, value judgements on the nature of income redistribution. This is not to imply, however, that redistributive effects should be ignored. On the contrary, their importance suggests the analyst has a valuable role to play in providing information on the distributional aspects of projects, and the application of a variety of distributional weights in a sensitivity analysis may help demonstrate to decision makers the impacts of various options.

Public Participation and Analysis

In a recent essay on impact assessment Tribe (1976) takes the view that the *process* of policy analysis is at least as important as the result itself. In other words, not only must justice be done, it must be seen to be done. It has been argued here that objective data only takes on meaning when value judgements are applied to it and that these might come from politicians and experts. There are many cases, however, where that is insufficient and the preferences of the public, or some segment of it, must be considered as part of the analysis. In recent years there has been a growing trend towards this in governmental decision making and one only has to look at the interest in motorway inquiries, or applications for new power stations, dams, or nuclear reprocessing facilities, to see it demonstrated.

Figure 6.2   *Simple model of public participation*

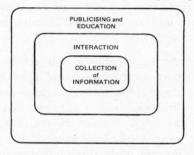

(after Hampton, 1977)

If the models in rational analysis, therefore, are to be drawn closer towards reality, perceptual or subjective indicators based on reports from individuals, i.e. the public, must be considered as a necessary complement to the analysis. These indirectly measured psychological variables reflect general feelings, expectations, and satisfactions of individuals related to the world as described by objective data, and support for or disagreement with the potential changes associated with proposed policy. These subjective measures help determine whether change is in a positive or a negative direction and help assess the priority and sensitivity of particular aspects of the policy in relation to the whole. The generation and measurement of these social and psychological variables is an important task of the analyst and has two benefits. Firstly, in the conceptual and research phases of analysis it assists in defining the dimensions of the policy problem. Better problem formulation and reformulation means a more complete and relevant data base and indicator selection. Secondly, in the analytic phase the information generated by public participation can provide, directly or indirectly, the value weights necessary for any aggregation that is required.

Public participation activities are of three types. Firstly, there is publicising and education, or the dissemination of information to the public; secondly, there is the provision and promotion of opportunities for interaction between the public and those responsible for developing the policy or programme; and thirdly, there is the collection of information which is useful to the policy analysis. In a revised version of Hampton's (1977) model of public participation these three activities are conceptually contained in a nesting of boxes (Figure 6.2). The centre box, collection of information, can only be reached by involvement in the outer boxes – publicising and interaction. In addition to these three activities, there are five dimensions of public participation which must be considered (Montgomery and Esman, 1971):

(1) Scope — the participation may be diffuse or specific, i.e. it may cover all aspects of a policy or just some.

(2) Scale — the problem scale may range from single issue to strategic, from local to national, from specific to abstract. Indications are that participation is easier at the local level.

(3) Size — for each of the three activities some participation group must be identified, i.e. those directly affected, or interested. Size may vary for each box – many more may receive information than interact. The size may be allowed to define itself.

(4) Frequency — participation may be recurring or one-time only. Participatory activities may need to recur at conceptual, research, and evaluative phases.

(5) Directness — interaction may range from face-to-face to mailed information, and response may vary according to the degree the participation group is affected by the proposed policy.

The information collected as a result of a participation exercise can be used to value weight in two ways. First, some researchers argue that such subjective information, sometimes in conjunction with expert opinion, can be used directly to structure an explicit mathematical weighting scheme which in turn can be applied to objective data (Gordon and Niedercorn, 1978). Although such an approach may tend to involve unsupportable causal assumptions and assume a monolithic public instead of one made up of diverse and competing groups, it cannot be dismissed out of hand. For although it is no doubt wise to be wary of those who would quantify the unquantifiable, it is unwise to avoid quantifying the quantifiable. Rank ordering is certainly possible and, as in the planning balance sheet, weights can be associated with different sectors of the public. Again this is best done in a sensitivity analysis framework. The other approach to using this information is to provide it as a complement to the objective data and allow the two kinds of information to be synthesised by the decision maker. This indirect approach avoids many theoretical problems but does carry with it the danger that the decision maker will ignore the information or do the synthesis badly. That, however, is the stuff of political debate and if this seems the best approach the analyst can only exhort that all the relevant opinions be considered.

In either case, measuring many of these subjective aspects is difficult, but the importance of doing so cannot be under-rated and the methodology is steadily improving. The simple surveys of straight-forward questions which suffer from problems such as respondents' strategic behaviour, are now mostly superseded by survey formats using the Likert scale of measuring respondents' satisfactions-dissatisfactions on a five or seven point continuum. This gives a relative intensity of preferences if not interval scales. Other techniques are being developed which may yield interval data, distinguish between personal judgements and judgements about a wider com-munity, and force the respondent to consider simultaneously costs and benefits – a problem for simpler surveys. Such techniques as Clark's (1974) 'budget pies' for assessing citizen preferences in US urban expenditure or the use of priority evaluation games in the UK for evaluating community preferences in environmental and transport planning (Hoinville et al., 1972) may well be applied with other rational techniques. Such a priority evaluation scheme was recently used by London Transport as part of its planning for the rejuvenation of underground stations (Woudhuysen and Law, 1979).

Finally, a criticism is often levelled at participation exercises that they are elitist in that only a small, interested segment of the popula-tion wish to be involved. For example, in environmental matters, the argument is often made that the policies involved (e.g. noise and air pollution abatement, scenic amenity) are basically relevant only to the middle class (Beckerman, 1974). This attitude is partly founded on the casual observation that it is the better-off who participate in public inquiries and argue the case for conservation against motor-ways or new coal mines. However, the most recent research can find no evidence to support this allegation (Pearce, 1978). In any event, as Collins (1978a, p. 45) points out:

'Given the constraints of the framework of government ... and the likely level of resources that could be devoted to public participation over a protracted period it is unreasonable to expect participation to rise above the consensus-building level for anything but a fraction of the population.'

This question of elitism does amplify the point that the three activities of public participation must be actively promoted by those administrators and analysts who hope to realise its value, and that promotion includes providing reasonable access to information at a useful time in the planning process. The value of participation is that it provides information essential for the clarification of most policy problems, and increases the incentives for the public to co-operate with, and appreciate, the policy process. The quality of the information collected and the level of appreciation of the policy process by citizens will be proportional to the amount of publicising and interaction which occur, that is, participation is based on sharing information, which in turn really means sharing power. Unfortunately, some governmental bodies may well resist public participation for this reason. The links between publicising and education, and information collection, are nevertheless quite clear.

Conclusion

One final problem must be mentioned: that of the difference between problem assessment and project assessment. No technique can assess the usefulness of a particular project if, in fact, that project is one of a number of otherwise unexplored options related to a larger problem. In other words, rational techniques work best if the proper problem is being addressed. For example, assessing the relative locational advantages for a new airport is best done in light of a more general transport plan. Similarly, studies of the environmental impact of mining coal in undisturbed agricultural or grazing land will best be undertaken in light of a larger scheme for the development of energy resources. This is a restatement of the problem of unspecified objectives and problem scale but worth additional emphasis for, although policy making sometimes is not or cannot be rational enough to look at the 'larger' problem, it is worthwhile as an ideal.

Part II explores each category of these rational techniques in some detail, including a discussion of the important and contentious issues, and an examination of the similarities and differences between techniques which might be used to aid in integrating two or more analyses of the same problem.

Bibliography: Part I

Ackoff, Russell L., 1976. 'Does Quality of Life Have to be Quantified?' In *Operational Research Quarterly*, Vol. 27, pp. 289–303.

Allison, Graham T., 1971. *Essence of Decision: Explaining the Cuban Missile Crisis*. Boston: Little Brown & Co.

Arrow, Kenneth J., 1954. *Social Choice and Individual Values*, second edition. New York: Wiley.

Barnes, Jack (ed.), 1975. *Educational Priority – Curriculum Innovation in London's EPA's*. London: Her Majesty's Stationery Office.

Barron, Iann and Curnow, Ray, 1979. *The Future with Microelectronics*. London: Francis Pinter.

Beckerman, W., 1974. *In Defence of Economic Growth*. London: Jonathan Cape.

Beer, Anne, 1977. 'Environmental Impact Analysis' In *Town Planning Review*, Vol. 48, pp. 389–96.

Bish, Robert L., 1976. 'The Assumption of Knowledge in Policy Analysis' In *Problems of Theory in Policy Analysis*, Gregg, Phillip M. (ed.), Lexington, Mass: D. C. Heath and Co.

Bisset, R., 1978. 'Quantification, Decision Making and Environmental Impact Assessment in the United Kingdom' In *Journal of Environmental Management*, Vol. 7, pp. 43–58.

Blalock, Herbert M., 1975. 'Indirect Measurement in Social Science – Some Non-Additive Models' In *Quantitative Sociology – International Perspectives on Mathematical and Statistical Modelling*. Blalock et al. (eds.), New York: Academic Press.

Boucher, Wayne I. (ed.), 1977. *The Study of the Future: An Agenda for Research*. Washington: Natural Science Foundation.

Brand, Jack, 1975. 'The Politics of Social Indicators' In *British Journal of Sociology*, Vol. 26, pp. 78–90.

Brent, Robert J., 1979. 'Imputing Weights Behind Past Railway Closure Decisions Within a Cost-Benefit Framework' In *Applied Economics*, Vol. 11, pp. 157–70.

Brooks, Harvey, 1976. 'Environmental Decision Making: Analysis and Values. In Tribe et al., 1976.

Brown, C. V. and Jackson, P. M., 1978. *Public Sector Economics*. London: Martin Robertson.

Bunn, D. W., 1977. 'Policy Analytic Implications for a Theory of Prediction and Decision' In *Policy Sciences*, Vol. 8, pp. 125–34.

Bunn, D. W., 1978. 'Screening Methods in Policy Analysis' In *Socio-Economic Planning Sciences*, Vol. 12, pp. 329–31.

Buxton, M. J. and West, R. R., 1975. 'Cost-Benefit Analysis of Long-Term Haemodialysis for Chronic Renal Failure' In *British Medical Journal*, 17 May, pp. 376–9.

Canadian News Facts, 1978. 'Guaranteed Income Experiment Ended' p. 1884.

Capps, B., 1977. 'Performance Measurement: A Cautious Welcome' In *Municipal and Public Services Journal*, Vol. 85, pp. 1009–10.

Carley, Michael and Walkey, Anna, 1978. *Some Key Elements in Social Impact Assessment.* Paper, Canadian Conference on Social Impact Assessment. Banff.

Carley, Michael, 1979. 'Social Theory and Models in Social Indicator Research' In *International Journal of Social Economics*, Vol. 6, pp. 33–45.

Catlow, J. and Thirlwall, C. G., 1976. *Environmental Impact Analysis.* London: Department of the Environment.

Cazes, B., 1971. 'Opportunities and Pitfalls of Future-Oriented Research' In, Urban, G. R. (ed.), *Can We Survive Our Future?* New York: St Martins Press.

Churchman, C. West, 1975. 'On the Facility, Felicity and Morality of Measuring Social Change' In *Social Accounting: Theories, Issues and Cases.* Seidler, L.J. and Seidler, L.L. (eds.). Los Angeles: Melville Publishers.

Clark, Brian D., Chapman, K., Bisset, R. and Wathern, P., 1978. 'Methods of Environmental Impact Analysis' In *Built Environment*, Vol. 4, pp. 111–21.

Clark, Terry N., 1973. 'Community Social Indicators: From Analytical Models to Policy Applications' In *Urban Affairs Quarterly*, Vol. 9, pp. 3–36.

Clifford, Sue, 1978. 'EIA – Some Unanswered Questions' In *Built Environment*, Vol. 4, pp. 152–60.

Cochrane, A. L., 1972. *Effectiveness and Efficiency.* Nuffield Provincial Hospitals Trust.

Coleman, James S., 1972. *Policy Research in the Social Sciences.* Morristown N.J.: The General Learning Press.

Collins, Neil, 1978. 'Limits of Participation' In *Local Government Studies*, Vol. 4, pp. 39–56.

Cupps, D. Stephen, 1977. 'Emerging Problems of Citizen Participation' In *Public Administration Review*, Vol. 37, pp. 478–87.

Cutt, James, 1975. 'Policy Analysis: A Conceptual Base for a Theory of Improvement' In *Policy Sciences*, Vol. 6, pp. 223–98.

Davies, Bleddyn, 1977. 'Social Service Studies and the Explanation of Policy Outcomes' In *Policy and Politics*, Vol. 5, pp. 41–60.

De Meyer, F. and Plott, C. R., 1970. 'The Probability of a Cyclical Majority' in *Econometrica*, Vol. 38, pp. 345–54.

Dimock, M. E. and Dimock G. O., 1953. *Public Administration.* Chicago: Holt, Rinehart and Winston.

Dror, Yehezkel, 1968. *Public Policymaking Re-examined.* Scranton, Pa: Chandler Publishing.

Dror, Yehezkel, 1971a. *Ventures in Policy Sciences.* New York: American Elsevier.

Dror, Yehezkel, 1971b. *Design for Policy Sciences.* New York: American Elsevier.

Duncan, Otis Dudley, 1969. 'Social Forecasting – The State of the Art' In *The Public Interest*, Vol. 17, pp. 88–118.

Economist, The 1978. 'America's Invigorating Paralysis' Vol. 269, 23 December, pp. 52–5.

Edwards, John, 1975. 'Social Indicators, Urban Deprivation and Positive Discrimination' in *Journal of Social Policy*, Vol. 4, pp. 275–87.

Edwards, Michael, 1977. *The Ideological Function of Cost-Benefit Analysis in Planning.* University of London: Town Planning Discussion Paper No. 25.

Einhorn, H. J. and McCouch, W., 1977. 'A Simple Multiattribute Utility Procedure for Evaluation' In *Behavioural Science*, Vol. 22, pp. 270–82.

Enthoven, Alain C., 1970. 'The Systems Analysis Approach' In *The Administrative Process and Democratic Theory*, Gawthrop L.C., (ed.) Boston: Houghton Mifflin and Co.

Epping Forest District Council, 1977. *Performance Measurement in Local Government.*

Etzioni, Amitai, 1967. 'Mixed Scanning: A "Third " Approach to Decision Making' In *Public Administration Review*, Vol. 28, pp. 385–92.

Finsterbusch, Kurt and Wolf, C. P., 1977. *Methodology of Social Impact Assessment.* Stroudsburg, Pa: Dowden, Hutchinson and Ross.

Fischoff, Baruch, 1977. 'Cost-Benefit Analysis and the Art of Motorcycle Maintenance' In *Policy Sciences*, Vol. 8, pp. 177–202.

Fisher, Gene H., 1977. 'Cost Considerations in Policy Analysis' In *Policy Analysis*, Vol. 3, pp. 107–14.

Forcese, Dennis P. and Richer, Stephen, 1973. *Social Research Methods.* Eaglewood Cliffs, New Jersey: Prentice-Hall.

Foster, C. D. and Beesley, M. E., 1963. 'Estimating the Social Benefit of Constructing an Underground Railway in London' In *Journal of the Royal Statistical Society*, Vol. 126, Series A, pp. 46–92.

Fowles, Jib, 1977. 'The Problem of Values in Futures Research' In *Futures*, Vol. 9, pp. 303–14.

Freeman, Howard E. and Bernstein, Ilene N., 1975. 'Evaluation Research and Public Policies' In Nagel, Stuart S. (ed.), 1975, pp. 9–25.

Fry, Brian R. and Tompkins, Mark E., 1978. 'Some Notes on the Domain of Public Policy Studies' In *Policy Studies Journal*, Vol. 6, pp. 305–13.

Gershuny, J. I., 1978. 'Policy Making Rationality: A Reformulation' In *Policy Sciences*, Vol. 9, pp. 295–316.

Glennerster, Howard, 1975. *Social Service Budgets and Social Policy.* London: George Allen and Unwin.

Goldstein, Michael S., Marcus, Alfred C. and Rausch, N. P., 1978. 'The Non-Utilisation of Evaluation Research' In *Pacific Sociological Review*, Vol. 21, pp. 21–44.

Gordon, Ian, 1978. *On Measuring or Not Measuring Local Welfare.* The Regional Studies Association, London: paper presented to the Conference on Social Indicators in Planning and Policy.

Gordon, Ian, Lewis, Janet and Young, Ken, 1977. 'Perspectives on Policy Analysis' In *Public Administration Bulletin*, Vol. 25, pp. 26–35.

Gordon, Peter and Niedercorn, John H., 1978. 'A Procedure for Fully Evaluating the Anticipated Impacts of Selected Public System Innovations on Various Environments using Citizen-Generated Information Inputs' In *Socio-Economic Planning Sciences*, Vol. 12, pp. 77–83.

Haefele, Edwin T., 1977. 'Towards a New Civic Calculus' In Wingo and Evans, 1977. pp. 268–79.

Hakim, C., 1978. *Social and Community Indicators from the Census.* London: Office of Population, Censuses and Surveys.

Hampton, William, 1977. 'Research into Public Participation in Structure Planning' In Sewell and Coppock, 1977.

Haveman, Robert H. and Weisbrod, Burton A., 1975. 'Defining Benefits of Public Programs: Some Guidance for Policy Analysts' In *Policy Analysis*, Vol. 1, pp. 169–96.

Haveman, Robert and Watts, H. W., 1976. 'Social Experimentation as Policy Research: A Review of Negative Income Tax Experiments' In *Evaluation Studies Review Annual*, Vol. 1. Glass, G.V. (ed.). London: Sage Publications.

Hill, Morris, 1968. 'A Goals-Achievement Matrix for Evaluating Alternative Plans' In *Journal of the American Institute of Planners*, Vol. 34, pp. 19–28.

Hoinville, Gerald and Prescott-Clark, Patricia, 1972. *Traffic Disturbance and Amenity Values*. London: Social and Community Planning Research.

Holroyd, P., 1978. 'Change and Discontinuity: Forecasting for the 1980's' In *Futures*, Vol. 10, pp. 31–43.

Hy, Ronn, 1976. 'Futures Research and Policy Studies' In *Policy Studies Journal*, Vol. 4, pp. 416–24.

Jeffers, John N. R., 1978. *An Introduction to Systems Analysis with Ecological Applications*. London: Edward Arnold.

Jenkins, W. I., 1978. *Policy Analysis: A Political and Organisational Perspective*. London: Martin Robertson.

Johnston, Denis F., 1978. 'Social Indicators and Social Forecasting' In Fowles, Jib. (ed.), *Handbook of Futures Research*. Westport and London: Greenwood Press.

Kramer, Fred A., 1975. 'Policy Analysis as Ideology' In *Public Administration Review*, Vol. 35, pp. 509–17.

Kirk, J. H. and Sloyan M. J., 1978. 'Cost-Benefit Study of New Covent Garden Market' In *Public Administration*, Vol. 56, pp. 35–50.

Ladd, John, 1975. 'Policy Studies and Ethics' In Nagel, Stuart S. (ed.). pp. 177–84.

Land, Kenneth C., 1975. 'Theories, Models and Indicators of Social Change' In *International Social Science Journal*, Vol. 27, pp. 7–37.

Laszlo, E., 1972a. *Introduction to Systems Philosophy – Towards a New Paradigm of Contemporary Thought*. Gordon Publishing.

Laszlo, E., 1972b. *The Systems View of the World*. New York: Brazilier.

Lee, Norman and Wood, Christopher, 1978a. 'EIA – A European Perspective' In *Built Environment*, Vol. 4, pp. 101–10.

Levine, James, Musheno, Michael and Palumbo, Dennis, 1975. 'The Limits of Rational Choice in Evaluating Criminal Justice Policy' In Nagel, Stuart S. (ed.), 1975, pp. 89–104.

Lewis, Janet and Flynn, Rob, 1979. 'The Implementation of Urban and Regional Planning Policies' In *Policy and Politics*, Vol. 7, pp. 123–42.

Lichfield, N., 1971. 'Cost-Benefit Analysis in Planning: A Critique of the Roskill Commission' In *Regional Studies*, Vol. 5, pp. 157–83.

Lilienfield, Robert, 1978. *The Rise of Systems Theory: An Ideological Analysis*. New York: Wiley-Interscience.

Lindblom, Charles E., 1968. *The Policy Making Process*. Englewood Cliffs, N.J.: Prentice Hall.

Lineberry, R. L., 1979. 'Pricing the Welfare State?' Paper presented to Symposium on Decentralisation and Diversity, Policy Studies Institute, London.

Little, I. M. D. and Mirrlees, J. A., 1974. *Project Appraisal for Developing Countries*. London: Heinemann Educational Books.

Local Government Operational Research Unit, 1976. *Development Plan Evaluation and Robustness*. London: Department of the Environment.

Longbottom, D. A., 1977. *Resource Allocation Techniques for Public Services*. Durham University Research Paper No. 2.

Lonsdale, Alan J., 1978. 'Judgement Research in Policy Analysis' In *Futures*, Vol. 10, pp. 213–24.

Luft, Harold S., 1976. 'Benefit Cost Analysis and Public Policy Implementation. In *Public Policy*, Vol. 24, pp. 437–62.

Lyden, Fremont J. and Miller, Ernest G. (eds.), 1978. *Public Budgeting: Program Planning and Evaluation*, 3rd edition. Chicago: Rand McNally College Publishing.

Luce, R. D. and Raiffa, H., 1957. *Games and Decisions*. New York: Wiley.

Majone, C. and Wildavsky, A., 1978. 'Implementation as Evolution' In *Policy Studies Review Annual*, Vol. 2, Beverley Hills and London: Sage.

Maynard, Alan, 1979. *Pricing the Welfare State?* Paper presented to Symposium on Decentralisation and Diversity, Policy Studies Institute, London.

McHale, John and McHale, M. V., 1976. 'An Assessment of Futures Studies Worldwide' In *Futures*, Vol. 8, pp. 135–45.

Meade, J. E., 1955. *Trade and Welfare*. London: Oxford University Press

Meltsner, Arnold J., 1976. *Policy Analysts in the Bureaucracy*. Berkeley: University of California Press.

Meltsner, Arnold J., 1979. 'Don't Slight Communication: Some Problems of Analytical Practice' In *Policy Analysis*, Vol. 5. pp. 367–92.

Merewitz, Leonard and Sosnick, Stephen H., 1971. *The Budget's New Clothes: A Critique of Planning – Programming – Budgeting and Cost-Benefit Analysis*. Chicago: Rand McNally College Publishing.

Mishan, E. J., 1974. 'Flexibility and Consistency in Project Evaluation' In *Economica*, Vol. 41, pp. 81–96.

Mishan, E. J., 1976. *Elements of Cost-Benefits Analysis*, Second edition. London: George Allen and Unwin.

Montgomery, John D. and Esman, Milton J., 1971. 'Popular Participation in Development Administration' In *Journal of Comparative Administration*, Vol. 3, pp. 358–82.

Moore, Terry, 1978. 'Why Allow Planners To Do What They Do? A Justification from Economic Theory' In *Journal of the American Institute of Planners*, Vol. 44, pp. 387–98.

Nagel, Stuart S. (ed.), 1975. *Policy Studies and the Social Sciences*. Lexington, Massachusetts: D. C. Heath and Co.

Nagel, Stuart and Neef, Martin, 1978. 'Finding an Optimum Choice, Level, or Mix in Public Policy Analysis' In *Public Administration Review*, Vol. 38, pp. 404–12.

Nash, Christopher, Pierce, David and Stanley, John, 1975. 'Criteria for Evaluating Project Evaluation Techniques' In *Journal of the American Institute of Planners*, Vol. 41, pp. 83–9.

Nelkin, D., 1977. *Technical Decisions and Democracy: European Experiments in Public Participation*. Beverley Hills and London: Sage Publications.

Nijkamp, Peter, 1977. 'Stochastic Quantitative and Qualitative Multicriteria Analysis for Environmental Design' In *Regional Science Association Papers*. Morgan D. Thomas (ed.), Vol. 39, pp. 175–99.

Olsen, Marvin E. and Merwin, Donna, 1977. 'Towards a Methodology for Conducting Social Impact Assessments Using Quality of Life Social Indicators' In Finsterbusch and Wolf (eds.).

Olson, Mancur, 1973. 'Evaluating Performance in the Public Sector' In *The Measurement of Economic and Social Performance*, Milton, Moss (ed.). New York: National Bureau of Economic Research.

Pearce, D. W., 1978a. *The Social Incidence of Environmental Costs and Benefits*. University of Aberdeen: Occasional Paper No. 78–08.

Pearce, D. W., 1978b. *The Valuation of Social Cost*. London: George Allen and Unwin.

Pedersen, Kjeld Møller, 1977. 'A Proposed Model for Evaluation Studies' In *Administrative Science Quarterly*, Vol. 22, pp. 306–17.

Pigou, A. C., 1924. *Economics of Welfare*, Second edition. London: Macmillan.

Poland, Orville F., 1974. 'Programme Evaluation and Administrative Theory' In *Public Administration Review*, Vol. 34, pp. 333–8.

Prest, A. R. and Turvey, R., 1965. 'Cost-Benefit Analysis: A Survey' In *The Economic Journal*, Vol. 75, pp. 683–735.

Quade, E. S. and Boucher, W. I., 1968. *Systems Analysis and Policy Planning: Applications in Defense.* New York: American Elsevier.

Rawls, John, 1972. *A Theory of Justice.* Oxford: Clarendon Press.

Rein, Martin and White, Sheldon H., 1977. 'Can Policy Research Help Policy?' In *The Public Interest,* Vol. 49, pp. 119–36.

Reynolds, James F., 1975. 'Policy Sciences: A Conceptual and Methodological Analysis' In *Policy Sciences,* Vol. 6, pp. 1–27.

Rittel, Horst W. J. and Webber, Melvin M., 1973. 'Dilemmas in a General Theory of Planning' In *Policy Sciences,* Vol. 4, pp. 155–69.

Rokeach, Milton, 1973. *The Nature of Values.* Glencoe: The Free Press.

Schmid, A. Allan, 1975. 'Systematic Choice among Multiple Outputs of Public Projects Without Prices' In *Social Indicators Research,* Vol. 2, pp. 275–86.

Scioli, Frank P. and Cook, Thomas J., 1975. *Methodologies for Analysing Public Policies.* Lexington, Mass: D. C. Heath and Co.

Seidler, L. J. and Seidler, L. L. (eds.), 1975. *Social Accounting: Theories Issues, and Cases.* Los Angeles: Melville Publishing.

Self, Peter, 1970. 'Nonsense on Stilts: Cost-Benefit Analysis and the Roskill Commission' In *The Political Quarterly,* Vol. 41, pp. 249–60.

Self, Peter, 1972. *Administrative Theories and Politics.* London: George Allen and Unwin.

Self, Peter, 1974. 'Is Comprehensive Planning Possible and Rational?' In *Policy and Politics,* Vol. 2, pp. 193–203.

Self, Peter, 1975. *Econocrats and the Policy Process.* London: Macmillan.

Sen, Amartya, 1975. 'The Concept of Efficiency' In *Contemporary Issues in Economics.* Parkin M. and Nobay A. (eds.). Manchester University Press.

Sewell, W. R. Derrick and O'Riordan, Timothy, 1976. 'The Culture of Participation in Environmental Decision Making' In *Natural Resources Journal,* Vol. 16, pp. 1–22.

Sewell, W. R. Derrick and Coppock, J. T. (eds.), 1977. *Public Participation in Planning.* London: John Wiley and Sons.

Shapiro, S. P., 1979. 'Environmental Protection for Whom?' In *Social Policy,* Vol. 10, pp. 24–9.

Simon, Herbert A., 1957. *Administrative Behaviour,* Second edition. Glencoe: The Free Press.

Simon, Herbert A., Smithburg, Donald W. and Thompson, Victor A., 1958. *Public Administration.* New York: Knopf.

Smith, Brian, 1976. *Policy Making in British Government.* London: Martin Robertson.

Smyth, R. B., 1976. 'Evaluation – Where Next?' In *Town Planning Quarterly,* Vol. 44, pp. 24–9.

Sondheim, Mark W., 1978. 'A Comprehensive Methodology for Assessing Environmental Impact' In *Journal of Environmental Management,* Vol. 6, pp. 27–42.

Stanley, John K., 1977. 'An Evaluation of Residential Area Improvement Strategies from the Residents Viewpoint' In *Socio-Economic Planning Sciences,* Vol. 2, pp. 147–53.

Stern, George J. A., 1976. 'SOSIPing, or Sophistical Obfuscation of Self-Interest and Prejudice' In *Operational Research Quarterly,* Vol. 27, pp. 915–29.

Strauch, Ralph E., 1975. 'Squishy Problems and Quantitative Methods' In *Policy Sciences,* Vol. 6, pp. 175–84.

Strauch, Ralph E., 1976. 'A Critical Look at Quantitative Methodology' In *Policy Analysis,* Vol. 2, pp. 121–44.

Stuart, M., 1978. 'Reports Mountain Grows' In *The Guardian,* 27 November.

Tribe, L. H., 1976. 'Ways Not to Think About Plastic Trees' In Tribe et al., 1976, pp. 61–91.

Tribe, L. H., Schelling, C. S. and Voss, J., 1976. *When Values Conflict – Essays on Environmental Analysis, Discourse and Decision.* Cambridge, Mass: Ballinger Publishing.

Tullock, Gordon, 1967. 'The General Irrelevance of the General Possibility Theorem' In *Quarterly Journal of Economics*, Vol. 81, pp. 256–70.

Tullock, Gordon and Wagner, Richard E., 1976. 'Rational Models, Politics and Policy Analysis' In *Policy Studies Journal*, Vol. 4, pp. 408–17.

Ukeles, Jacob B., 1977. 'Policy Analysis: Myth or Reality?' In *Public Administration Review*, Vol. 37, pp. 223–28.

United Nations, 1975. *Towards a System of Social and Demographic Statistics.* ST/ESA/STAT/SER.F/18. New York: Department of Economic and Social Affairs.

United Nations Environmental Programme, 1979. *Guidelines for Assessing Industrial Environmental Impact and Criteria for the Siting of Industry.* Nairobi: UNEP.

Walker, Warren E., 1978. *Public Policy Analysis: A Partnership Between Analysts and Policymakers.* Los Angeles: Rand paper 6074.

Waters, W. G. II, 1976. 'Impact Studies and the Evaluation of Public Policies' In *Annals of Regional Sciences*, Vol. 10, pp. 98–103.

Weiss, Carol H., 1972. *Evaluation Research – Methods of Assessing Program Effectiveness.* Englewood Cliffs, N.J.: Prentice Hall.

Weiss, Carol H., 1977. 'Research for Policy's Sake: The Enlightenment Function of Social Research' In *Policy Analysis*, Vol. 3, pp. 531–46.

Wildavsky, Aaron, 1966. 'The Political Economy of Efficiency' In *Public Administration Review*, Vol. 26, pp. 292–310.

Wildavsky, Aaron, 1969. 'Rescuing Policy Analysis from PPBS' In *Public Administration Review*, Vol. 29, pp. 189–201.

Williams, Alan, 1972. 'Cost-Benefit Analysis: Bastard Science? and/or Insidious Poison in the Body Politick?' In *Journal of Public Economics*, Vol. 1, pp. 199–225.

Williams, Alan and Anderson, Robert, 1975. *Efficiency in the Social Services.* London: Basil Blackwell.

Wilner, Daniel, 1974. *Evaluation: The State of the Technical Art.* Washington: Paper presented at the National Conference on Evaluation in Alcohol, Drug Abuse, and Mental Health Programs.

Wingo, Lowden and Evans, Alan, (eds.), 1977. *Public Economics and the Quality of Life.* Baltimore and London: The Johns Hopkins University Press.

Wolf, C. P., 1974. *Social Impact Assessment: The State of the Art.* Milwaukee: Environmental Design Research Association.

Woudhuysen, J. and Law, H., 1979. 'Underground Transport: How To Do It Right' In *Design*, No. 371, pp. 42–7.

Wynne, N., 1975. 'The Rhetoric of Consensus Politics: A Critical Review of Technology Assessment' In *Research Policy*, Vol. 4, pp. 108–58.

Zapf, Wolfgang, 1975. 'Systems of Social Indicators: Current Approaches and Problems' In *International Social Science Journal*, Vol. 27, pp. 479–98.

PART II

PART 3.1

7　Cost-Utility Techniques

In Chapter 5 a number of rational techniques were grouped under the generic heading 'cost-utility' and it was suggested that most were related in some way to the most well-known of the techniques – cost-benefit analysis. We noted that the cost-benefit approach evolved from the work of the economist A. C. Pigou, who argued that neo-classical equilibrium economics could no longer ignore the concept of social costs which might cause public welfare to differ from private welfare. This difference reflected an imperfect working of the market economy and a possible role for state intervention in the workings of that economy. The kind of government intervention indicated in Pigou's argument often related to collective, or public, goods like police services, roads, defence, sewers, clean rivers, etc. These public goods cannot be bought and sold like private goods as the benefits they confer are spread across the population at large and cannot be limited to those people willing to pay for them.

The implications of the provision of these public goods, and of the concept of social cost, for public resource allocations decisions are twofold. First, that social costs include side-effects of production and consumption activities which do not involve any corresponding payments. These are termed externalities, and they may be positive or negative, that is, costs or benefits. They must be considered in any policy decision. Secondly, the valuation of social costs and benefits may not have an analogue in the market mechanism which gives private sector prices, and even where such an analogue does exist the prices indicated may still need to be adjusted for market related distortions.

Cost-utility analysis attempted to fill the need for resource allocation which took into account externalities and public sector pricing. Cost-benefit analysis (CBA), the first of the cost-utility techniques, involves the prediction and valuation, in money terms, of the losses and gains in economic welfare, or social costs and benefits, which are incurred by society if a project or programme is undertaken. The main tasks of the economist doing a CBA are to identify the right costs and benefits to be considered in the analysis, and to estimate the various prices to be assigned to those. If market prices are unavailable, or inappropriate, the CB analyst spends a considerable amount of effort developing surrogate, or 'shadow', prices which are used to value costs and benefits.

CBA is generally used in comparing projects or programmes competing for the same resources and in determining whether any one of these contributes a net economic benefit to public welfare, that is, whether a project meets a social welfare criterion. The best known of these criterion is that of Pareto optimality: a resource allocation pattern is worthwhile if at least one person is made better off while no one else is made worse off. While the Pareto criterion seems unexceptionable enough in principle, in practice it is not very workable in that in virtually every case of resource allocation in the public sector there are net gainers and net losers – at the end of the day somebody is worse off because of various transfers of resources.

This limitation in the Pareto criterion led to the formulation by Kaldor (1939) and Hicks (1939) of a normative welfare criterion which now forms the conceptual basis for much CBA. The Hicks–Kaldor test argues that social welfare is increased if either a Pareto improvement is made or if the net gainers in the allocation pattern *could* compensate the net losers to the extent that they would be no worse off after the reallocation of resources – a potential Pareto improvement. The emphasis is on the could, and compensation need not occur. This is essentially an efficiency criterion and purposefully ignores the specific consideration of distributional equity. This stance is now maintained most notably by Mishan (1974) who argues that the net losers will be compensated in the long run by the diversity and redistributive effect of the overall government programme. A different perspective is argued by Little (1957) (and others) who add to the Hicks–Kaldor criterion the proviso that the worth of any reallocation of resources must also be judged on its redistributive effects as otherwise the resulting distribution of income is implicitly seen as a necessarily good distribution. An extension of this line of argument is that, within the CBA itself, special weighting should be given to costs and benefits accruing to particularly disadvantaged groups in society (Nash et al., 1975b). However, if net losers belong to future generations, then questions of redistribution may become very difficult. Given these differing perspectives on the relevant social welfare criterion to be used in the CBA, we can say the immediate purpose of a CBA is usually to determine if social welfare is greater with a proposed reallocation of resources than without, and may include consideration of who should be compensated, by whom, and by what means.

CBA requires that benefits and cost be converted by money terms.

Arguments that some things in life are beyond money (Ackoff, 1976) are countered by noting that money provides a very convenient unit for measurement, that many things are costed in any event, and that where they are not they are given an implicit value by the very act of resource allocation (Pearce, 1978b). This emphasis on monetarisation means that CBA is most useful in projects involving long-range capital expenditures with benefits susceptible to money measures. In many cases, however, it is impossible to measure benefits or it is otherwise not necessary to do so, where end benefit (e.g. crime reduction) is an agreed objective.

Where benefits are not monetised CBA gives way to the related cost-effectiveness analysis (CEA) which compares non-monetary benefits to monetary and non-monetary costs. The benefits are usually measured in various physical units and the analysis tries to identify the best mix of inputs (least costs) which accomplish or satisfy the stated objectives (benefits) in terms of unit costs of outputs. CEA is very useful for human resource and social service programmes which generally lack money measured outputs, and where the problem is either to appraise different ways of meeting objectives or to determine optimum programme size. This might be the case, for example, where benefits are related to health, security, or equality. Bebbington (1978), for example, in examining UK local authority research requirements finds that one problem in six is specifically a cost-effectiveness problem. CEA, he notes, is particularly well suited to the problem often faced by government departments in a recession: how to maintain standards while reducing expenditure. CEA, unlike CBA, generally involves fixed benefit but otherwise the techniques are very similar, especially in the measurement of costs. The measurement of non-monetary benefits in CEA is much the same as in output studies in evaluation research, which are considered in Chapter 10.

Measuring Costs and Benefits

Two concepts of cost are important in CBA and these have been termed financial costs and resource costs, sometimes called budget and economic costs respectively. Financial costs are closely related to the ordinary usage of the term cost and are the monetary values of the actual goods and services used in carrying out a particular policy, conducting a programme or delivering a service. These are the costs of material, manpower, facilities, information, administration, and other overheads which often have market values and are easily expressed in monetary terms. Resource costs, on the other hand, involve 'opportunities foregone' and refer to the benefit which might have been gained had the resources been employed in their next best alternative use – the lack of this benefit is a project cost. For example, the opportunity cost of a flood control scheme is the value of the resources which might have been put to their next best use, say in water pollution control. The examination of resource costs and benefits must include consideration of the externalities associated with a project, and the extent that these externalities are to be incorporated in the analysis is an issue discussed later. For CBA, of course resource costs and benefits must be expressed in monetary terms.

Where market prices are distorted or absent costs and benefits are usually determined by developing 'shadow prices' in one of three ways. The first is an inferred behaviour approach. This involves establishing an analogue for the non-existent market by finding out the value people place on one good for which they do not pay money by inferring it from the price they pay for a different good which they value equally. Alternatively, this approach generalises from one set of observations of consumer behaviour to many more. It is used most widely in transport studies to value trade-offs in journey time against money and in recreational studies where the value of an amenity (e.g. a National Park) is inferred from the costs people are willing to pay to get there. For many situations, however, finding a surrogate market entails many difficulties. For example, trade-offs may be unclear: for some people (the 'Sunday driver') the very act of journeying has an amenity value in itself. On the other hand, willingness to journey to a National Park may well be a function of the location of alternative types of recreation: a person who lives on the sea may feel less of a compunction to travel to the mountains than does a person who lives near neither.

A second means of pricing costs and benefits is what Pearce (1978b, p. 27) terms the alternative cost approach. This involves finding the minimum money expenditure necessary to remove a social cost or to provide a social benefit. For example, removing a certain pollutant from a lake might cost a minimum of x. One cost then of the development of a factory which added more pollutants to that lake could be deduced from x. A problem with this approach, however, is that in many cases the value of x will not be clear. Pearce warns that what may appear at first glance to be an alternative cost is often only partial compensation for disbenefits. For example, the provision of soundproofing to homes near an airport mitigates only the cost of noise inside a building and says nothing about exterior noise, or even what happens when a window is opened.

The third approach to valuation is the direct one – to ask people in a survey. And although economists have tended to shun this in favour of the inferred behaviour approach, it has received some attention especially by market researchers and planners. This approach requires two assumptions: first, that the respondent has sufficient knowledge about his situation to answer with a relative degree of accuracy and secondly, that the respondent is honest and does not engage in strategic behaviour of one sort or another. The attitude survey is the most common of these techniques and can provide important information on relative values for costs and benefits, but with no facility for translation into money values. Recently other techniques such as planning games and 'budget pies' have been developed by which respondents must consider costs and benefits simultaneously, trade-off money values for various government services, and so indicate 'prices'. These techniques are still fairly experimental and their value depends greatly on the knowledge and honesty assumptions being fulfilled. Nevertheless, in cases where no other method of shadow pricing is possible, the use of questionnaires is always preferable to no information at all, and usually preferable to guesswork. Mishan (1976), for example, warns that the economist in earnest about developing the CBA technique will give serious thought to the possibilities of surveys.

Direct and Indirect Costs and Benefits

One important distinction in CBA is between direct and indirect effects, sometimes called primary and secondary. Direct effects are increases or decreases in well-being, or real value of output, resulting from a particular resource allocation. The most obvious direct effect is the benefit of greater physical production, for example, electricity from a hydroelectric project. Direct effects may also arise from changes in quality of service delivery, for example, reduced journey times in transport schemes, or the provision of new services or amenities, for example, recreational fishing and boating on the lake backed up by the dam in the hydroelectric project. This latter effect may also involve direct costs like forestry resources flooded or recreational amenities lost due to valley flooding.[1] Indirect effects are indirectly generated by the resource allocation and are usually taken to describe income multiplier effects induced by the allocation, and other effects stemming from the allocation. Around the newly created lake, for example, hotels and restaurants may be constructed as a result of the

---

[1] Another version of this example is found in Haveman and Weisbrod (1975).

demand created by the recreational activity – the profits associated with these can be considered indirect effects.

The extent to which indirect effects enter into the CBA calculations is a matter of some contention among economists and the history of the argument is documented elsewhere (Sassone and Schaffer, 1978, pp. 38–40). One thing worth remembering is that the distinction is in a sense arbitrary in that what is really being considered is a spectrum of costs and benefits ranging from the most direct to the most indirect. Otherwise a general rule of thumb on inclusion or exclusion depends on the employment situation in the economy. If the increasingly unlikely condition of full employment exists then indirect effects are excluded from the CBA calculus on the grounds that they are transfer payments, that is that any resources used in promoting indirect effects must be diverted from somewhere else in the economy and the overall benefit remains unchanged. In the more likely situation of under-utilised labour resources in the form of national or regional unemployment, however, indirect effects may indeed generate benefit in excess of the second-best alternative (which might be workers doing nothing) and would have to be considered in the CBA. The extent of this consideration would have to be based on some evaluation of the opportunity costs foregone. For example, if construction workers building the resorts around the above lake were previously unemployed then their wages would be an indirect project benefit, as well as a direct cost, and the end resource cost of their labour would be nil.

Related to the question of transfer payments is the distinction between real (sometimes termed rather confusingly 'technological') effects and pecuniary effects. A real effect is one which results in a change in social welfare, consumption or production opportunities, consumer satisfaction, or unit costs for a given level of output. A pecuniary effect, on the other hand, is a change in some people's welfare at the expense of others. It is a redistribution of income and does not reflect any net gain in social welfare. As such it may be ignored in the classic CBA unless some specific social judgement is made that such a transfer payment confers real benefit on society.

Boundaries of Analysis

A different but related distinction must be drawn between external and internal effects, and making this distinction defines the scope of the analysis. Internal effects accrue directly or indirectly to the agency, administrative unit, or target or client population of that unit or agency. External effects are those which fall on anyone not encompassed by the definition of the internal boundary and are unexpected benefits received for which no payment is made, or costs imposed with no direct compensation. For example, in the assessment of the location of a new airport, foreign travellers may receive certain benefits without payment, just as local residents may suffer cost (noise) without compensation. Collectively the defined external effects are externalities.

The boundary definition may take a number of forms (Haveman and Weisbrod, 1975). A national perspective defines all effects on persons within a country as internal. Boundaries might also distinguish one region or area such as a town or a river valley from the rest of a country, or the client group of one agency from the remainder of citizens. Finally, a boundary might be drawn between those in receipt of direct effects and those in receipt of indirect effects. This, however, would ignore externalities and as such have only limited private sector application, if at all.

These boundary distinctions determine the scope of the analysis carried out. At one end of a continuum is the general, or system-wide, analysis which attempts to take into account the wide variety of interdependencies in an economy and consider variables which might be relevant rather than those which are obviously relevant. Such interdependencies may exist in geographical aspects, for example, in pollution control where river water quality is affected by the variety of water intake and sewage treatment facilities upstream from an area under consideration. Cost considerations are also highly interdependent. Pollution control equipment for a single installation might be highly expensive, if required for a number of installations the price may drop. In the social services field interdependencies between agencies should be considered, for example, increased health services for homeless alcoholics might have considerable effects on policing patterns. At the extreme, in a system-wide CBA, costs and benefits and indirect effects would be calculated for society as a whole. In fact, in most pluralistic societies, what is important is the calculation of costs and benefits as they affect various sectors of the population and the general CBA includes many relevant groups with a cost-benefit equation for each (Roth, 1978).

The likely case is that the CBA will be partial, or specific, and consider the interdependencies of only some variables, i.e., a number of indirect effects will be ignored. In many situations this is obviously the more practical and cost-effective approach. The most obvious difficulty with the partial approach is the danger of ignoring relevant externalities. The potential importance of externalities depends to a large extent on whether they support or conflict with the appraisal based on the direct effects. If they are supportive then it may make little difference if they are underplayed. If they are conflicting, however, their measurement may be critical for a fair assessment (Stewart, 1978, p. 156). Another difficulty is that if the analysis is partial in the sense that it is regional or local then there may be data problems especially if the project boundaries, which might be chosen on geographical grounds (a river basin) does not conform to existing political units or statistical units for which data is available. And if the analysis is confined to a particular region care must be taken to ensure that ignored effects external to the study region, or 'spillovers', would in fact be inconsequential to the outcome of the analysis. Finally, the level of analysis, and the significance of externalities, will vary with the magnitude of projects in question. Small projects are more unlikely to have significant externalities and at the partial or specific CBA level with small projects the analysis may well proceed to something like an actual cost-benefit ratio. With any undertaking with a large number of interdependencies and significant externalities, however, the CBA will serve to enlighten the problem, but hardly to indicate a decision. This range from partial to general CBA is along the continuum from issue to strategic analysis discussed in Chapter 3.

Tangible and Intangible Effects

Except perhaps for consideration of income distribution, no issue has generated more disagreement and spawned more alternatives to CBA than the distinction between tangible and intangible costs and benefits. Tangible benefits to the CB analyst are those which can be valued in monetary terms with prices or shadow prices. The definition of intangibles is unfortunately open to considerable dispute and most definitions are really about two different concepts. These are:

(a) effects which cannot be measured in money terms but can or might be quantified, and
(b) effects which cannot be measured or quantified.

Haveman and Weisbrod (1975) prefer the term intangible for (a) and immeasurable for (b). *Cost-Benefit Analysis – A Handbook* (Sassone and Schaffer, 1978) on the other hand, calls (a) uncommensurables and (b) intangibles. Roth (1978) prefers unpriceables for (a) and immeasurables for (b) and this is probably the best terminology. In any event the question of how to deal with (a) and (b) in CBAs, which are supposed to deal with money values, is of great and unresolved contention and its echo reverberates throughout rational analysis in the form of the quantification – qualification issue discussed in the last chapter. A few economists argue that intangible effects, like income distributional effects, are outside the scope of CBA and should be understood by decision makers as such. The reasoned response to this line is that they then may well be ignored altogether in the decision or severely undervalued in the face of a priced data. Most analysts follow the approach suggested by Haveman and Weisbrod (1975) that (i) any such effects be described as explicitly as possible, and where feasible in quantitative units and (ii) that sensitivity analysis be used to establish potential maximum and minimum values for unmeasured effects and their impact on net benefits, and (iii) that the CBA be presented in such a way as to indicate how valuable the intangibles will have to be to make a project economically worthwhile, that is, the CBA will include a contingency calculation.

Finally, it is worth noting that as various dimensions of 'quality of life' assume increasing importance in our lives it is likely that the issue of intangibles will become more, rather than less, important in CBA and related techniques. One issue which falls on the borderline between the tangible and intangible is the valuation of life itself. Some argue that life cannot be valued in monetary terms. Others, however, counter reasonably that such cost versus life valuations are done regularly, if implicitly, by government in resource allocation decisions and in the setting of various health and safety guidelines. Investment in health care is an obvious example, others are highway upgrading programmes or the setting of airline safety standards. In each case some trade-off between cost to government or private industry and the possibility or probability of injury or death is made. The attachment of a probability figure to a possible occurrence is called risk assessment, which is considered shortly. Mishan (1976) contains a useful discussion of the evaluation of accidents and death in CBA.

The Discount Rate

Most public sector investments will have the costs and benefits spread out over a number of years with costs incurred early in the project life and benefits accruing later. This is true of capital intensive projects like power plants as well as in the social services, for example, in health and education. A problem arises in that most people value benefits in the present higher than those in the future, while future costs are valued lower than present costs. That the present value of costs and benefits should be different from their value at the time they occur is generally accepted as is the need for a formula for reducing benefit value by an increasing amount the more years into the future they occur. For example, a benefit of £100 next year may be worth only £90 to us this year. What is contentious, however, is the choice of a discount rate for converting future value into net present value, that is deciding what rate will accurately reflect the value of £100 next year in this year. Too low a rate overvalues future benefit, and socially inefficient projects may result, while too high a rate unfairly reduces the estimated value of the public investment.

There are basically two schools of thought on the choice of a discount rate (Brown and Jackson, 1978, p. 167). One is the 'social opportunity cost of capital' school which argues that the role of the discount rate is to be a measure of the next best alternative use to which the resources employed in the project might otherwise have been put. Within this school some economists take the view advanced by Baumol (1969) that the rate of return on investment in the private sector accurately reflects the opportunity costs in the economy and that this is an appropriate discount rate for a public sector project. Other economists argue that public sector investments should be judged by a social discount rate which reflects the higher social return on public investment attributable to beneficial externalities which do not occur in private investments (Marglin, 1963). This may be true for some public investments and not for others. In either case, the identification of a single rate of return for a particular sector of the economy can be most difficult.

A second school of thought, the 'social rate of time preference' school, stresses the need for the discount rate to reflect society's evaluation of the relative desirability of receiving benefit and cost at different periods in the future. The analyst's task is to determine what these evaluations mean in terms of a discount rate. The main problem with this approach is that it tends to weigh heavily in favour of current generations and downgrades the values of future generations. This is especially the case in projects with a long operating life, or those that generate pollutants which will be inherited by future generations, such as projects in the transport or energy fields. In some cases, these future valuations can be altered substantially so that they do play a significant role in the decision process (Brown and Jackson, 1978). But in some projects this problem of inter-generational time preference may overwhelm the CBA logic altogether. Pearce (1979), for example, argues that in projects which generate substantial amounts of nuclear waste, the application of a discount rate so under-values the risk of contamination to later generations that CBA is not appropriate for such decisions.

There is no simple answer to the choice of a discount rate. Even where one is agreed, it may vary over time and this must be accounted for in the CBA. Ultimately the discount rate is based on value judgements on the relationships of the present to the future and among social and economic institutions in society. Whose values are acceptable is as open to debate as in any other issue and the discount rates of environmentalists may well be as valid as any chosen by economists. The choice of discount rate is therefore a political act. Probably the best approach is for CB analysts to suggest a range of possible discount rates and then run a sensitivity analysis to demonstrate what effect, if any, the different rates have on the project appraisal calculations. The same approach should be used in estimating the project life to which the discount rate is applied, especially where the costs are initially very high and benefits may be realised over long time periods, as the results of the CBA will be sensitive to varying the project life. This was the situation recently in a study of some proposed electrification plans by British Rail (Hope, 1979), where it was found that the combination of a discounted cash flow with the arbitrary assumption that railway electrification equipment had only a 30 year life heavily biased against its acceptance. Instead the analysis was reworked to compare the costs and benefits of electric versus diesel trains in perpetuity. This showed electrification to offer a much more favourable return on investment especially given possible changes in fuel prices. In any case, it is always important that decision makers be aware of the sensitivity of alternate assumptions as to the discount rate and project life.

Cost-Benefit's Reformist Offspring

Cost-benefit, in attempting to develop a quantitative welfare function with an emphasis on monetary values, is open to much criticism in a world of multi-dimensional and conflicting forces. It has been criticised for ignoring societal goals, for overvaluing efficiency, for over-emphasising money at the expense of qualitative and subjective aspects of the quality of life, for ignoring social and environmental costs and benefits and other intangibles, for aggregation and reductionism, and for ignoring the complexity of the decision making process. Each of these critiques is reflected in some alternative but related technique. Many moved far enough away from the approach and methodology of CBA to warrant their own classification, for example, social indicator and quality of life research, evaluation research, and social and environmental impact assessment. Even in these cases, however, many concepts of CBA are incorporated into the various approaches, for example, the concept of direct and indirect effects in environmental impact studies. Other techniques are reformist – they have continued to use a CBA framework. These, we have seen, attempted to deal in the main with the nefarious problems of aggregation, some by attempting to improve the aggregative qualities of CBA, others on the opposite tack of promoting disaggregating techniques.

Disaggregated Cost-Utility

The best-known of the disaggregated techniques is Planning Balance Sheet Analysis (PBSA) developed over the last twenty-five years by Nathaniel Lichfield and devised as a means of introducing the rigour of social CBA into the urban and regional planning process. PBSA attempts to elucidate the prospective consequences of planning proposals to provide information to decision makers and to aid political debate. As Lichfield (1971, p. 174) points out:

> 'Planning analysis unhappily has lacked the rigorous tools which would enable it to pursue this complex path (consideration of costs, benefits and externalities) and come up with a decision which was demonstrably the best in the public interest, that is having the maximum net advantage to the community as a whole. It was in the recognition that cost-benefit analysis techniques could be adopted for this purpose, without any loss to the objectives of the planners, that led to the formulation of the (PBS) technique.'

PBSA follows out of modern welfare economics and, in a reaction against the problems of aggregative techniques like CBA, leaves decision makers to determine the manner in which individual welfares should be summed together. Lichfield further argued that CBA needed modification if it was to be useful in planning for two reasons (Lichfield et al., 1975). First, CBA was usually applied to projects in a single sector of activity, for example, water resources or airport development and as a consequence analysis focused only on the costs and benefits accruing to those directly involved in that sector. Most planning problems, on the other hand, are multi-sectoral with many divergent groups affected in many ways which would not always be amenable to monetarisation or even quantification. CBA, it was felt, under-represented these intangibles in presentations to decision makers by simply placing them in a prose text accompanying the main numerical analysis. PBSA, on the other hand, incorporates this information within the same visual framework as the money figures and this, it is argued, helps decision makers give intangibles their due regard in choosing a preferred option.

Secondly, Lichfield felt that CBA ignored questions of distributional equity which were very important in planning decisions. PBSA, on the other hand, sets out the incidence of costs and benefits against various groups in society. This process begins with the identification of the 'producer/operators' who are responsible for establishing and running the projects under consideration. Each of these producer/operators are paired with a group of individuals who will consume the goods and services of the producers in real or notional transactions. These transactions are not confined to the market nor do they merely involve benefits. Costs, too, are represented as passing from producer to consumer in these transactions. The end result of the PBSA is seen as a comprehensive set of social accounts which cover both resource costs and outputs. Measurements in the balance sheet are based on opportunity costs and consumer willingness to forego alternative goods and services for benefits or to receive goods and services in compensation for costs. This information is gathered as much as possible through observation and analysis of revealed preferences rather than by survey research. Where prices or shadow prices are not available, other quantified units of measurement are used including notional point systems or symbols.

The PBSA approach goes some way towards meeting the criticisms of CBA regarding the identification of the incidence of income redistribution in project analysis, and avoids problems of value weighting by leaving the ultimate weighting to the decision makers after analysis. In the identification of the incidence of redistribution PBSA still faces the difficulty of capturing in some way the nature of interpersonal comparisons and the distributional effects embodied in what might be substantial and indirect externalities, especially in multi-sectoral planning decisions like those found in regional land use planning. As for the multifold problems of aggregation PBSA by-passes these by opting for presentation of data in a clearly disaggregated format even while recognising that such a format may impose on the decision maker the need to digest large amounts of information and make explicit trade-offs between monetary and intangible aspects of projects. Nash et al. (1975b) suggest that disaggregated approaches like PBSA would be of even more assistance to decision making if a sensitivity analysis was conducted on the effect of varying value judgements on such matters as equity.

Finally, Hill (1968b) has a point when he argues that benefits and costs have only instrumental value in that they must be judged in relation to some societal objective, and that the relevancy of the inclusion of various costs and benefits in the analysis is also judged in the light of these objectives. Lichfield recognised the lack of specific objectives as a valid shortcoming in his approach and in later writing counselled the elucidation of community objectives, not going so far however, to suggest extensive attempts to measure progress towards objectives. This in any event was not the *raison d'etre* of PBSA which was rather to demonstrate the incidence of costs and benefits on various sectors of the society.

There have been other similar techniques suggested for avoiding the pitfalls of CBA and disaggregation including Stern's 'multivariate cost-benefit analysis' (1976) and Goeller's 'system impact assessment' (1974). Both are similar variations of PBSA and add little to that approach. Stern, for example, misjudges PBSA's commitment to disaggregation and suggests much the same format as PBSA.

Aggregating Cost-Utility

After PBSA certainly the next most well known reformist technique is Hill's Goals-Achievement Matrix Analysis (GAM). This is a highly rational approach which conforms closely to the steps of classic rational analysis in that it concentrates on the step by step assessment of optional means of meeting present goals or objectives. Hill (1968b) outlines the steps of GAM analysis as follows:

(1) Planning objectives are formulated at the outset and defined in operational terms.

(2) Alternative courses of action are specified.

(3) For each objective a cost-benefit account is prepared which considers monetary effects, quantified but non-monetary effects, and intangibles. For each objective and course of action costs and benefits are compared and aggregated where possible.

(4) A weighting scheme is developed which reflects the community's valuation of each objective and the incidence of costs and benefits associated with each alternative. This reflects distributional considerations in that sectors of the public are identified who are specifically affected by costs or benefits. Both objectives and weights are to be developed by a variety of tactics including surveys and consultations with politicians, experts, and community interest groups. Indirect approaches suggested include revealed preference analysis of consumer behaviour and previous government decision making. The weights applied to the objectives are interpreted as the community's desired distribution of benefits, or 'equity'.

(5) If the achievement of objectives cannot be measured in a straightforward manner, transformation functions are de-

Figure 7.1 Simple goals achievement matrix

Goal Description	I			II			III			IV		
Relative Weight	2			3			5			4		
Incidence	Relative Weight	Costs	Benefits	Relative Weight	Costs	Benefits	Relative Weight	Costs	Benefits	Relative Weight	Costs	Benefits
Group a	1	A	D	5	E	–	1	–	N	1	Q	R
Group b	3	H	–	4	–	R	2	–	–	2	S	T
Group c	1	L	J	3	–	S	3	M	–	1	V	W
Group d	2	–	–	2	T	–	4	–	–	2	–	–
Group e	1	–	K	1	–	U	5	–	P	1	–	–
		Σ	Σ		Σ	Σ		Σ	Σ			

(from Hill, 1968b)

veloped which demonstrate possible trade-offs between outcomes measured in different units, and facilitate adding such
measures of achievement on a single scale. Money is the
recommended single scale where possible. These transformations will be discussed further. The weighted indices of goals-
achievement are then summed and the preferred plan among
the alternatives is that with the largest index. Figure 7.1 is a
simple goals-achievement matrix.

Before discussing the GAM approach further it is worth looking at
a highly logical extension of this matrix approach – the Plan Evaluation and Robustness Program (PERP) developed for the UK's
Department of the Environment (Local Government Operational
Research Unit, 1976). PERP is highly logical because it is a GAM
developed into a computer programme designed to assist in evaluating
development plans. The strict parameters guiding programming help
at once to demonstrate the sheer theoretical cleanliness of the GAM
approach while highlighting the enormous practical difficulties associated with such an endeavour. Figure 7.2 outlines the steps involved
in the PERP which, like GAM, evaluates the effectiveness of different
planning options in relation to objectives and, in addition, analyses
the impact of uncertainty in these results.

The first step in the use of PERP, as in GAM, is to define a
comprehensive set of objectives, which are reasonably independent of
one another, and can be expressed numerically, at least in terms of
relative degree of achievement. Secondly, an evaluation matrix is
constructed, which is simply objectives versus alternative planning
strategies. Into the cells of this matrix a series of raw performance
scores are inserted. These scores will give some indication of levels of
performance of each alternative or strategy on a particular objective.
The scores could be sufficient for evaluation at this stage, for example,
if they were in monetary units arising out of a cost-benefit analysis.
In that case, the programme would jump to steps 8–12 in Figure
7.2. More often, however, the raw performance units will be some
combination of subjective assessments of relative levels of achievement
of an alternative such as 'objective 50 per cent achieved' and secondly,
numerical data expressed in a variety of units such as x acres affected,
x db reduction in traffic noise, x £s expended, etc.

If the latter is the case the user of PERP is faced with the following question: what is the relationship between a raw performance
score and the actual level of benefit of that alternative to the community at large? The level of benefit is termed a utility value and

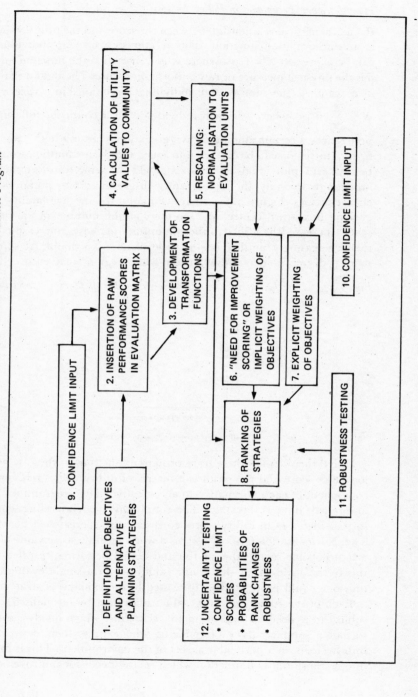

Figure 7.2 The ultimate GAM – Plan Evaluation and Robustness Program

4. CALCULATION OF UTILITY VALUES TO COMMUNITY

5. RESCALING: NORMALISATION TO EVALUATION UNITS

3. DEVELOPMENT OF TRANSFORMATION FUNCTIONS

2. INSERTION OF RAW PERFORMANCE SCORES IN EVALUATION MATRIX

6. "NEED FOR IMPROVEMENT SCORING" OR IMPLICIT WEIGHTING OF OBJECTIVES

7. EXPLICIT WEIGHTING OF OBJECTIVES

10. CONFIDENCE LIMIT INPUT

9. CONFIDENCE LIMIT INPUT

1. DEFINITION OF OBJECTIVES AND ALTERNATIVE PLANNING STRATEGIES

8. RANKING OF STRATEGIES

11. ROBUSTNESS TESTING

12. UNCERTAINTY TESTING
* CONFIDENCE LIMIT SCORES
* PROBABILITIES OF RANK CHANGES
* ROBUSTNESS

the mathematical relationship between the score and the utility value is a transformation function. This relationship for one individual can be expressed $w = f(p)$, where w is welfare, f is the function and p is the physical measure or raw performance score. The total welfare in a region is the sum of each individual's relationship, expressed $W = \sum_{i=1}^{N} fi(pi)$ where i is each individual. To account for differing preferences, a certain amount of disaggregation is possible in two ways: firstly, the region can be divided into zones and the assumption would be that each individual within a zone held the same transformation function or secondly, the region can be disaggregated by population characteristics. Figure 7.3 is such a function for the availability of parking in a town centre. We see how, as the number of parking spaces increases the utility to the community increases, increasingly, then decreasingly until it begins to level off. (No doubt, at some point it decreases increasingly, as the whole region is paved over).

Figure 7.3   Hypothetical relationship between number of parking spaces and utility

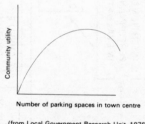

(from Local Government Research Unit, 1976)

PERP then applies these transformation functions to the raw performance score and the result is a matrix of utility values relating a component of each alternative to an objective. The programme can also rescale data at this stage. This simply involves converting scores so that increases in utility scores correspond to increases in benefit. The 'Normalisation Option' assigns a worst possible score value of 0, a best possible score value of 100 and actual performance rated on this 0–100 scale. If all the utility values are in a single evaluation unit one could proceed directly to step 8, the ranking of strategies.

Each of the scores or utility values may then be normalised and subject to a 'need for improvement' technique, which involves some sort of a sample survey of residents who express their desire for improvement in a particular aspect of the environment. This is built into a transformation function which relates needs for improvement to performance levels, i.e., as a performance score increases the need for improvement decreases. The assumption the authors make is that if achievement is relatively unimportant a low need for improvement score will be registered, thus implicitly weighting objectives. Otherwise a weighting set must be applied which expresses the varying importance of different objectives. A variety of ways of developing weighting sets are suggested including social surveys, analyses of house prices, consultation with experts, etc. The utility values in evaluation units are multiplied by these weights to give a matrix of weighted scores. The columns in the matrix are summed to lead us to the ranking of strategies, which gives us an overall effectiveness score for each planning alternative, the most effective being the desirable plan.

The second part of PERP tests for uncertainty in the accurate estimation of overall scores at present and in the future. This is done in two ways. Firstly, confidence limits are the bounds within which the scores or weights are likely to fall with a 95 per cent probability. The result of this input is a table showing the effect of these uncertainties on the ranking of strategies, for example, a total score of 60 might have a 95 per cent probability of falling within the 57 to 63 range. Finally the programme can calculate a robustness measure. This does not involve probability of change but rather is a measure of the least amount the scores or weights must change before there is a reversal of ranking between two strategies.

The difficulties associated with the goals-achievement matrix approach are numerous. Firstly, it assumes that policy objectives are clear cut and amenable to operationalisation which they often are not. Nor does it assist in their determination or refinement. To be fair however, Hill (1968a) has stated that GAM is designed to be used in one functional sector of activity at a time where the assumption no doubt is that objectives are fairly well agreed and defined. It is the developers of PERP who push the GAM approach over into multi-sectoral development planning where they rather naively assume clear operationalised objectives. PBSA was of course specifically designed for multi-sectoral analysis but it wisely leaves the need for operationalised objectives at a fairly general level.

Secondly, where PBSA presents decision makers with distributional effects and leaves them to then form judgements as to their equity, GAM requires a set of equity and goal achievement weights in advance of analysis. In theory this seems like a reasonable step but as we have noted in the previous chapter there are serious difficulties associated with value-weighting. As Nash et al. (1975a) points out, the studies required for adequate quantitative value-weighting schemes are so complex and expensive that most schemes end up reflecting no more than the analysts' own value judgements. Thirdly, the idea of developing useful transformation functions is theoretically attractive but, like value-weighting, highly difficult to obtain. And the simplification of community preferences, however valid, into functions carries with it the danger of glossing over the highly political nature of the satisfaction of preferences. The utility value of parking spaces has much to do for example with one's values on the public vs. private transport mix. And yet Hill (1968b, p. 27) states 'the goals-achievement matrix is not very useful if weights cannot be objectively determined or assumed' – an unlikely prospect.

Fourthly, GAM and PERP ignore the likely situation of interrelated utility values, where one change in an alternative affected a variety of objectives in different ways and different directions. This would be especially true in areas of social policy, for example, where a change in the unemployment benefit rate would have a host of ramifications affecting different planning objectives of different government departments. Finally, such highly aggregated schemes like CBA, reduced to a single figure, run the risk of compounding small errors. Although at some points Hill suggests GAM does not aim for single figure reductionism he also states 'the key to decision-making by means of the goals-achievement matrix is the weighting of objectives, activities, locations, groups or sectors in urban areas. By the application of relative weights it is possible to arrive at a unique conclusion' (Hill, 1968b, p. 27).

Therefore while the GAM approach is attractive in the abstract, its usefulness is severely limited by these difficulties and the assumptions necessary for it to be carried out. However, in the form of the PERP programme with its facility for sensitivity analysis, it would allow one to examine quickly the implications of changing objectives and value-weightings, assuming these were somehow determined in the first place. In addition, GAM does make one set out a list of clearly defined objectives, even if it does not help formulate them.

Decision Analysis: Preferences and Uncertainty
Recently a series of techniques have evolved from systems analysis and the behavioural sciences which attempt to deal in a positive and quantitative manner with the impacts of uncertainty and value judgements on decision making. The typical goal of such analyses is the rank ordering of project alternatives based on measures of total utility. Mechanically the decision theory techniques are similar to

those of the matrix approach. Applications of this method have been attempted in a number of areas including land use (Gardiner and Edwards, 1975), water pollution (O'Conner, 1973), and airport location (Keeney and Raiffa, 1976). Unlike CBA, but like both PBSA and GAM, decision analysis (or multiattribute theory) does not try to evolve a common monetary denominator for analysis, but rather selects the relevant dimensions (or attributes) of alternatives and evaluates each alternative on each dimension. The evaluations themselves are often preference rankings based on surveys. These judgements are aggregated to produce a ranking. Although conceptually the tendency is towards aggregation some decision analysts do recognise the limitations of attempts at optimality.

It is worth noting here a distinction commonly drawn in the economic literature between risk and uncertainty (Mishan, 1976). Risk assessment involves the analysis of a large amount of data of past occurrences of a series of events, which enables probabilities of occurrence to be assigned to the same events in the future. Such analysis allows insurance companies, for example, to set automobile insurance rates based on the characteristics of the driver and the vehicle. Risk assessment is also used to construct 'event trees' of the probability of possible sequences of equipment failure in complex man/machine operations such as power stations. It does not, of course, establish the bounds which constitute an acceptable level of risk. The various risk assessments are readily incorporated into the cost-benefit analysis. Uncertainty, on the other hand, usually means an ignorance of the exact probability distribution for future events, or even of the nature of the future events themselves. For example, the political situation that will exist in Iran in 1985 is uncertain whereas the probability of the risk of hurricanes hitting the eastern seaboard of the US in 1985 can be estimated from past data.

This distinction is not a hard and fast one. With uncertainties, for example, it is sometimes possible to predict that the likelihood of a future event falls with a range of probabilities and to incorporate this information into a sensitivity analysis. In this field of decision analysis, which often relies on relatively more available *subjective* assessments of probabilities in a specific project oriented environment, the use of the term uncertainty covers what economists would call risk.

The basic paradigm of decision analysis involves five steps (Keeney and Raiffa, 1976). The first is pre-analysis in which the problem is identified, and viable alternative solutions given. In the second step the anatomy of the problem is structured in a decision tree (Figure 7.4) with *decision* nodes and *chance* nodes. These nodes identify points

Figure 7.4   Partial decision tree

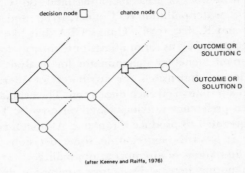

(after Keeney and Raiffa, 1976)

in time where choices must be made, where events not under the decision maker's control will take place, or when further information may become available. The third step is an uncertainty analysis where probabilities are assigned to the various branches emanating from the chance nodes. These probabilities are based on stochastic models, expert opinion (Nijkamp, 1977), public opinion sampling (Stanley, 1977), or the decision maker's subjective assessment (Keeney and Raiffa, 1976). The fourth step is for the decision maker to assign utility values to different paths through the decision tree. Finally, an initial optimal strategy is identified which indicates what the first choice in the decision strategy should be and what choice might be made at future decision nodes.

The basic elements of decisions which this approach manipulates are described by Keeney and Raiffa (1976, p. 27) in the following manner:

	Single attribute	Multiple attribute
Certainty	1	2
Uncertainty	3	4

Attributes are those properties or dimensions which describe a problem. A single attribute may be sufficient (e.g. pedestrian fatalities reduced), but usually a problem requires a multi-attribute assessment. The set of attributes selected are expected to meet the following criteria: (i) to cover completely all important aspects of the problem (ii) to be operational (iii) to be decomposable into simplified units (iv) to be non-redundant to avoid double counting and (v) to be minimal, to keep the problem as simple as possible. As in PBSA or GAM the measurements themselves are based on monetary and non-monetary indicators and preference rankings for subjective data; the difference being that probability of attribute occurrence is a standard part of the analysis. Where preference rankings are required the decision analyst may make use of simple hypothetical questions involving easy-to-comprehend probability distributions to attempt to get at the decision makers underlying value judgements across a range of attributes.

Without delving into the complex mathematics of decision analysis we can note that, like GAM, it encompasses many of the classic steps of rational problem solving, with the proviso that subjective preference ranking becomes essential to the analysis rather than optional, as it is often treated in CBA. Conceptually, it differs little from the other matrix approaches and is therefore subject to the same imposing limitations. The intention of decision analysis to assess subjective values and systematically include them in the decision process is worthwhile, but a basic assumption of a unitary decision maker is hardly tenable in complex, pluralist societies. Such an assumption suggests that the subjective values and derived utility function of the identified decision maker be that person politician, bureaucrat, or dictator, is paramount over all other value sets in the society. Some multi-attribute theorists, however, seem quite at home with the fact that the subjective trade-offs (or rankings) of different groups within society may be difficult to reconcile, if at all. Nijkamp (1977), for example, argues that even extensive public participation exercises are no guarantee of problem resolution and the best the analyst can do is to help derive the conditions under which compromise solutions may be acceptable.

As for most cost-utility techniques the ability of decision analysis to indicate anything like 'the best choice' is inversely proportional to problem scale. At the neighbourhood level for example, Stanley (1976) demonstrates the applicability of aggregating preferences for various options for residential neighbourhood improvement schemes. Beyond this scale of analysis difficulties mount rapidly and this approach, like PBSA, is most useful where it helps to elucidate the scope of the problem, attempts to anticipate uncertainty, and provides substance for political debate over alternatives.

Where decision analysis is unique is in its attention to the relationship between preferences and uncertainty. With regard to much social cost-benefit analysis, for example, Stewart (1978, p. 162) has recently noted that:

'The *ex post* out-turn may differ from the *ex ante* expectations for all sorts of reasons, including changes in technology, economic changes, wrong specification of relationships, and managerial capacity. Hirschman (1977) provides a fascinating account of many such changes in projects surveyed in his *Development Projects Observed*. Almost invariably predictions proved wrong in the cases he surveyed. Where the outcome was reasonably close to expectations this normally proved to be due to cancelling out of errors. The lessons from his studies would be that flexibility and managerial capacity – particularly capacity to react to change – are the critical elements to look for in choice of projects, rather than the sort of factors sorted out by social cost-benefit analysis.'

This suggests that decision analysis, instead of concentrating on optimal paths, could be most useful in helping to sensitise decision makers and administrators to the problems of uncertainty and how these problems affect their preferences and management style. Decision makers and administrators prepared for the possibilities of changing circumstance, setbacks, or new and potentially disturbing information, and used to weighing alternatives in terms of probable outcomes, will more likely have the obviously important 'capacity to react to change'.

Conclusion

The cost-utility techniques, especially CBA, are in wide use in numerous sectors and often provide good value for money up to the point where they help to clarify the political choices among alternatives. With a tendency to monetarisation in CBA and quantification in the remaining techniques it is useful to reiterate that the application of rational techniques is a subjective activity. The choice of one technique over another, therefore, is not a matter of which is 'correct' but rather a reflection of the value set which determined the problem definition and the alternatives under review. As we noted in the last chapter making this explicit is the moral responsibility of the analyst and cannot be avoided by any guise of neutrality. And since clarification of political choice rather than optimisation should be the goal of analysis, a high degree of aggregation or single indices must be avoided. The results of an analysis are best presented in a disaggregated format like that of the Planning Balance Sheet with its attention to the distribution of costs and benefits to various societal groupings. The attention to uncertainty and underlying value judgements demonstrated in decision analysis should also be integral to any techniques which seeks to expose the relevant issues in aid of choice.

Notes on further reading

The best comprehensive introduction to cost-benefit analysis is Anderson and Settle (1977). More difficult for the non-economist is Sassone and Schaffer (1978) and Mishan (1971). The latter work is summarised in the more accessible Mishan (1976) work.

The concept of 'quality of life' from the economist's perspective is examined in Wingo and Evans (1977) – especially worthwhile are articles by Wingo, Culyer, and Donnison. Articles by Amin, Mirrlees, Sadik, and Stewart in the same issue (Vol. 6, 1978) of *World Development* explore practical limitations to CBA, especially concerning income distribution. The volume by Pearce (1978b) deals with the problems associated with measuring non-marketed intangible goods. Nash, Pearce and Stanley (1975a, b) is a lucid exploration of the important role of values in cost-benefit analysis.

Lichfield, Kettle and Whitbread (1975) and Hill (1968a) are the best guides to their own techniques.

A judicious reading of parts of Keeney and Raiffa (1976) provides the best introduction to decision theory and multi attribute analysis, however, some parts are very formidable mathematically. Rowe (1977) is by far the most complete dissection of the concepts of risk and uncertainty.

References

Ackoff, Russell L., 1976. 'Does Quality of Life have to be Quantified?' In *Operational Research Quarterly*, Vol. 27, pp. 289–303.

Amin, Galal A., 1978. 'Project Appraisal and Income Distribution' In *World Development*, Vol. 6, pp. 139–52.

Anderson, Lee G. and Settle, Russell F., 1977. *Benefit-Cost Analysis: A Practical Guide*. Lexington, Mass.: Lexington Books.

Baumol, William J., 1969. 'On the Discount Rate for Public Projects' In *The Analysis and Evaluation of Public Expenditure*. Washington: Government Printing Office.

Baumol, William J. and Oates, Wallace E., 1979. *Economics, Environmental Policy and the Quality of Life*. Englewood Cliffs, N.J.: Prentice Hall.

Bebbington, A. C., 1978. *The Experimental Value of Social Intervention* University of Kent mimeo.

Brown, C. V. and Jackson, P. M., 1978. *Public Sector Economics*. Oxford: Martin Robertson.

Edwards, Michael, 1977. *The Ideological Function of Cost-Benefit Analysis in Planning*. University College, London: Town Planning Discussion Paper No. 25.

Fischer, David W., 1974. 'On the Problems of Measuring Environmental Costs and Benefits' In *Social Science Information*, 13(2) pp. 95–105.

Fischoff, Baruch, 1977. 'Cost-Benefit Analysis and the Art of Motorcycle Maintenance' In *Policy Sciences*, Vol. 8, pp. 172–202.

Fischoff, Baruch, Slovic, Paul, and Lichtenstein, Sarah, 1979. 'Weighing the Risks' In *Environment*, Vol. 21, pp. 17–38.

Fisher, Gene H., 1977. 'Cost Consideration in Policy Analysis' In *Policy Analysis*, Vol. 3, pp. 107–44.

Foster, C. D. and Beesley, M. E., 1963. 'Estimating the Social Benefit of Constructing an Underground Railway in London' In *Journal of the Royal Statistical Society*, Vol. 126. Series A, pp. 46–92.

Gardiner, P. C. and Edwards, W., 1975. 'Public Values: Multiattribute-Utility Measurement for Social Decision Making' In *Human Judgement and Decision Processes*. Kaplan, M. and Schwartz, S. (eds.). New York: Academic Press.

Goeller, B. F., 1974. *System Impact Assessment: A More Comprehensive Approach to Public Policy Decisions*. R-1446-RC. Santa Monica: The Rand Corporation.

Haveman, R. H. and Weisbrod, B. A., 1975. 'Defining Benefits of Public Programs: Some Guidance for Policy Analysts' In *Policy Analysis* Vol. 1, pp. 169–96.

Hayden, F. Gregory, 1977. *Time Analysis for Social Planning and Project Evaluation: An Alternative to the Temporal Misguidance of Neo-classical Time-Stream Discounting*. University of Nebraska, Lincoln: Faculty Working Paper No. 50.

Hicks, J. R., 1939. 'The Foundations of Welfare Economics' In *Economic Journal*, Vol. 49, pp. 696–712.

Hill, Morris, 1968a. 'A Goals-Achievement Matrix for Evaluating Alternative Plans' In *Journal of the American Institute of Planners*, Vol. 34, pp. 19–28.

Hill, Morris, 1968b. *Public Investment Allocation*. University of Pennsylvania: PhD Dissertation.

Hirschman, A. D., 1977. *Development Projects Observed*. Washington: The Brookings Institution.

Hope, Richard, 1979. 'No Sparks on BR's live wires' In *The Guardian*, 5 June.

Johnson, Ronald W. and Pierce, John M., 1975. 'The Economic Evaluation of Policy Impacts, Cost-Benefit and Cost-Effectiveness' In Scioli and Cook, 1975.

Kaldor, N., 1939. 'Welfare Propositions of Economics and Inter-personal Comparisons of Utility' In *Economic Journal*, Vol. 49, pp. 549–52.

Keeney, Ralph L. and Raiffa, Howard, 1976. *Decisions and Multiple Objectives: Preferences and Value Trade-offs*. New York: John Wiley and Sons.

Knetsch, Jack L. and Fleming, William F., 1977. 'Resource Development Alternatives: An Evaluation Strategy' In *Annals of Regional Science*, Vol. 11, pp. 39–50.

Krutilla, John V. and Fisher, A., 1975. *The Economics of Natural Environments – Studies in the Valuation of Commodity and Amenity Resources*. Baltimore: Johns Hopkins Press.

Layard, Richard (ed.), 1972. *Cost Benefit Analysis*. London: Penguin Modern Economics Readings.

Lewis, David C., 1978. *Cost Benefit Analysis and the Determination of Best Environment Options*, University of Warwick Working Paper Collection: School of Management, Discussion Paper No. 12.

Lichfield, N., 1971. 'Cost-Benefit Analysis in Planning: A Critique of the Roskill Commission' In *Regional Studies*, Vol. 5, pp. 157–83.

Lichfield, N. Kettle, P. and Whitbread, M., 1975. *Evaluation in the Planning Process*. Oxford: Pergamon.

Little, I. M. D., 1957. *A Critique of Welfare Economics* (second edition). Oxford: Clarendon Press.

Local Government Operational Research Unit, 1976. *Development Plan Evaluation and Robustness*. London: Department of the Environment.

Luft, Harold S., 1976. 'Benefit Cost Analysis and Public Policy Implementation' In *Public Policy*, Vol. 24, pp. 437–62.

Marglin, S. A., 1963. 'The Social Rate of Discount and the Optimal Rate of Investment' In *Quarterly Journal of Economics*, February, pp. 95–112.

Mirrlees, J. A., 1978. 'Social Cost-Benefit Analysis and the Distribution of Income' In *World Development*, Vol. 6, pp. 131–8.

Mishan, E. J., 1971. *Cost-Benefit Analysis*. London: George Allen and Unwin.

Mishan, E. J., 1974. 'Flexibility and Consistency in Project Evaluation' In *Economica*, Vol. 41, pp. 81–96.

Mishan, E. J., 1976. *Elements of Cost-Benefit Analysis*. Second edition. London: George Allen and Unwin.

Nash, Christopher, Pearce, David, and Stanley, John, 1975a. 'Criteria for Evaluating Project Evaluation Techniques' In *Journal of the American Institute of Planners*, Vol. 41, pp. 83–9.

Nash, Christopher, Pearce, David and Stanley, John, 1975b. 'An Evaluation of Cost-Benefit Criteria' In *Scottish Journal of Political Economy*, Vol. 22, pp. 121–34.

Newton, Trevor, 1972. *Cost-Benefit Analysis in Administration*. London: George Allen and Unwin.

Nijkamp, Peter, 1977. 'Stochastic Quantitative and Qualitative Multi-criteria Analysis for Environmental Design' In *Regional Science Association Papers*. Thomas, Morgan D. (ed.). Vol. 39, pp. 175–99.

O'Conner, M. F., 1973. *The Application of Multiattribute Scaling Procedures to the Development of Indices of Water Quality*. Chicago: Report 7339, Center for Mathematical Studies in Business and Economics, University of Chicago.

Pearce, D. W., 1978a. *The Social Incidence of Environmental Costs and Benefits*. Aberdeen: Occasional Paper No. 78–08, University of Aberdeen.

Pearce, D. W. (ed.), 1978b. *The Valuation of Social Cost*. London: George Allen and Unwin.

Pearce, D. W., 1979. 'Social cost-benefit and nuclear futures' In *Energy Economics*, Vol. 1, pp. 66–71.

Peskin, Henry M. and Seskin, Eugene P. (eds.), 1975. *Cost-Benefit Analysis and Water Pollution Policy*. Washington: The Urban Institute.

Prentice, R. C., 1977. *Decision Analysis as Exploration*. Durham University Business School, Research paper series No. 4.

Prest, A. R. and Turvey, R., 1965. 'Cost-Benefit Analysis – A Survey' In *The Economic Journal*, Vol. 75, pp. 683–735.

Ratcliff, Donald, 1974. 'Cost-Benefit Analysis and the Personal Social Services' In *Policy and Politics*, Vol. 2, pp. 237–48.

Roth, William, 1978. *The Economic and Political Context of Cost-Benefit Analysis*. Wisconsin University: Institute for Research on Poverty. Discussion Paper 497–78.

Rowe, William D., 1977. *An Anatomy of Risk*. New York: Wiley-Interscience.

Sadik, Abdul-Karim T., 1978. 'A Note on Some Practical Limitations of Social Cost-Benefit Analysis Measures' In *World Development*, Vol. 6, pp. 221–5.

Sassone, Peter G. and Schaffer, William A., 1978. *Cost-Benefit Analysis: A Handbook*. New York: Academic Press.

Scioli, Frank P. Jr. and Cook, Thomas J., 1978. *Methodologies for Analyzing Public Policies*. Lexington, Mass.: D. C. Heath.

Self, Peter, 1975. *Econocrats and the Policy Process*. London: Macmillan.

Stanley, J. K., 1974. 'A Cardinal Utility Approach for Project Evaluation' In *Socio-Economic Planning Sciences*, Vol. 8, pp. 329–38.

Stern, George J. A., 1976. 'SOSIPing, or Sophistical Obfuscation of Self-Interest and Prejudice'. *Operational Research Quarterly*, Vol. 27, pp. 915–29.

Stewart, Francis, 1978. 'Social Cost-Benefit Analysis in Practice: Some Reflections in Light of Case Studies Using Little-Mirrlees Techniques' In *World Development*, Vol. 6, pp. 153–65.

Williams, Alan, 1972. 'Cost-Benefit Analysis: Bastard Science? and/or Insidious Poison in the Body Politick?' In *Journal of Public Economics*, Vol. 1, pp. 199–225.

Williams, Alan and Anderson, Robert, 1975. *Efficiency in the Social Services.* London: Basil Blackwell.

Wolfe, J. N., 1973. *Cost-Benefit and Cost Effectiveness.* London: George Allen and Unwin.

Wingo, Lowden and Evans, Alan (eds.), 1977. *Public Economics and the Quality of Life.* Baltimore and London: The Johns Hopkins University Press.

8 Studying Environmental and Social Impact

Both environmental impact assessment (or analysis) (EIA) and social impact assessment (SIA) are based on two assumptions: (1) that the future can be predicted, or guessed at, with enough reliability to make it worthwhile considering potential changes which might be caused by the introduction of new projects or new technology and (2) that policy makers will understand the assessment and respond by modifying the decisions that they might otherwise have made (Peterson and Gemmell, 1977). And although numerous problems of causation, social complexity, and pluralism may weigh against these two assumptions they are reasonable insofar as they form the basis for most attempts at policy analysis.

There are dimensions of impact which are common to both EIA and SIA. Firstly, there are direct and indirect impacts. Direct, or primary, impacts are immediately related to the proposed project or programme. Indirect, or secondary or tertiary, impacts are induced by, or associated with, proposed change and are the 'second-order' effects of direct impacts. The distinction is very similar to that of direct and indirect costs and benefits in cost-utility analysis. For example, a direct impact of a decision to build a refinery at a particular remote location may be the migration of a large construction crew to that location. Indirect impacts will stem from the multiplier effects associated with the crew taking up residence – economic impacts such as increased local spending on goods and services, environmental impacts such as pressure for housing construction on agricultural land, and social impacts such as increased demand for health and social services. In most cases the indirect impacts will far outweigh the direct in magnitude and must be considered in conjunction with the direct. The main point, however, is not any rigid distinction between direct and indirect impacts. Rather it is the importance of the inter-relationships among impacts, and the need to specify cut-off points for the consideration of multiplier effects. These will be of decreasing relevance to the policy analysis as they become more indirect.

Secondly, there is gross and net impact. Gross impact is the projected future environment with the proposed change examined in light of the existing environment without the change. Net impact is the projected future environment with the proposed change minus the projected future environment without the proposed change (Corwin et al., 1975). The importance of this distinction is that the study of net impact considers only direct impacts associated with the project in question, and treats indirect impacts such as population growth induced by a project, as exogenous factors which would have occurred in any event. This may be a valid approach when considering a small scale project but will increasingly cause the analysis to deviate from reality as problem scale increases – the larger the problem the more important it is that gross impact be the focus of study.

Thirdly, impacts may be socially concentrated or dispersed. Concentrated impacts are those associated with a particular locale or affecting a particular segment of the population, while dispersed impacts are spread thinly over a wider range (Corwin et al., 1975). The more concentrated the impacts the more likely that opposition or pressure groups will play an important role in reaching the development decision. The relevance of a particular rational technique to the policy analysis may also be affected by the degree of impact concentration. SIA with its joint emphasis on objective data and public participation is more suitable to problems with concentrated impacts than, for example, cost-benefit analysis which better evaluates problems with dispersed impacts affecting society generally but not a particular segment of the population (Sassone, 1977).

Fourthly, impacts have duration in that they occur over time and may cease to occur at some point. For example, noise and heavy traffic associated with the construction of a major facility will cease when construction is complete. Finally, impacts have geographical scale which range from on-site, through local, regional, and national up to global. Again the specification of cut-off points for consideration of impacts related to scale is essential for the analysis. For example, the construction of a refinery on a green field site may be favoured locally by those who stand to benefit from increased trade and employment prospects, disfavoured regionally by those who stand to lose a recreational or amenity site, and yet favoured again nationally by those considering the energy or investment implications of the project.

Environmental Impact Methodology

As many as 50 differing methodologies for studying environmental impact have been identified (Canter, 1977). Most are variations of the following types which, while not entirely distinct, are helpful in differentiating the many approaches to EIA. Some include social impact assessment as an integral part of the EIA but the danger of this is that the treatment of the socio-economic aspects of a project can be very superficial in an otherwise good EIA.

Overlays

Conceptually one of the simplest methodologies is transparent overlay mapping, a common technique in land use planning wherever the chief concern is locating a project or a route alignment in physical space (Clark et al., 1978a, p. 116). The geographical area under concern is divided into grid cells, and demographic information and various physical characteristics are represented graphically on transparent maps divided into the spatial units. These maps are overlayed to help communicate the location, geographical scale, and degree of concentration or dispersion of impacts. The use of computer programmes extends the range of this technique in that a large number of environmental factors can be coded and displayed and the project location based in part on those spatial units which possess the most advantageous mix of environmental indicators. The major disadvantage of overlay mapping is that it is really only useful for locational problems in that it ignores a number of dimensions of impact including duration and the inter-relationship between direct and indirect impacts. An added problem may be that the type of data displayed will be biased towards that already available from existing government survey maps (Sondheim, 1978).

Cross Impact Techniques

A second approach to EIA is the use of cross impact techniques, which range from simple lists of the environmental parameters which might be considered in analysis, to complex scaling-weighting checklists which attempt to relate objective data to various subjective evaluations of the differential weights which might be assigned to the environmental factors. Some of the most common cross-impact methods are the various uses of matrices which are double checklists with possible project associated activities along one axis and potentially impacted environmental characteristics or conditions along the other. The matrix approach differs from the simple checklist in that some attempt is made to relate causally (if only in a very inexact fashion) particular activities to the specific impact produced by those activities and to assess these as to magnitude. A number of cross impact strategies for EIA are explored below. In the next chapter a more specific use of the term cross impact is discussed in relation to futures studies.

The Matrix Approach

A well-known matrix approach is that of Leopold et al. (1971) of which there are numerous variations. The Leopold Matrix itself involves 100 specified actions which might cause impact on one axis related to 88 environmental factors on the other. The cells of the matrix represent the inter-relationship between activity and impact and where impact is expected, the cell is bisected by a diagonal line. Two figures are contained in each cell. A magnitude figure is based on objective data and is described by numerical values of one to ten. An importance figure, also on a one to ten scale, represents the expert opinion of some inter-disciplinary team as to the relative importance of this interaction compared to the other impacts in the matrix. Variations of the Leopold matrix have been attempted for many types of EIA's including studies of the construction of oil production platforms in Scotland (Polytechnic of Central London, 1973), power stations in Israel (Hill and Alterman, 1974) and port facilities in Canada (Environment Canada, 1974).

The advantages of the matrix approach are that it is a comprehensive, wide-ranging screening technique for impacts, and it is a good means of displaying information for ready communication to policy makers and the public. The disadvantages are, firstly, the many associated with subjective ranking described in Chapter 6. Secondly, that an enormous range of information must be considered: in the matrix described above, which might even be expanded, there are 8,800 cells, each potentially containing measures of magnitude and importance. In spite of the large amount of information displayed the matrix approach is not predictive as much as descriptive, and the data may not be used to fullest advantage. Thirdly, the matrix approach is a poor vehicle for considering the impact dimensions of concentration, deviation and geographical scale. Finally, in North America researchers have attempted to identify a single standardised matrix to cover a diversity of problems, but an individual matrix for each separate project, and even parts of projects, might well be more relevant and easier to handle (Beer, 1977). This however, suggests the obvious problem that some impacts could be overlooked or conveniently ignored.

Related to the Leopold Matrix is a technique known as Project Appraisal for Development Control (PADC) and suggested for the assessment of major industrial planning applications in the UK. This approach integrates one or more impact matrices into the development application process. It attempts to resolve two recurring problems in assessing proposals, namely, the difficulty of obtaining sufficient detailed information from prospective developers, and the lack of a framework for the systematic appraisal of proposals (Clark et al., 1978a, p. 116). PADC requires that all prospective developers submit a 'Project Specification Report' giving detailed information on the project and its processes, including construction and operational phases, and using an impact matrix to ensure comprehensiveness. A series of technical advice notes are available to aid in assessing scale and significance of impacts – these notes cover such areas as hydrology, visual intrusion, water pollution, transport, etc. The PADC approach suffers from the same limitations as other matrix techniques but has the decided advantage that it perceives the use of a matrix as part of a wider development control process which includes such activities as public hearings on development applications. In addition the proposers of PADC stress the need to consider all the important dimensions of impact rather than only those amenable to the matrix approach.

Scaling-Weighting Techniques

The limitations of the matrix approach spawned two variations. The first are the attempts to establish scaling-weighting checklists, sometimes called indexing schemes. The most well known is the highly quantified Batelle system developed for evaluating water resource projects (Dee et al., 1973). This system is based on a checklist organised into 4 categories, 17 components, and 78 socio-environmental parameters. The steps involved include translating environmental data or parameter estimates into commensurate units by way of a series of transformation functions which yield an 'environmental quality' scale. These scale values are multiplied by importance values which are determined by the use of the Delphi technique on a panel of laymen or specialists, and a composite score is developed with and without the project. The Batelle system is thus very highly aggregated and complex, and although occasionally suggested as highly systematic, it may suffer from problems of hidden value judgements and implied causation resulting in arbitrary weights which are wholly dependent on the composition of the weighting panel. This may be acceptable when dealing with strictly environmental factors such as amounts of petrochemical oxidents in the air, but quite unsuitable for the social measures it proposes such as 'social interaction', or even for borderline measures such as noise.

A similar technique is recently developed by Sondheim (1978) which takes much the same panel weighting approach but attempts to deal with the inherent limitations in the Batelle system by stating specifically that the approach is highly subjective and dependent on the composition of the weighting panel. The emphasis is then on the structuring of the weighting panel for each project so as to reflect the diversity in the community necessary for sound political dialogue. The approach is seen as offering guidelines rather than answers to decision makers while retaining the systematic advantages of rational analysis.

Tree Diagrams

A second variation of the matrix approach is the application of network analysis to EIA in an attempt to explicitly identify second and higher order impacts by using variations of tree diagrams to indicate the flow of impacts through the environmental system. The object is not to show the impact directly resulting from project action, as in the matrix, but to show the path of the primary impact through other parts of the system. Impact trees can be a simple series of successive relationships in a chain (Figure 8.1) or may form a branching 'tree' of impacts (Figure 8.2). The successive orders of impacts may disappear quickly if they cannot be traced but alternatively, cut-off points may need to be specified or one might trace impacts into absurdity. The use of the network diagram is, in many cases, a symbolic display of hypothesised causation rather than any specifically quantified formula especially as it moves from strictly biophysical impacts to socio-economic impacts. As such it is best used in conjunction with other objective and subjective information. It is, however, quite a useful manner of demonstrating to policy makers and the public the types of linkages which need to be thought about and debated prior to any development decision.

Dynamic Simulation Modelling

The most recent of EIA techniques involves the use of various dynamic simulation procedures which structure causal models to reflect interactions between environmental variables. The simulation model is designed to imitate, in an approximate fashion, the features of a complex system. It is a potentially sophisticated forecasting tool which expresses mathematically relationships and inter-relationships among influencing factors and events in an environmental system over time. The conceptual structure of a dynamic model is simple in that it is an iterative cycle which takes values for variables in the present (T_1), and processes them through some model which contains for-

Figure 8.1 Impact chain

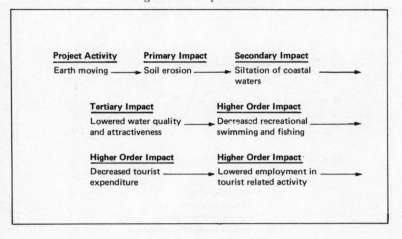

Figure 8.2 'Tree' of impacts

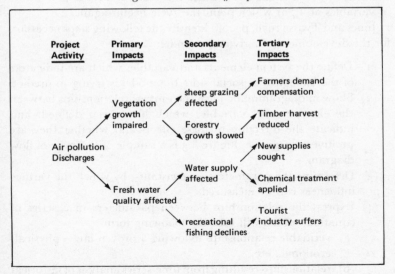

Figure 8.3 Simplified schematic of causal effects in dynamic model

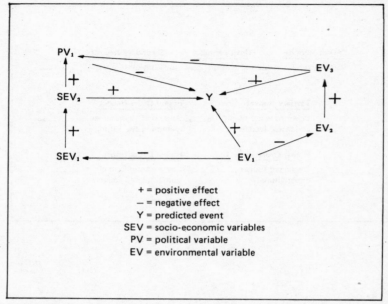

+ = positive effect
− = negative effect
Y = predicted event
SEV = socio-economic variables
PV = political variable
EV = environmental variable

mulae for rates of change over time. The result is a set of new values of variables at T_2 at which point the cycle begins again.

Jones and Twiss (1978, p. 208) identify the following steps necessary for the development of a dynamic model:

(1) Define the system elements and variables which are indicators of the biological or social state the model is trying to predict;

(2) Show in diagrammatic form the mutual relationships between the elements and variables which have been defined, and indicate the direction of these effects and whether they are positive or negative. Figure 8.3 is a sample of this type of flow diagram;

(3) Determine the parameters, or constants, by which the various influences can be measured;

(4) Express the relationships between parameters in a series of equations which will take the following form:
  (a) verifiable relationships following a proven law – physical, economic, etc.,
  (b) relationships resulting from time-series analysis of historical data
  (c) qualitative or subjectively determined relationships;

(5) Simulate on the computer;

(6) Test the model by using past data to forecast the present.

The techniques of simulation range from the qualitative to the numerical. Qualitative simulation models may only require the user to specify whether the relationship between relevant system variables is positive, negative, or nil, or they may be more complex and require data on the relative magnitude of interaction effects. The data may also be objective or subjective and the computer is used to evaluate the dynamic implications of the specified relationships. As more and more objective data becomes available the model moves closer to the pure numerical simulation made up of a series of differential equations.

The potential advantages of the simulation approach are great and it promises further methodological development in the long run. The disadvantages are, at present, it is expensive and time consuming, and it requires a large amount of data to be processed by computer. Also the actual specification of the model at any sophisticated level can be very difficult because of the complexity of the systems to be simulated and the difficulty of establishing the quantitative relationships between variables.

Social Impact Assessment

Social impact assessment techniques attempt to expand the study of natural, or biophysical, environmental impacts to include the social and socio-economic impacts that may be associated with a new programme, policy, or project. These impacts, or alterations in living conditions, include changes in psychological and physiological factors, community processes, and changes in the production, distribution and consumption of goods and services. Sometimes such considerations are included in the EIA but often they are glossed over. In addition to the question of 'which impacts?' SIA is also concerned with 'who gains and who loses?', that is, which groups in society gain benefit or suffer disbenefits. SIA also considers the issue of mitigation – the easing or transferring of the burden of disbenefits. The literature of SIA generally falls into two camps: theoretical attempts at specifying an assessment system or model, and the practical issuance of SIA reports related to a particular development. The former are as yet simple, and the latter *ad hoc* and not entirely systematic.

Models of Social Impact Assessment

In Chapter 5 many of the steps which might be associated with SIA were outlined. Wolf expands on this formulation with a model of interaction between some policy or project and the concurrent and subsequent socio-economic impact (Figure 8.4). In this Wolf model (1974, p. 11) the direct impacts (A) represent some change in the variables describing the initial condition. The continuing effect of readjustment and adaptation to change is represented by (B) and the nature of this will vary from group to group. In addition, the direct impacts themselves may result in a reaction which changes the planned project (C). This often takes the form of public opposition. Moreover the project is the result of some more general policy and has a 'history' in that it is the solution to some pre-existing concern or issue (D). This history conditions public receptiveness at the points of impact and adaptation (E). Finally, and as we noted in Chapter 6,

Figure 8.4   Wolf's model of social impact assessment

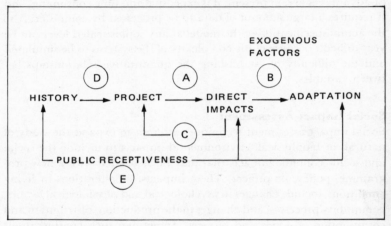

exogenous variables, random or systematic, add to the difficulty of isolating project-associated change from other changes in the socio-economic environment. Wolf's simple model is a good reflection of the flow of interactions which SIA must contend with but does not begin to tackle the problem of measuring change.

One of the most comprehensive theoretical approaches to SIA proposes to use a set of social indicators to measure predicted social impacts. This is the model of Olsen and Merwin (1977) which relates direct demographic and economic impacts through indirect impacts (social structural change and public service alterations) to changes in social well-being resulting in collective responses. These in turn feedback to policy decisions, as in Wolf's model. And in spite of the fact that Olsen and Merwin (1977, p. 49) recognise the enormous theoretical difficulties past researchers have had in developing quality of life indicators, they do go on to propose '50 factors, or community characteristics, that are essential components of the quality of social life in the United States and other western societies'. These factors are transformed to a standard score by the establishment of preferred values which may be specified by 'qualified experts', or the public as a whole, and these standard scores are subjectively value weighted by an elaborate scheme of interviews with various segments of the population.

Olsen and Merwin's recognition of the difficulties of causation, the necessity for subjective value weighting, and their attempt to structure this highly aggregated model and relate it to SIA, is certainly worthwhile. The model is, however, a long way from having the widespread practical significance the authors would ascribe to it in that it suffers from the problems of aggregation, especially where it attempts to ascribe widely applicable positive or negative valuations to the social indicators. In addition, the model is predicated on further dynamic systems models which 'will provide a means for predicting with considerable accuracy the most probable consequences that would result from any proposed development project' (p. 53). As we have seen, however, these dynamic models, while having considerable potential, are at present far from useful in the social field except at a very low level of sophistication. Given all the potential problems of the Olsen–Merwin approach, it does at least recognise and make explicit the difficulties associated with ascribing causation to indirect social effects, and is probably most useful as an organisational model for practical efforts at collecting objective data relevant to the SIA.

One problem with SIA in the recent past has been some confusion over its supposed role in the policy making process. One school of thought perceives it as social scientific attempts at predicting the effects of change by applying the skills of various academic disciplines like sociology, anthropology, political science, etc. In other words, supplying needed information to enlighten decisions. Others, however, see the most important tasks of SIA as mobilising public involvement in the decision process – a participatory role. Carley and Walkey (1978) explore these dual roles, and argue that valid, and valuable, SIA can ill afford to ignore either. They suggest that the opinions and reactions of residents in the study area, and other individuals concerned with the project, are essential to an understanding of the objective data generated by social scientific analysis. Such opinions and reactions result, not from a public relations exercise, but rather from concerted public participation in the assessment process, which means the essential two-way flow of information and interaction discussed in Chapter 6. The public response and the attitudinal information generated by such a process is important for bringing the SIA closer to the elusive social reality which, as we have seen, is only very partially mirrored by rational analysis. Public participation also helps all the actors in the decision process put some measures of priority, positive or negative direction, and sensitivity, to the various factors in the assessment problem. Most importantly it promotes the intensive public debate which leads to healthy policy decisions. This perspective attempts to combine the social scientific and participatory roles of SIA.

A similar case is put by Conner (1978), who approaches the issue from the participation perspective. He suggests a joint venture or co-operative model for the participation role of SIA as opposed to the usual adversary model. This co-operative model is based on the early and continued involvement of the community in the assessment process. In this model of development the community, in Conner's words, 'is an active, informed partner rather than a patient or victim' (p. 5). The model is an exhortation to SIA and decision making which is open and informed by participation, which is again seen as an essential complement to social scientific analysis. This exhortation to openness and public involvement is certainly worthwhile although Conner's model is perhaps somewhat misguided if he is suggesting that SIA ultimately brings harmony to political decision making. Such decision making will always involve adversaries as long as pluralistic, divergent, and often irreconcilable, value stances exist in an impact area. Conner is right, however, if he is arguing that participation can help some divergent values coalesce towards a decision.

An even stronger stance is taken by Torgerson (1979) who argues that the predominant tendency in most current efforts at SIA can be characterised as *elitist* in that they have a technocratic orientation, with the analyst assuming the role of an expert engaged in detached scientific inquiry. Such elitist impact assessors emphasise objective data, ignore social conflict, and give only a token nod to public involvement in the process. Torgerson suggests this elitist stance arises out of a functionalist orientation in sociology, that is, one based on the assumption that communities have monolithic, discernible social goals, the degree of attainment of which can be measured. This orientation is rejected by Torgerson who argues that social systems may well be about the systematic promotion of certain value stances at the expense of others, that is they are about pluralistic rather than monolithic social processes. Instead, a *participatory* mode of SIA is proposed which recognises the value orientation of the SIA researcher, and the necessarily ambiguous, or subjective, nature of studies of social phenomena which means intuitive judgements will always be present in the analysis. In this participatory mode active public participation is viewed as essential to the SIA process, and the right of affected parties. Such participatory impact assessment is itself an educative social process which may change society. The final assessment arises, not from some formula-derived single numerical figure, but from inter-group conflict and co-operation over development proposals.

Many of Torgerson's arguments and warnings about SIA are similar to those advanced more generally in this book. He counsels a high degree of suspicion of the role and value of rational analysis. His emphasis on participation is not just strong but in fact constitutes the cornerstone of his argument for an SIA process which becomes almost one with the pluralist political process itself. This is an embracing and laudatory role for SIA. It is worth noting, however, simply as a matter of balance, that the political process is in turn enlightened by the objective and subjective data gathered as part of the SIA process, and such routine data collection procedures also serves a valuable role in the complex mosaic that constitutes political decision making.

Practical Social Impact Assessment

In the more practical vein of SIA, the methodology is virtually all *ad hoc* – SIA still might be called a problem area without a well defined approach (Sassone, 1977). Most SIA's consist of an objective data base and projections related to socio-economic and demographic impacts and possibly subjective data gathered by interviews with the public, experts and politicians. Most SIA's deal at minimum with the following types of impact:

(1) Demographic impacts including labour force and population shift, employment multiplier effects, displacement and relocation problems, and changes in population make-up.

(2) Socio-economic impacts especially changes in income and income multiplier effects, employment rates and patterns, and taxation and rates.

(3) Institutional impacts including demands on local financial and administrative services, for example, in the fields of housing, water, sewers, schools, police, criminal justice, health and welfare, recreational facilities, and others; and especially changes in capital and operating budgets.

(4) Psychological and community impacts especially changes in intangible aspects of life, for example, social integration, community and friendship networks, sense of place, and community cohesion.

To date most SIA is directed at resource development or large scale construction projects. Around various facets of the development of the UK's North Sea oil and gas reserves, for example, social impact has been examined in many geographical areas and related to such diverse aspects of development as secondary industry, small businesses, health patterns, migrating workers and leisure. In North America social impact studies have also been addressed to such diverse topics as bridge building, tidal power, transmission line corridors, coal mining, and new communities. Less attention has been paid to SIA for human services planning and programmes but there is no reason for this not to occur (Grigsby and Hruby, 1978). In whatever field is addressed, impact assessments are generally fashioned in an *ad hoc*, but fairly comprehensive manner, based on the demands of the project and the general creativity of the investigator as opposed, for example, to a cost-benefit analysis which is most usually conducted to a similar format in many differing projects.

A different, more limited and rigorous approach to SIA is taken by the Argonne National Laboratory in their Social and Economic Assessment Model (SEAM). This is a computerised simulation model designed to estimate some socio-economic changes which accompany energy and industrial developments (Stenehjem, 1978). SEAM can provide annual estimates of the following data for any county or group of counties in the continental United States:

(a) Population projections by age, sex, and race.
(b) Direct employment requirements of most types of energy-related facilities.
(c) Secondary employment requirements created by new energy or industrial facilities.
(d) Locally available work force from impact and adjacent counties.
(e) Numbers and characteristics of in-migrating worker households attracted by the new facility.
(f) Housing needs and subcounty spatial allocation of the new population.
(g) Public service requirements and costs due to the new population.

To date the SEAM model has been used in a number of studies. In one case it was used to forecast the incremental public costs of new and expanded coal mines in over 200 US counties by 1985, under two differing projected levels of coal extraction. In another study, SEAM was used to study the changes which might occur in a single county in Virginia in which two new coal mines were to be developed (Argonne National Laboratory, 1978). In this case, advisory groups of local residents were established to provide the researchers with important local data, and to examine critically the forecasts of the model. The forecasts were then presented to public meetings for further feedback. The main purpose of the exercise was to avoid as many possible negative impacts of the mine development as possible.

Quite a different approach to SIA is taken by Freudenburg (1978) who argues that in the past SIA has often ignored or glossed over the study of the informal social networks and relationships which go a long way towards defining the nature of the community affected. Ignoring these relationships has meant that very important social consequences of development (i.e. impacts) have also been ignored by SIA researchers. Freudenburg is especially interested in 'boom-towns' which experience rapid development due to new energy ex-traction and power generation projects. In these boomtowns, for example, he suggests that rapid change destroys, or irrevocably alters, mechanisms of social control and social caring which had previously characterised the town. This may lead not only to a diminishing quality of community to many people, but more specifically to sub-stantial increases in 'social pathology rates, such as crime, drug abuse, etc. Why these important changes and impacts in informal social networks are ignored is a matter of conjecture. The reason is un-likely to be malicious, but rather some combination of time and re-source constraints and the sheer difficulty of so doing. Certainly it is not possible for all SIAs done by a consultant-researcher to include continuous monitoring or lengthy visits to the affected community over a period of many years. On the other hand, Freudenburg is right that these are vitally important issues and that the patterns and lessons that emerge in one boomtown (or in any other assessment problem) should give us guidance in similar future developments. This points to an important role for the academic community interested in SIA: the long-term study and monitoring of the social impact of large development in communities where such development is taking place.

One case where this very role has been taken up is in Huntly, New Zealand where a team in the University of Waikato is studying the socio-economic impacts generated by the process of locating, designing, and constructing a large power station in a small town made up of a variety of socio-economic and racial groupings. The Project Huntly began in 1975 and has a main objective of gathering information which would assist planning for similar future projects (Fookes, 1979, 1978). This is a *monitoring* project now entering its fifth year of study of such topics as land and housing, local authority administration, demography, traffic generation, provision of services, recreation, employment, community attitudes and stress, and minority racial groups. Of special interest in a lengthy project of this type is the ability to compare resident expectations with actual events for a variety of population sub-groups. In addition, Project Huntly has established a data base of 98 variables which may prove useful for testing for some causal relationships between construction activity and postulated impacts. Project Huntly is also paying attention to the concept of monitoring itself and should provide valuable information on the possibilities and pitfalls of this important aspect of SIA.

Issues in Impact Assessment

With most impact assessments it is essential that analysts recognise and take into account the pluralistic nature of the decision process. This is especially important in SIA and we have noted a move in this direction from a number of different quarters. EIA, on the other hand, may avoid the issue where biophysical impacts are taken as population-wide impacts, but this should not always be assumed to be the case. As Shields (1975, p. 280) notes:

'The impacts of high technology projects affect different people in different ways at different times. Some people lose a great deal, others gain, and others most probably fall somewhere in between, gaining in some ways but losing in others.'

The continued recognition of this pluralism will be helped by the institutionalising of SIA in the development process – but only in a form, as Torgerson (1979) warns, which promotes active public participation which begins before commitments to a project have been made.

Some people say the main problem with assessment is simply that these techniques obstruct new development, are overly pessimistic, and generally slow down progress. If, however, the results and responses they generate are taken as fuel for pluralist debate then this information, while certainly not pleasing all factions, can hardly be obstructionist in concept and any substance to that charge must lie in the misapplication of the techniques. As for pessimism and progress

– one man's pessimism is another's healthy scepticism and the optimal rate of progress depends, of course, entirely on one's definition of progress. Again it is a pluralist issue. Recently civil engineers' professional societies on both sides of the Atlantic noted how impact assessment was a 'useful tool' which could 'raise the consciousness of practitioners … so that issues are expanded and considered' (Howie, 1978, p. 22).

An issue second only to the one of pluralism is the question of how to integrate and indicate trade-offs between types of impacts: the social, the economic, and the natural environment. Johnston (1975, p. 153) notes that major political battles are fought along these lines:

'Does economic progress impose too many social and environmental costs? Does environmental pollution require too many economic sacrifices? Are social programs too expensive economically?'

The only final answer will come from intelligent political debate which will be fostered if impact researchers construct their work so as to indicate what and where trade-offs are possible, and what the relative magnitudes of these might be. Integration between discrete types of rational analysis will be helped by an understanding of the nature of the policy making process such as has been advocated here. Lastly, a satisfactory mix of techniques and the timing of their use is probably best judged on site, and from experience.

For environmental impact studies the biggest problem is just that: sheer size of output. Attempts to describe complex ecosystems with virtually infinite inter-relationships result in descriptions of extreme complexity, and even limiting the EIA to the more significant impacts still often results in massive surveys. A single power station project in the US, for example, may generate 2,500 pages of EIA, much of it of only marginal significance to decision makers if they bother to decipher it at all. The issue is not one of the failure of comprehensiveness as much as one of synthesis and communication. Many statements of environmental impact have no method of separating the serious issues from the trivial and yet this is essential if decision makers are to comprehend and utilise EIA's. Some environmentalists may argue that EIA's are undiscriminating because researchers wish to camouflage the critical issues but more likely the problem is the opposite: a fear of synthesis and selection which is reflected in the reluctance to downgrade the non-critical issues (Bardach and Pugliaresi, 1977). If environmental impact analysts accept that they, too, are part of the political debate rather than disinterested professionals they might overcome such reluctance.

In social impact assessment a lack of methodological rigour results in an *ad hoc* project by project approach which has the apparent advantage that each SIA is tailored (ideally) to the decision needs of policy makers concerned with *a* particular project. This advantage may be offset, however, by four disadvantages: (i) that lack of any systematic methodology can hide endogenous value judgements which do not reflect any political consensus on the part of concerned parties; (ii) lack of methodological rigour hampers efforts to advance the state of the art by the systematic application of empirical methods in such difficult areas as prediction of impacts, or the isolation of exogenous demographic variables; (iii) that it is difficult to compare or contrast different projects or different SIA's; and (iv) that it is difficult to integrate potentially important theoretical work and successful methodological approaches from other disciplines into the SIA approach. Aside from the relative newness of the social impact assessment field the main reason for this state of affairs is that most impact studies have to be concerned with the immediate needs of policy making rather than methodological development. Finally, the complex and multi-faceted nature of the decision process should be reflected in SIA which stresses equally the importance of good data collection and thorough public participation.

Notes on further reading

The literature on environmental impact assessment is voluminous. The best place to start is with Hammond, Macinko and Fairchild (1978) which is a substantial and perceptive review of the literature of EIA with over 3,400 references discussed at some length by 26 authors.

General introductions to EIA techniques are found in Corwin et al. (1975) and Canter (1977) from a North American perspective, and Catlow and Thirlwall (1976) from the UK perspective. Good articles on the practical use and limitations of EIA include Bardach and Pugliaresi (1977) on the US experience and Clifford (1978) and Beer (1977) on the UK's. Clark et al. (1978b) is a good review of basic methodology.

Holling (1978) is a comprehensive overview of environmental systems modelling. Tribe et al. (1978) provides a thought-provoking discussion on the philosophical and value aspects of environmental analysis.

The literature of social impact assessment is scanty by comparison. Finsterbusch and Wolf (1977) is an interesting compendium of articles especially those of Peterson and Gemmell, and Sassone. Runyon

(1977) describes a number of methodological techniques which might be applied to SIA, and Flynn (1976) comments on the methodological weakness of most current SIA. The latter article is in the *Social Impact Assessment* bulletin – the only periodical devoted solely to SIA, although *Environment and Behaviour* also takes up the topic. Finally, Torgerson (1979) is a serious and lengthy consideration of the philosophy and the politics of SIA in a policy making perspective, and an important contribution to this fledgling field.

References

Argonne National Laboratory, 1978. *Energy and Environmental Assessments*, No. 5.

Bardach, Eugene and Pugliaresi, Lucien, 1977. 'The Environmental Impact Statement vs. the Real World' In *The Public Interest*, Vol. 9, pp. 22–38.

Beer, Anne, 1977. 'Environmental Impact Analysis' In *Town Planning Review*, Vol. 48, pp. 389–96.

Bisset, R., 1978. 'Quantification, Decision Making and Environmental Impact Assessment in the United Kingdom' In *Journal of Environmental Management*, Vol. 7, pp. 43–58.

Boyer, Jeanette C., Mitchel, Bruce and Fenton, Shirley, 1978. *The Socio-Economic Impacts of Electric-Transmission Corridors – A Comparative Analysis*. Faculty of Environmental Studies, Ontario: University of Waterloo.

Burkhardt, D. F. and Ittelson, W. H., 1978. *Environmental Assessment of Socio-Economic Systems*. New York and London: Plenum Press.

Burnett, Pat, 1977. 'Perceived Environmental Utility under the Influence of Alternative Transportation Systems: A Framework for Analysis' In *Environment and Planning* A, Vol. 9, pp. 609–24.

Canter, Larry W., 1977. *Environmental Impact Assessment*. New York: McGraw Hill Book Company.

Carley, Michael and Walkey, Anna, 1978. 'Some Key Elements in Social Impact Assessment' Canadian Conference on Social Impact Assessment, Banff, Paper.

Catalano, R., Simmons, S. J. and Stokols, D., 1975. 'Adding Social Science Knowledge to Environmental Decision Making' In *Natural Resources Lawyer*, Vol. 8, pp. 41–59.

Catlow, J. and Thirlwall, C. J., 1976. *Environmental Impact Analysis* London: Department of the Environment.

Chalmers, James A., 1977. 'The Role of Spatial Relationships in Assessing the Social and Economic Impacts of Large-Scale Construction Projects' In *Natural Resources Journal*, Vol. 17, pp. 209–22.

Cheremisinoff, P. N. and Morresi, A. C., 1977. *Environmental Assessment and Impact Statement Handbook*. Ann Arbor: Ann Arbor Science Publishers.

Clapham, W. B. Jr., and Pestel, R. F., 1978. *A Common Framework for Integrating the Economic and Ecological Dimensions of Human Ecosystems. II: Processes and Problem Chains Within the Natural Stratum*. Luxemburg: International Institute for Applied Systems Analysis.

Clark, B. D., Chapman, K., Bisset, R. and Wathern, P., 1976. *Assessment of Major Industrial Applications*. London: Department of the Environment.

Clark, B. D., Chapman, K., Bisset, R. and Wathern, P., 1978a. 'Methods of Environmental Impact Analysis' In *Built Environment*, Vol. 4, pp. 111–21.

Clark, B. D., Chapman, K., Bisset, R. and Wathern, P., 1978b. *Environmental Impact Assessment in the USA: A Critical Review*. Research Report 26. London: Department of the Environment.

Clark, Michael, 1978. 'Environmental Impact Assessment: An Ideology for Europe' In *Town and Country Planning*, pp. 395–99.

Clifford, Sue, 1978, 'EIA – Some Unanswered Questions' In *Built Environment*, Vol. 4, pp. 152–60.

Conner, D., 1978. 'The Community – Partner or Patient in Social Impact Assessment' In *Constructive Citizen Participation*, Vol. 6, pp. 3–5.

Corwin, R. et al., 1975. *Environmental Impact Assessment*. San Francisco: Freeman, Cooper & Co.

Culhane, Paul J., 1975. 'Note: The Academic Research Group as a Model for Social Impact Assessment' In *Environmental Sociology*, Vol. 7, pp. 17–20.

D'Amore, Louis J., 1978. 'An Executive Guide to Social Impact Assessment' In *Business Quarterly*, Vol. 43, pp. 34–45.

D'Amore, Louis J. and Rittenburg, Sheila, 1978. 'Social Impact Assessment: A State of the Art Review' In *Urban Forum*, Vol. 3, pp. 8–10, 12.

Dee, et al., 1973. 'Environmental Evaluation System for Water Resource Planning' In *Water Resources Research*, Vol. 9, pp. 523–35.

Environment Canada, 1974. *An Environmental Assessment of Nanaimo Port Alternatives*. Ottawa: Environment Canada.

Finsterbusch, Kurt and Wolf, C. P., 1977. *Methodology of Social Impact Assessment*. Stroudsberg, Pennsylvania: Dowden, Hutchinson and Ross.

Finsterbusch, Kurt and Barker, Michael, 1977. *Social Impact Assessment Manual for Highways*. Maryland State Highway Administration.

Fitzsimmons, S. J., Stuart, L. I. and Wolf, C. P., 1975. *Social Assessment Manual: A Guide to the Preparation of the Social Well Being Account*. Cambridge Mass.: Abt Associates Inc.

Flynn, Cynthia, 1976. 'Science and Speculation in Social Impact Assessment' In *Social Impact Assessment*, No. 11/12, pp. 5–14.

Fookes, T. W., 1978. *Social and Economic Impact of the Huntly Power Station*. New Zealand: School of Social Sciences, University of Waikato.

Fookes, T. W., 1979. *Monitoring Social and Economic Impact: Huntly Case Study*. New Zealand: School of Social Sciences, University of Waikato.

Freudenburg, W. R., 1978. A *Social* Social Impact Analysis of a Rocky Mountain Energy Boomtown. Paper presented to the annual meeting of the American Sociological Association, September, San Francisco.

Griffith, Carl, 1978. 'A Welfare Approach to SIA' In *Social Impact Assessment*, No. 34, pp. 9–12.

Grigsby, J. E. and Hruby, M., 1978. 'Linking Social Impact Assessment and Human Services' In *Social Impact Assessment*, No. 25, pp. 3–10.

Hammond, K. A., Macinko, G. and Fairchild, W. B. (eds.), 1978. *Sourcebook on the Environment*. Chicago and London: University of Chicago Press.

Haussmann, F. C. (ed.), 1978. *Techniques and Methods for Social Impact Assessment*. Institute for Environmental Studies, University of Toronto.

Hill, M. and Alterman, R., 1974. 'Power Plant Site Evaluation: The Case of the Sharon Plant in Israel' In *Journal of Environmental Management*, Vol. 2, pp. 179–96.

Holling, C. S. (ed.), 1978. *Adaptive Environmental Assessment and Management*. Chichester: John Wiley and Sons for the International Institute for Applied Systems Analysis.

Howie, Will, 1978. 'Impact Analysis: a US Growth Industry' In *New Civil Engineer*, 12 January.

Johnson, Ronald W. and Pierce, John M., 1975. 'The Economic Evaluation of Policy Impacts, Cost-Benefit and Cost-Effectiveness Analysis' In Scioli and Cook (eds.), *Methodologies for Analysing Public Policies*. Lexington: D. C. Heath.

Johnston, R. A., 1975. 'Assessing Social and Economic Impacts' In Corwin et al.

Jones, Harry and Twiss, Brian C., 1978. *Forecasting Technology for Planning Decisions*. London: Macmillan Press Ltd.

Kneese, Allen V. and Bower, Blair T. (eds.), 1972. *Environmental Quality Analysis: Theory and Method in the Social Sciences*. Baltimore and London: The Johns Hopkins Press.

Lee, Norman and Wood, Christopher, 1978a. 'EIA – A European Perspective' In *Built Environment*, Vol. 4, pp. 101–10.

Lee, Norman and Wood, Christopher, 1978b. 'The Assessment of Environmental Impacts in Project Appraisal in the European Communities' In *Journal of Common Market Studies*, Vol. 16, pp. 189–210.

Leopold, L. et al., 1971. *A Procedure for Evaluating Environmental Impact*. Washington: US Geological Survey.

Olsen, Marvin E. and Merwin, Donna J., 1977. 'Toward a Methodology for Conducting Social Impact Assessments Using Quality of Social Life Indicators' In *Methodology of Social Impact Assessment*. Finsterbusch, K. and Wolf, C. P. 1977.

O'Riordan, T. and Hey, R., 1976. *Environmental Impact Assessment*. London: Saxon House.

Pearce, D. W., 1978a. *The Social Incidence of Environmental Costs and Benefits*. Aberdeen University: Occasional Paper No. 78–08.

Peterson, George L. and Gemmell, Robert S., 1977. 'Social Impact Assessment: Comments on the State of the Art' In *Methodology of Social Impact Assessment*. Finsterbusch, K. and Wolf, C.P. 1977.

Polytechnic of Central London, 1973. *Impact: A Study of the Effects of Proposed Oil Platform Construction in the Western Highlands*. London.

Runyon, Dean, 1977. 'Tools for Community-Managed Impact Assessment' In *Journal of the American Institute of Planners*, Vol. 43, pp. 125–35.

Sassone, Peter G., 1977. 'Social Impact Assessment and Cost-Benefit Analysis' In *Methodology of Social Impact Assessment*. Finsterbusch, K. and Wolf, C. P. 1977.

Shields, Mark, 1977. *Social Impact Assessment: An Analytic Bibliography*. US: Fort Belvoir, VA: US Army Institute for Water Resources.

Sondheim, Mark W., 1978. 'A Comprehensive Methodology for Assessing Environmental Impact' In *Journal of Environmental Management*, Vol. 6, pp. 27–42.

Stenehjam, E. J., 1978. *Summary Descriptions of SEAM: The Social and Economic Assessment Model*. Argonne National Laboratory, Illinois.

Torgerson, Doug, 1979. *Industrialisation and Assessment: Social Impact as a Social Phenomenon*. Report to the Northern Social Research Division. Ottawa: Department of Indian and Northern Affairs.

Tribe, L. H., Schelling, C. S. and Voss, J., 1978. *When Values Conflict – Essays on Environmental Analysis, Discourse and Decision*. Cambridge, Mass.: Ballinger Publishing.

U.S. General Accounting Office, 1978. 'Assessing Social Programme Impact Evaluations: A Checklist Approach' Washington: PAD–97–2. GAO.

Waters, W. G. II., 1976. 'Impact Studies and the Evaluation of Public Policies' In *Annals of Regional Science*, Vol. 10, pp. 98–103.

Wolf, C. P. (ed.), 1974. *Social Impact Assessment: The State of the Art*. Milwaukee: Environmental Design Research Association.

Wolf, C. P., 1975. 'Social Impact Assessment in a Cross-Cultural Perspective' In *Environmental Sociology*, Vol. 6, pp. 18–28.

Wood, Christopher, 1977. 'Environmental Impact Assessment in the UK: A Review' In *Landscape Research*, Vol. 2, pp. 11–16.

9 Social Forecasting and Futures Studies

In Chapter 5 we noted that social forecasting could be described as the use of quantitative techniques for prediction, and futures research as attempts to generate possible alternative visions, or scenarios, of the future by making use of a variety of quantitative and qualitative techniques. Futures research, therefore, may be viewed as encompassing social forecasting. Three types of futures research have been identified: trend extrapolative, qualitative, and dynamic modelling (Chambers et al., 1971). Trend extrapolative research is social forecasting in that it is always quantitative and projects patterns and changes in patterns based on historical data. Qualitative research, on the other hand, relies on human judgement and rating schemes, and usually manipulates qualitative information in a quantitative fashion. Qualitative research is often undertaken when objective data is scarce – a common situation. The dynamic modelling approach is also quantitative and expresses mathematically relationships between variables in a specified system. This results in a prediction of a future occurrence given some other occurrence, rather than simply an extrapolative projection.

Each of these types of futures research has four dimensions:

(1) The operative sector in which the forecast is being made – technological, economic, social or cultural, etc.
(2) The range of the projection – short, medium or long term.
(3) The particular technique chosen, based in part on the first two dimensions.
(4) The reflexive effects of forecasting in which forecasts reflect and influence attitudes and values, and may even act as self-fulfilling prophecies (McHale, 1976, p. 236).

As to the techniques themselves, they are numerous and varied. Over a decade ago Jantsch (1967) noted over 100 methods and many more have appeared in various guises since, especially related to business and technology forecasting. Here we describe only the most common of each type of futures techniques. The references at the end of the chapter suggest further sources which describe many of the other, more specialised, techniques.

Trend Extrapolation

Of the quantitative techniques many are concerned with extrapolating contemporary historical trends into the immediate future in order to estimate minimum and maximum curves representing the growth or decline of some activity. Such techniques implicitly assume that factors which influenced past phenomena will continue to have the same or a similar effect in the future, and that the direction and rate of this effect can be estimated. For all techniques but the most simple, this assumption is not that trends themselves will necessarily continue into some uneventful future, but rather that certain factors are operating to produce certain effects and that, unless one has reason to believe that these factors will cease to operate as they have in the past, one might assume their continuation. As such, all trend extrapolations are implicitly tentative and based on an assessment of the likely stability of the pattern of influencing factors (Ferkiss, 1977, p. 21). The key factor is the current rate of change of the important factors and changes in these rates of change – whether the rates are accelerating or decelerating. Once this is known various mathematical techniques are used to develop projections based on the analysis of time-series or chronologically ordered points of raw data. The analysis tries to identify regular or systematic variation in the series of data, seasonal variation, cyclical patterns repeating every few years, trends in the data, and the growth rate of those trends (Chambers, 1971, p. 50).

The most common of the time series techniques are curve fitting methods which attempt to draw out, with least error, the curve which best represents the discrete plotted points. These often make use of some form of least squares regression. This relatively unsophisticated approach is sometimes useful for short term forecasting. Attempts, however, to extend it even to the medium term have often resulted in fallacious forecasts which in turn may cause a mismatch between social need and capital expenditure. For example, the recent difficulties in projecting fertility rates and school enrolments provide a good example of the problems which might be caused by reliance on the assumption that trends will continue to move in the same direction over time. To overcome these limitations a few more sophisticated curves are postulated. Jones and Twiss (1978), in their excellent revue of technology forecasting techniques for business, describe three such curves which may have applicability to public policy:

(1) Growth, or S-curves, which recognise that trends mature, or begin to level off, as finite physical limits or points of decreasing utility are reached, for example, train speeds or number of automobiles per household.

(2) Quantified analogies which suggest that similar events separated in time may follow somewhat parallel development patterns. These can be projected and used to anticipate events and problems associated with the introduction of legislated social change. For example, the introduction of government medical insurance in a country previously without such a scheme might be compared with the prior introduction of similar schemes in other countries.

(3) Substitution curves which suggest that a new product or programme will replace the use of an old product or programme at a rate which can be predicted given some historical data on which to base a prediction. For example, the introduction of birth control clinics will probably replace some visits to family doctors at a specified rate.

No matter how sophisticated these extrapolative techniques, however, they do more or less assume a continuous situation, which while likely over the short term, is not over the long term. As such, the techniques which are useful for social forecasting in the immediate future do quite poorly in the longer term, unless data patterns are exceptionally stable. These techniques cannot begin to predict contextual changes, turning points, or discontinuities which influence, upset or overthrow trends, nor do they impute any causal relationship whatever between stimulating factors and the phenomena under study. Potential discontinuities are only developed in qualitative techniques, and postulated causation in dynamic models.

Qualitative Techniques

The trend extrapolative techniques then are limited for anything but short-term forecasting and, in any event, require historical data which is often quite scarce. A variety of qualitative techniques have sprung up in response to the demand for future projections given the limitations of extrapolation. These techniques are qualitative in that they rely on human judgements and criticism gathered by the asking of questions of opinion and value. They are not so much concerned with

predicting *a* future as with generating a number of plausible alternative futures. These alternatives will demonstrate a range of event
occurrences and possible trend fluctuations which policy makers may
wish to anticipate so as to meet with the appropriate plans. The
primary purpose of these qualitative techniques then is not so much
to predict the future as to facilitate exploration of possible networks
of critical events.

Scenario writing

One of the best known (if only for its notoriety) methods of generating
possible alternatives for the future is scenario writing. The chief pro-
ponent of this approach has been Herman Kahn of the Hudson
Institute. Scenario writing has been defined as a 'technique which
attempts to set up a logical sequence of events in order to show how,
starting from the present (or any other given) situation, a future state
may evolve step by step' (Tydeman and Mitchell, 1977, p. 12).
Scenario writing is a completely subjective activity and may involve
no more than the imagining of various sequences of future events by
some 'bright' individual. At its best it is a careful examination of the
crucial issues in society in the hope of grasping the nature of any
paradigm shifts which might occur. Naturally enough, scenario
writing is open to criticisms of prejudice, hidden value judgement,
and even theatricality, and can have no more function than to sensitise
author and readers to the possibility of alternative futures (Fowles,
1976, p. 260).

Delphi Technique

A well known and popular qualitative technique is the Delphi
technique developed by Helmer and Dalkey at the Rand Corporation
in the 1960s. This approach makes use of panels of anonymous experts
for forecasting in the hope of avoiding the psychological and person-
ality problems of group interaction which may hinder face-to-face
dynamics, for example, domination of a meeting by the strongest
personality or reputation. Delphi is, in Helmer's (1972, p. 15) words
'a systematic method of collecting opinions from a group of experts
through a series of questionnaires, in which feedback of the group's
opinion distribution is provided between question rounds while pre-
serving the anonymity of the responses'. As these rounds progress the
panel's membership, which may number from 7 to 100 or more, are
expected to consider the degree their estimates differ from group
consensus and to revise the estimates if they choose. In this way, a
consensus of expert opinion arises. Delphi is suggested for use where

objective data is lacking and to obtain forecasts of the time scale or schedule of future events, subjective probability estimates of some occurrence, subjective but quantitative estimates of future activity levels, and new factors which may influence the future state of techno-logical or social developments (Jones and Twiss, 1978, p. 6). The Delphi methodology has evolved considerably over the years but all variations retain the basic characteristics of anonymity and iterative, interactive forecasting. Recently a computer assisted Delphi has been developed which enables direct but anonymous interaction, larger panels, and participation over an undetermined time period (Boze-man, 1977, p. 545).

Studies of the usefulness of Delphi show conflicting results. A number render favourable conclusions such that different panels produce similar forecasts and that a significant number of events do indeed take place as predicted (Ament, 1970). Others are critical, especially of Delphi's lack of a theoretical base. Sackman (1974 and 1976), in a study for the Rand Corporation where Helmer developed Delphi, finds that it is not empirically linked to objective and independently verifiable external validation criteria and should be replaced by rigor-ous questionnaire techniques. Probably the biggest limitation to Delphi is the fact that consensus of opinion is reached not by a comparison of arguments of substance but 'due to whatever person-ality factors cause one sort of individual to hold his ground and another to compromise' (Fowles, 1976, p. 261). In spite of these limitations, however, there is some role for expert forecasting, especially related to changing technology (for example, in the aerospace industry) and Delphi may be helpful as one of a number of inputs to a policy decision.

Cross Impact Analysis

One problem with Delphi is that future events are treated as discrete occurrences rather than in inter-related networks of possible events. The cross impact technique attempts to overcome this limitation by assessing, in a subjective, judgemental manner like Delphi, the prob-ability of the future occurrence of an event given the recurrence of a pattern of earlier events or changes in trends. This is done by developing an initial list of potential events along with (obviously subjective) estimates of their occurrence. Then estimates of the prob-ability of various combinations of events occurring, usually displayed in matrix form, are used to adjust the initial probabilities. For example, events X and Y may have a low probability of occurrence when considered independently. If event X does take place, however, the probability of Y may increase considerably. In this case X might be the development of a lightweight electrical storage battery by 1985 and Y the widespread use of electric vehicles by 1990.

Cross impact is therefore concerned with events over time: given X what is then the likelihood of Y? A computer is almost always used in cross impact to assess the changing probabilities in each cell of the matrix through a series of potential sequences of event-occurrences related to trends. Three levels of sophistication are noted in cross impact studies:

Level 1   estimates which events will occur by time T
Level 2   estimates which events will occur by time T and the order of their occurrence
Level 3   estimates which events will occur by time T and the actual time of their occurrence (Enzer and Alter, 1978, p. 231).

In spite of its high degree of quantification, cross impact, dependent as it is on subjective judgements, is of course open to the same criticisms as Delphi, especially concerning the lack of a theoretical base. As Fowles notes 'like Delphis ... quasi-models such as cross impact analysis also operate on unproven notions about the nature of society' (Fowles, 1976, p. 261). Also cross impact, like Delphi, relies on asking questions and this means there is no assurance about what respondents actually mean when they answer the question 'If.... then....? or if they even understand the conditional nature of the question. For these reasons it is no doubt wise to think of cross impact, not as a predictive technique, but rather as allowing:

'A heightened awareness of situations which may arise to thwart otherwise well conceived policy choices and an understanding of the follow-up actions that may be taken after initial choices are made.' (Enzer, 1976, p. 14).

Gaming

A technique with some value as an educational, or sensitising, device is role playing in what have been described as 'serious games'. Here participants assume a role and a position on some postulated future issue. The role is played out in interaction with others in the game, often utilising a computer for instantaneous analysis of the cross impact of various decisions. This computer feedback often forms the basis for the next round of the game. These games are common in strategic military planning, in technology assessment, and are sometimes used in town planning exercises. A number are described in Zuckerman and Horn (1973). While the games have no research value and are not predictive, they are useful for bringing potential but competing resource users face to face in a mock political situation and they sometimes help people understand others' perceptions and reactions to potential events.

Counterfactual Analysis

Similar to gaming is this recent and unique approach to studying the future. The authors of counterfactual analysis, Baer and Fleming (1976), take the stance that usual futures techniques (like cross impact) postulate some hypothetical event in the future and then attempt to place that event in the context of numerous other events in future – all hypothetical and relying on a myriad of assumptions, implicit and explicit. They argue that this constitutes an entire system of unknowns with virtually unlimited possibilities for compounding error. Rather they suggest that a proposed policy be imagined as occurring in the recent past and then 'counterfactual' alternative events be developed by taking the known sequence of events and asking how they might have differed had the proposed policy been in effect. Thus, alternative policy impacts can be suggested based on an analysis which has other variables, such as demographic changes, as realistic conditions in that they have already occurred. The known course of events (say policy A) is compared with one or more counterfactual courses of events (say policy B or C). At points of time (say 1970) when a different outcome to past development would likely have occurred given policy B or C different outcomes can be suggested and these in turn will influence outcomes later in time. A first round of analysis establishes a plausible range of policy impacts and subsequent iteration, by computer simulation if applicable, and with increasingly sensitive estimates of impacts, generates increasingly refined estimates of counterfactual outcomes.

For example, policy A may be the actual building of a motorway in 1970 which is compared with the hypothetical policy B of extended public transport. Given that many other social and demographic factors are held constant (as actually occurred), then the two policies can be compared over a range of actual and hypothetical impacts. Such impacts could include settlement patterns, traffic levels, air pollution levels, public expenditure levels, etc. The authors emphasise that counterfactual analysis cannot be used for prediction but rather is designed to serve as a basis 'for informed and rigorous speculation, providing both an understanding and a feel for a sequence of events' in the spirit of Vickers' (1965) term 'policy appreciation'. It is probably most useful in the short to medium term where the variables of the immediate past approximate most closely the policy situation which is to be appreciated.

Dynamic Modelling

Neither the trend extrapolative nor the qualitative techniques make any attempt to establish systematically and quantitatively the causal linkages between various factors which influence future events. This task is left to the dynamic modelling approach, which attempts to simulate some system of inter-related variables. The basic steps in dynamic modelling have been described in the previous chapter. The dynamic model in futures research may make use of a number of trend extrapolations, but postulates causation among variables rather than using the more pragmatic approach of fitting a curve to data without attempting to specify why. The conceptual basis for dynamic modelling in futures research may be found in econometric models and economic input–output models which are based on a system of inter-dependent regression equations, the parameters of which are usually estimated simultaneously.

The most well known simulation in futures research has been the Club of Rome report *The Limits to Growth* developed by Meadows et al. at the Massachusetts Institute of Technology (1972). This was a global model with the variables of population growth, food supply, resource depletion, capital investment and pollution. This model was thoroughly criticised by the Science Policy Research Unit (1973) at Sussex University in the UK for making a number of fallacious assumptions about demographic change and technological progress – assumptions which reflected the value judgements of the researchers. This problem of endogenous value judgements is as common in futures research as in other techniques if not more so. Chapter 8 suggested that the questions used in the dynamic modelling process had to reflect (i) proven physical relationships (ii) tested postulated relationships from the social sciences or (iii) qualitative judgements as to relationships. In modelling environmental impact, quantification of bio-physical variables can be based on (i) and (ii). In any futures research with a high component of social variables, however, the necessary theoretical work required for (ii) will probably be lacking and models will have to rely on qualitative judgements. As such they can be regarded as no more than quasi-models which 'operate on unproven notions about the nature of society' (Fowles, 1976, p. 261). This lack of a theoretical base is, of course, in addition to the practical problems associated with dynamic modelling such as data availability and processing costs. So these kinds of simulations, while having considerable potential, will in the foreseeable future be more profitably confined to limited (sectoral) aspects of larger problems rather than grandiose global modelling attempts.

Issues in Futures Studies

The broadest objection to many attempts to study the future is that it is impossible – that prediction must be based on verifiable historical data extrapolated, but that extrapolation is only of short-term value given the possibility of unforeseeable events or discontinuities in trends. In addition, the argument goes, the number of variables which must be considered rises exponentially the further into the future one attempts to peer. Hence, as one author sums up this line of thought (without concurring with it), 'prediction is a worthless activity and is nothing more than speculation. However trapped out it may be in mathematical paraphernalia, any man's guess is as good or bad as another's' (de Hoghton et al., 1971, p. 14). But this line of reasoning, which may have some validity, begs the real question which is absolutely central to all attempts to manage man and resources – what does tomorrow hold, what are the range of possibilities we should try to meet if we are to manage the present and immediate future creatively? The need for some sense of the future is an essential and natural need of all man-influenced systems and the value of futures studies is not so much prediction as the development of a range of alternative futures, or boundaries which can help set the limits for consideration, discussion and debate, and management.

This boundary setting is part of a two dimensional process: first, it helps to confine the expenditure of management energy to the possible future in avoidance of the improbable. For example, it is unlikely that we need to plan in any way for the disappearance of the nation state in the next 25 years. At the same time, given those boundaries, futures studies help to alert management to the possibilities and probabilities of the future and expand range of the debate on the allocation of present day resources. For example, consideration of the alternative futures associated with technological change (micro-processors), legal change (mining of the sea), or political change (devolution and regional autonomy) are essential activities for policy makers today. And even where a particular scenario may be based on value-laden assumptions, for example, Meadows' Club of Rome world model, the ensuing debate about those assumptions can raise and help to clarify many important issues. In short, like many rational techniques, futures research is more about fuelling public-debate about important policy issues than it is about predicting any one future.

If, however, there is an exception to this it is undoubtedly with the trend extrapolative techniques which are about social forecasting rather than alternative futures. Here we do well to remember that we are talking more about projection of historical data, and not prediction which implies causality. These type of forecasts, however fraught with methodological difficulty, are essential for the short-term data needs of management in the allocation of expenditure. They are not very useful, however, for long-term policy making which is a highly political activity and in any event, their reliability appears to fall drastically in the medium term. Methodology for extrapolation is steadily improving and the further references cite a number of works which explore these developments. Of particular note are various quantitative schemes for conducting sensitivity analyses which relate changes in assumptions to the degree of change in projections. This can result in a number of possible projections (or scenarios) clearly associated with differing assumptions. As time goes on real change associated with the various assumptions can be monitored closely to allow projections to be steadily revised and transmitted to management, for example, a high, medium and low projection of school place needs based on differing assumptions as to fertility. In such a way too the forecaster, rather than becoming overly associated with a particular forecast, is associated with the process of continually revising projections based on the most recent data. Related to sensitivity analysis are methods of threshold analysis, which suggest that discontinuities will arise in trends at points where various physical thresholds like traffic flows, or those dictated by policy like public transport fares, are reached. These thresholds can be treated as assumptions associated with particular trend patterns, but much more empirical work remains to be done on validating the projected impact of different thresholds.

Finally, if there has been one major hindrance to methodological development in quantitative social forecasting it is a lack of attention to the *de post facto* examination of forecasts themselves as a check on the structure and accuracy of the forecasting models. This is certainly the case, for example, in transport forecasting (Robbins, 1978; Mackinder, 1979) and most probably in other fields as well. The reasons for this are no doubt partly institutional in so far as many forecasters are planners rather than model builders per se. By the time the forecast year is reached the policy problems of short term future are far more pressing than any examination of past mistakes, especially in times of public expenditure restraint. This, however, does not diminish the patently obvious advantages of *de post facto* studies of forecasting efforts and closer ties between academic researchers and policy planners is perhaps one key to improved social forecasting.

For most qualitative techniques there should be no pretence about prediction – generation of possible alternative futures is their sole *raison d'etre*. The main problem is that they are usually based on judgements by experts, politicians, the public, etc., and so suffer from all the problems associated with value judging discussed in Chapter 6. To date, there has been little exploration of the critical issue of the way in which personal values can influence judgement in studies of the future. Even if it is accepted that it is, say, a necessary evil to rely on opinion, there is no understanding of the basis upon which those judgements stand, i.e. what is the rationale behind them. The rationale may be difficult to make explicit, or 'value weighters' may consciously or unconsciously have a distorted basis for their opinions. Hammond et al. (1977, p. 359) on self-reporting, suggest that if there is anything that psychologists have learned it is that introspective reports of cognitive activity have little meaning and it may be suspect to take such judgements at face value.

The most promising approach to this problem is from the behavioural sciences and is termed 'judgement research'. This approach views most qualitative futures techniques, for example cross impact or Delphi, as asymmetrical in their concern for the outcome of judgements. They lack a balancing 'something' which is a model of the inputs to judgements, that is, the more basic values, beliefs and assumptions about causality which underlie opinions invariably made up of some mix of rationality and intuition. The argument for studying these underlying assumptions is that policy analysis based on judgements may be of limited value to the decision maker unless the 'bases underlying the judgements are made explicit' (Lonsdale, 1978, p. 222). A judgement model is proposed which is used alongside other futures techniques to make them more symmetrical in the attempt to simulate reality. The judgement model requires researchers to ask 'what if' questions about cognitive systems and uses quantitative indicators as proxy variables representing underlying variables. This is a form of sensitivity analysis about judgements in that questions are asked about how different parties' judgements would change if certain problem parameters changed. Asking such questions, it is argued, helps to foster exploration of the underlying values system upon which particular judgements are based. This judgement approach, combined with other rational techniques, helps shed light on the best compromise the policy maker can hope for given the configuration of critical value conditions and outcome of judgements, and helps those concerned to understand better the nature of their own cognitive processes. Again, the intention is not prediction as much as a deeper appreciation and understanding of the interplay of trends, external events, and potential policies, and of the range of alternative futures (Lonsdale, 1978, p. 217).

Finally, in simulations by dynamic modelling the main problem, lack of theoretical development, has been discussed previously. Many analysts see this type of modelling as holding out the best promise for futures research, at least in the long run. Although any but the simplest socio-cultural models are too complex to be grasped by a single human brain, rapid increases in capacity and dexterity of computers may result in programmes capable of reliable modelling of large scale social change (Fowles, 1976, p. 262). In addition, dynamic models have the methodological advantage that work on them is proceeding in a variety of disciplines in addition to futures research, for example, in social indicator research (Land, 1975) and environmental impact research (Holling, 1978). The one chink in the armour of the hopes for dynamic modelling at a societal scale is the possibility that the assumption that societies are coherent systems may not hold. To speak, for example, of 'post-industrial society' assumes a definable and perceivable interdependence among various aspects of the society and predictable relationships among causes and events in that society. As Ferkiss (1977, p. 26) asks:

'What happens to prediction if none of this is true – if this inter-relatedness is not present in the same way all the time? ... suppose some things are more affected than others at different times in different contexts? What if there are major disfunctions in the social and cultural systems, and some interfaces occur without communication or influence?'

If that is indeed the case there will be no societal models of social change as there are econometric models of economic change. But we will never know without trying and even if such sophisticated modelling proves impossible the methodology will have at least developed to the point where subsystems, for example the educational or the health service subsystem, can be simulated reliably enough for good forecasting.

In conclusion, and although methodological development should proceed apace, the future of futures research should be much as Duncan (1969, p. 115) described that future ten years ago:

'There will be no pretence that we can gradually move toward the perfection of methods of anticipating what will actually occur, for such perfectability is not logically possible, aesthetically appealing or morally inspiring. What we may hope to improve, if not perfect, is our sense of responsibility for making known the implications of our knowledge.'

This responsibility of which Duncan speaks in conjunction with futures studies is of course the same sense of moral responsibility which was noted in Chapter 6 as an essential complement to all rational analysis.

Notes on further reading

Jones and Twiss (1978) is an excellent guide to the techniques of forecasting. The introduction to Ascher (1978) provides a stimulating discussion of the role of forecasting in the decision making process. Armstrong (1978) takes a humorous and rather idiosyncratic approach to forecasting and is most useful for an intensive bibliography – given that his comments can be more or less ignored.

On futures research, Linstone and Simmonds (1977) and Boucher (1977) both contain an interesting diversity of articles, in the latter the articles by the editor are especially worthwhile. Fowles (1978) has also edited an enormous collection of contributions from various authors – Part II is of most interest. Ferkiss (1977) is a good review of the applications and potential of futures research.

Linstone and Turoff (1975) is more or less the handbook of the Delphi technique. This should be read in conjunction with Sackman (1974 and 1976) and Hill and Fowles (1975) for a balanced perspective.

Fowles (1977) is an excellent article on the role of values in futures studies and Miles (1975) considers the inherent limitations of all attempts at prediction. Finally a perusal of the journal *Futures* is essential to a grasp of the subject.

References

Abt, Clark C., 1970. *Serious Games*. New York: Viking Press.

Ament, R. H., 1970. 'Comparisons of Delphi Forecasting Studies in 1964 and 1967' In *Futures*, Vol. 2, pp. 15–23.

Arrelbaum, Richard P., 1977. 'The Future is Made not Predicted: Technical Planners vs Public Interests'. In *Society*, Vol. 14, pp. 49–53.

Armstrong, J. Scott, 1978. *Long Range Forecasting from Crystal Ball to Computer*. New York: John Wiley & Sons.

Ascher, William, 1978. *Forecasting: an Appraisal for Policy-Makers and Planners*. Baltimore and London: The Johns Hopkins Press.

Baer, William C. and Fleming, Skye M., 1976. 'Counterfactual Analysis: An Analytical Tool for Planners' In *Journal of the American Institute of Planners*, Vol. 42, pp. 243–52.

Boucher, Wayne I. (ed.), 1977. *The Study of the future: An Agenda for Research.* Washington: National Science Foundation.

Bozeman, Barry, 1977. 'Epistemology and Future Studies: How Do We Know What We Can't Know?' In *Public Administration Review*, Vol. 37, pp. 544–9.

Chambers, J. C., Mullick, S. K. and Smith, Donald D., 1971. 'How to Choose the Right Forecasting Technique' In *Harvard Business Review*, Vol. 49, pp. 45–74.

de Hoghton, C., Page, W. and Streatfield, G., 1971. *... and now the Future. A PEP Survey of Futures Studies,* Vol. 37. London: Political & Economic Planning.

Duncan, Otis Dudley, 1969. 'Social Forecasting – The State of the Art. In *The Public Interest*, Vol. 17, pp. 88–118.

Encel S., Marstrand P. K. and Page W. (eds.), 1975. *The Art of Anticipation.* London: Martin Robertson.

Enzer, Selwyn, 1976. 'Interactive Cross-Impact Modelling' Paper M27, Center for Futures Research, University of S. California.

Enzer, Selwyn and Alter, Steven, 1978. 'Cross Impact Analysis and Classical Probability' In *Futures*, Vol. 10, pp. 227–39.

Ferkiss, Victor C., 1977. *Futurology: Promise, Performance, Prospects.* Georgetown University Washington: The Washington Papers, Vol. 5. Center for Strategic and International Studies.

Fowles, Jib, 1976. 'An Overview of Social Forecasting Procedures' In *Journal of the American Institute of Planners*, Vol. 42, pp. 253–63.

Fowles, Jib, 1977. 'The Problems of Values in Futures Research' In *Futures*, Vol. 9, pp. 303–14.

Fowles, Jib (ed.), 1979. *Handbook of Futures Research.* Westport and London: Greenwood Press.

Hammond, K. A., Mumpower, J. L. and Smith, Thomas H., 1977. 'Linking Environmental Models of Human Judgement: a Symmetrical Decision Aid' In *IEEE Transactions on Systems, Man and Cybernetics*, Vol. 7, pp. 358–67.

Harman, Willis W., 1978. 'Understanding Social Change – Some Comments on "Prediction and Social Change"' In *Futures*, Vol. 10, pp. 143–7.

Helmer, Olaf, 1977. 'Problems on Futures Research: Delphi and Cross Impact Analysis' In *Futures*, Vol. 9, pp. 17–31.

Hill, Kim Quaile and Fowles, Jib, 1975. 'The Methodological Worth of the Delphi Forecasting Technique' In *Technological Forecasting and Social Change*, Vol. 7, pp. 179–192.

Holling, C. (ed.), 1978. *Adaptive Environmental Assessment and Management.* Chichester: John Wiley & Sons for the International Institute for Applied Systems Analysis.

Jantsch, E., 1967. *Technological Forecasting in Perspective.* Paris: Organisation for Economic Cooperation and Development.

Jones, Harry and Twiss, Brian C., 1978. *Forecasting Technology for Planning Decisions.* London: Macmillan Press Ltd.

Land, Kenneth C., 1975a. 'Theories, Models and Indicators of Social Change' In *International Social Science Journal*, Vol. 27, pp. 7–37.

Linstone, Harold A. and Turoff, Murray (eds.), 1975. *The Delphi Method – Techniques and Applications.* Reading, Mass.: Addison-Wesley Publishing.

Linstone, Harold A. and Simmonds, Clive W. H., 1977. *Futures Research New Directions.* Reading, Mass.: Addison-Wesley Publishing.

Lonsdale, Alan J., 1978. 'Judgement Research in Policy Analysis' In *Futures*, Vol. 10, pp. 213–24.

Mackinder, I. H., 1979. *The predictive accuracy of British transport studies – a feasibility study*. Transport and Road Research Laboratory, Supplementary Report 483.

Martino, Joseph R., 1972. *Technological Forecasting for Decisionmaking*. American Elsevier.

McHale, John and McHale, M. C., 1976. 'An Assessment of Futures Studies Worldwide' In *Futures*, Vol. 8, pp. 135–45.

Meadows, D. H. et al., 1972. *The Limits to Growth*. New York: Universe Books.

Miles, Ian, 1975. *The Poverty of Prediction*. Farnborough & Lexington: D. C. Heath & Co.

Mitchell, R. B., Tydeman, J. and Curnow, R., 1977. 'Scenario Generation: Limitations and Developments in Cross Impact Analysis' In *Futures*, Vol. 9, pp. 205–15.

Robbins, J., 1978. 'Mathematical modelling – the error of our ways' In *Traffic Engineering and Control*. January.

Roberts, P. C., 1978. 'Futures Research in Government' In *Science and Public Policy*, Vol. 5, pp. 438–43.

Sackman, H., 1974. *Delphi Assessment: Expert Opinion, Forecasting and Group Procedure*. Santa Monica, California: Rand Corporation. R–1283–PR.

Sackman, H., 1976. 'A Sceptic at the Oracle' In *Futures*, Vol. 8, pp. 444–6.

Science Policy Research Unit, 1973. 'The limits to growth controversy' In *Futures*, Vol. 3, special issue.

Tydeman, J. and Mitchell, R. B., 1977. 'Subjective Information Modelling' In *Operational Research Quarterly*, Vol. 28, pp. 1–19.

Vickers, Sir Geoffrey, 1965. *The Art of Judgement*. New York: Basic Books.

Wheelwright, S. C. and Makridakis, S., 1973. *Forecasting Methods for Management*. New York: John Wiley & Sons.

Zuckerman, David W. and Horn, Robert E., 1973. *The Guide to Simulations – Games for Education and Training*. Lexington: Information Resources.

10 Evaluation Research

Dramatic growth in the past two decades in government expenditures on the public services has given rise to an interest in the *de post facto* examination of government programmes as a guide to the future. Evaluation research generally makes use of social science methodology in a manner that allows the empirical assessment of programme worth. This research attempts to answer such questions as: to what extent did the programme achieve its objectives, at what cost, was administration and implementation done well, and was the programme worth doing?

Three important purposes for conducting evaluation research have been identified (Freeman and Bernstein, 1975, p. 14). First, like social science in general, it can serve to change popular myths and beliefs, and challenge professional commitments. For example, recent research on teacher–pupil ratios make us rethink the popular notion that increasingly smaller classes are automatically better. Secondly, evaluation research provides measures of public accountability in the provision of social services and a means for identifying inefficient and ineffective programmes. This is the most common use of evaluation, for example, in studies of Educational Priority Area policies in the UK or similar projects, like HEADSTART, in the USA. Thirdly, evaluation research may form part of rational efforts to plan new programmes and refine social policies, either in the normal course of programme funding or as part of an administrative technique like Management by Objectives, which will be considered shortly.

Evaluation research can be distinguished from more academically oriented research (Weiss, 1972, p. 6) by the points that evaluation research: (i) is primarily intended for use in decision making and policy analysis and as such answers questions posed by the decision maker and not the researcher; (ii) is usually concerned with judging success or project worth relative to stated goals rather than being non-judgemental in character; (iii) often takes place in a policy setting where academic research procedures cannot be followed; (iv) is often marked by role conflicts between researchers and practitioners; (v) is usually not published, but typically is reported to those commissioning the research; (vi) may involve the researchers in allegiances to the organisation funding the research, and to improving efforts at social change.

Evaluation research tends to be concerned with either the impacts of programmes, the process of carrying out those programmes, or, in a more comprehensive fashion, both. Impact evaluation tries to gauge the extent to which a project effects a social change in a desired direction, and implies specified operationally defined objectives (Freeman and Bernstein, 1975, p. 13). The research is structured in such a manner so as to demonstrate that social changes are a function of the particular programme intervention and not other external factors. This type of evaluation research may take the form of controlled experiments on two or more population groups, longitudinal comparisons over time, or other quasi-experimental research designs. Where concern is more with efficiency than with effectiveness, evaluation may well be carried out within the framework of some cost-utility approach, like cost-effectiveness analysis, which stresses measures of output per unit input. Examples are the now somewhat discredited Planning Programming Budgeting System (PPBS) and the more recent emphasis on productivity measurement.

Evaluation which concentrates on the process of programme implementation rather than output, generally addresses two issues:

(1) Whether or not the practices and intervention efforts were undertaken as specified in the original conception and are consistent with the programme objectives and general principles embodied in the programme design.

(2) Whether or not the programme has been directed towards an appropriate or specified target population or target locality. (Freeman and Bernstein, 1975, p. 12).

Here the emphasis is on the manner by which formulated policy has been carried out and services have been delivered – on implementation and management technique. The concern is on 'how things get done' in the real world of conflicting programme objectives and organisational and institutional complexity. This has recently been termed implementation research.

Controlled and Quasi Experiments

This approach to evaluation research is marked by the attempted application of rigorous social scientific methodology to the evaluation of government programmes. Ideally, this means controlled experimentation with the allocation of individuals at random between a

control group and an experimental one, before and after measurements, and tests for statistical significance. When this is impossible,
which is very often, longitudinal studies using time series data is the
favoured method of evaluation and the most common. Finally, when
neither of these is feasible the researchers may fall back on any number
of simple statistical manipulation techniques for analysing data. These
latter evaluations are not experimental as such and rely a good deal
on common sense. They may result in faulty conclusions, usually as
a result of wrongly ascribing cause and effect. In many cases, however,
they are helpful, and given resources and time pressures, most appropriate for the evaluation at hand.

Attempts at evaluation by experimentation face a number of pitfalls
(Rivlin, 1971; Poland, 1974):

(1) Designing such research in a rigorous fashion is very difficult.
    There may be conflict between the desire for valid, reliable
    results which require long periods of research, and the equally
    urgent need to obtain results quickly and at a low administra-
    tive cost.

(2) There are time horizon problems – the interesting effects of
    various changes in social programmes may not show up for
    years or even decades. For example, benefits of programmes
    aimed at children may not reveal themselves until later stages
    in the life cycle.

(3) There may be moral dilemmas associated with giving new
    benefits to one group at the same time they are withheld from
    a control group – this may seem to be arbitrary behaviour on
    the part of government.

(4) Experiments on practical, manageable sample sizes do not
    necessarily reflect the changes in behaviour which might occur
    when new programmes are applied at a national level. Different
    locations where programmes are administered may differ
    greatly at the onset making post programme comparisons
    impossible.

(5) There are problems in implementing an experimental policy –
    different administrators may implement in different ways. The
    need to innovate or change social programmes to obtain better
    results while they are ongoing might make the experiment
    unreliable.

(6) If administrators are convinced of the worth of a programme
    they may try to influence the research accordingly, or, con-
    versely, to ignore the results. Proposals for experiments might

be a means of achieving delay in instituting real policy action, and reports on unsuccessful projects may well be suppressed.

(7) Isolation of programme variables from other external effects may be difficult and the broader the effects of the programme the more likely that external factors will influence dependent variables. Further the replication of social experiments is usually impossible – they are most often 'one-shot' attempts at evaluation.

Faced with such an array of difficulties one may wonder if evaluation by rigorous experimentation is worthwhile or even possible. The answer is yes, but a very qualified one. Haveman and Watts (1976, p. 440), as a result of their lengthy involvement in the New Jersey negative income tax experiments, suggest that controlled experimentation is only viable in cases where adequate behavioural models already exist, where high research standards can be met, and where programmes involve major, non-marginal shifts in the financing or delivery of social services. In these cases, it is likely that experimentation can add to the stock of knowledge, but powerful impacts on public policy are hardly expected. Public debate will be altered but not decided.

The Cost-Utility Approach to Evaluation
A quite different theme in evaluation research concentrates on efficiency and effectiveness and seeks to apply the principles of the cost-utility techniques to the evaluation of government programmes. The first and most well-known attempt at this emerged in the 1960s in the form of Planning Programming Budgeting Systems. PPBS in turn is an integral part of what has come to be known as corporate planning in the UK. PPBS can be described as a planning system in which government expenditure is evaluated by relating it to major policy objectives – by way of conducting an analysis of the costs and benefits of alternate routes to those objectives (Garrett, 1972).

PPBS is conducted in three stages. The first is the planning stage which requires that a management information system be set up which can transmit information on expenditure classified (possibly across administrative boundaries) according to the presumed output stemming from objectives. The second, programming, stage involves the allocation of resources to programmes in such a manner as to achieve the objective in the most effective and efficient manner. The third, budgeting, stage involves the integration of the PPBS plan into the management structure.

This last stage has been described as the weakest link in PPBS. Certainly a lot of the criticism directed at it might certainly have been tempered if the enthusiastic introduction of PPBS, federally in the USA and locally in the UK, had been done more judiciously and with an awareness of the inherent institutional limitations in such a highly rational approach. As with social experimentation PPBS as an evaluative technique would and has been resisted by those administrators who found that it was not in their personal interests to have programmes examined in great depth, and who found that cross-departmental analysis was inimical to their realistic objective of bureaucratic maintenance. The concentration on objectives required by PPBS is quite different from the day-to-day concern with process which occupies many administrators – the provision of service or the 'doing' aspects of their jobs. Indeed, some researchers concerned with implementation go as far as to argue that this type of goals-oriented rational approach embodies a kind of ideology or perception of the world itself quite distinct from the reality facing most administrators and this makes PPBS suspect as a model for decision making (Lewis and Flynn, 1979). Finally the information needs of PPBS are very great, and classification schemes complex, and these themselves may not appear to meet reasonable cost-benefit criteria for many administrators.

The bureaucratic problems of PPBS aside, there is another basic weakness where the concern is effectiveness rather than efficiency. The essence of the technical end of PPBS is described as 'a cost-benefit analysis ... which compares the costs of achieving the benefits from one programme with the cost of receiving equivalent benefits from an alternative programme' (Kahalas, 1978, p. 88). Or one might add, comparing the benefits and costs of one programme with the costs of doing nothing. If a PPBS emphasises effectiveness, that is attaining pre-established objectives, it is necessarily required that the objectives be identified, conceptualised and operationalised, and the results compared between alternatives. But the problems of defining objectives prior to measuring effectiveness are of course numerous and inter-programme comparisons are equally fraught with difficulty. For these reasons, evaluations of programme effectiveness within PPBS often gave way to methodologically and administratively simpler efficiency studies.

These types of efficiency studies, termed productivity or performance measurement, are considered shortly. First it is worth mentioning, but only briefly, some techniques related to PPBS which attempt to complement it and thus mitigate its deficiencies. Management by

Objectives (MBO) involves a process whereby senior administrators set overall objectives and each individual within the organisation translates those objectives into 'action plans' or objectives which guide his own activity (Kahalas, 1978). At the onset of the budget year superiors and subordinates examine these sub-objectives in light of the higher objectives and these are reviewed for progress throughout the year. The hope is that MBO fosters the development of reasonable operationalised objectives throughout a bureaucracy, and that involving all the actors in the development of those objectives encourages commitment to them thus lessening the tension between personal and organisational goals. In a simplistic way a commitment to MBO can only be 'good management' and provided it does not consume too many corporate resources it could well facilitate the development of operationalised objectives useful for budgeting.

Another technique related to PPBS is 'Zero-Based Budgeting' which involves the evaluation of all government programmes from the 'ground up' each fiscal year, by the usual variations of the cost-utility approach. The intention is to eliminate or cut back programmes which have become entrenched in the budgeting cycle beyond their effective life-span or in excess of their cost to benefit ratio. In this way administrators are responsible for justifying levels of expenditure on particular programmes on a regular basis. The most noted example of the use of the zero-based approach is by the then Governor of Georgia, Jimmy Carter, who used the technique to reduce budgets across 57 government agencies with reductions of from one to 15 per cent (Pyhrr, 1977). Generally, however, the costs in time and energy of annual re-evaluation has led to the introduction of rotating zero-base budgets in which some, but not all, programmes are examined each year. Like PPBS and MBO the zero-based approach is really about the provision of as much information as practicable for good resource allocation, the continued re-examination of organisational objectives, and marginal cost-cutting and re-allocation of funds within agencies. The techniques are not useful for wholesale shifts in resource allocations which can only occur subject to open political debate.

The rather over-enthusiastic and somewhat insensitive introduction of these approaches at the national level in the US and in local government in the UK engendered a considerable amount of vociferous criticism and many assumed that was the end of these overly trendy management and budgeting techniques. Nevertheless PPBS supporters, now much more reasonable in tone, continue to suggest real, if limited, advantage to such rational evaluation techniques. In the USA, there is considerable promotion of zero-base budgeting at the national and state level (Pyhrr, 1977). For budgeting UK public expenditure at the national level, Else and Marshall (1979) argue that the analytic concept of PPBS remains valid and worthwhile, provided it is introduced gradually and on a modest scale, unlike previous efforts. At the local government level in the UK, Thomas (1978) suggests that in spite of a variety of problems with the use of PPBS in a party political context, there are advantages such as clarification of expenditure alternatives, provision of management information, and 'a systematic framework within which ... political values can be applied' (p. 257). This accords with the 'real if limited advantage' argument put forward in this volume.

Performance Measurement

In addition to the desire for more systematic budgeting procedures the dramatic growth of public expenditure also gave rise to attempts to measure tangible improvements in public service delivery. Sometimes termed productivity measurement or performance auditing, at the extreme the various terms define anything from detailed work studies of the activities of individuals or small groups to measures of the effectiveness of policy (Epping Forest District Council, 1977). In actual practice performance measurement is almost entirely concerned with efficiency in terms of the conversion of organisational inputs to outputs. What few effectiveness measures (as opposed to efficiency) that do exist are usually citizen assessments of the quality of service delivery. Proponents of performance measurement studies argue that at any government level they can (i) help determine progress towards targets or goals set by public administrators; (ii) identify problem areas and help set priorities for efforts at improving productivity; (iii) help implement worker incentive schemes or so-called self-financing productivity deals (Hatry, 1972, p. 776). Comparison between local authorities may also help set priorities for allocating resources by central government to local government (as is done, for example, by the UK's Rate Support Grant) and focus attention on those services which perform consistently well so that they serve as examples for other authorities to emulate.

Considerable interest has been evinced in these studies, especially at the local government level. In the UK, for example, a study of five district councils has recently been completed by the District Audit Service (Epping Forest District Council, 1976). In the USA the Urban Institute has issued a variety of reports and guides to performance measurement. The approach is also quite topical given the increased attention in formal collective bargaining agreements to productivity clauses which stipulate changes in work rules and practices with the objective of achieving increased productivity and reciprocal worker gains (Horton, 1976). In this 'productivity bargaining' measurements of performance serve as both *ex ante* bargaining counters and *de post facto* checks on contract fulfilment, the latter often linked to varying wage payments.

The Urban Institute suggests the following criteria for selection of performance measures:

(1) Appropriateness and Validity. The measures should be quantifiable, in line with goals and objectives for that service, and be oriented towards the meeting of citizen needs and minimising detrimental effects.

(2) Uniqueness, Accuracy, and Reliability. Measures generally need not overlap, double counting should be avoided, but some redundancy may be useful for testing the measures themselves.

(3) Completeness and Comprehensibility. Any list of measures should cover the desired objectives and be understandable.

(4) Controllability. The condition measured must be at least partially under government control.

(5) Cost. Staff and data collection costs must be reasonable.

(6) Feedback Time. Information should become available within the time frame necessary for decision making (Hatry et al., 1977, p. 5).

Measures of performance take a number of forms. The most common is the ratio of input to output, with the amount or level of service delivery as the output measure, and employee hours or unit cost of service provision as the input measure. Examples of such measures are tons of refuse collected per workday, kilometres of street cleaning per monetary unit expended, or number of hours of recreational facility operation per monetary unit, etc. The assumption in each of these type of measures is that the *quality* of the output is held constant or improves as more efficient ratios are achieved (Hatry et al., 1977, p. 234). The output measures generally most easy to develop are those that cover services with the most tangible outputs. For example, refuse collection measures are much easier to come by than measures of police efficiency. In the latter case not only does some measure like 'number of arrests per employee hour' encourage perverse effects like inadequate investigation, but the objectives of policing programmes are undoubtedly subject to political debate. These type of problems, however, may reflect not so much any inadequacy in the general approach as the primitive methodology for measuring some service outputs.

Where output measures are unattainable it is common practice to fall back on personnel and equipment utilisation rates as substitute measures. These generally take the form of the ratio of the resource actually used to the amount potentially available (Hatry et al., 1977, p. 236). For example, in public transport a likely measure is percentage of trips late or cancelled because of unavailable personnel or vehicles compared to the scheduled amount, and for recreational facilities, number of scheduled hours closed for maintenance. These types of measures are best used as supplements to output measures.

Another supplement to these measures are those which come closest to measuring effectiveness – citizen evaluation of the quality of service provision. This generally takes the form of interviews of actual or past clients to ascertain the number satisfied with a service per monetary unit or employee hour expended. Such measures thus combine the traditional and somewhat suspect number of clients served with satisfaction levels. The Urban Institute suggests that this form of measure will be particularly important to those who believe that citizen, or client, satisfaction with services is a major product of government services. Although of considerable importance to evaluation even such citizen-generated measures must be taken judiciously. It is not infeasible for clients to be dissatisfied with a perfectly adequate service because of a variety of unmet needs which that service is not designed to fulfil. For example, police services cannot make up for inadequate social services. Conversely, a majority of citizens might be quite satisfied with environmental health services (for example, air emission regulations and inspections) which are in fact sub-standard and inefficient. Also citizen ratings may not translate easily into work activities – citizens may be concerned with the overall level of public transport provision, something a traffic supervisor can hardly do anything about. Nonetheless, these and other methodological problems considered, the citizen evaluation of services is a valuable addition to performance measurements.

As with many other types of evaluation, performance measurements only take on meaning with reference to something – usually other similar measurements. Hatry (1972) suggests three reference points: first, comparisons over time to provide information on trends and progress – this is the most common approach in government and with productivity deals. Secondly, comparisons can be made across jurisdictions, especially those with similar characteristics. This was the approach of the UK Epping Forest study which compared the activities of five district councils. Third, comparisons can be made among operational units within a particular service, for example, refuse collection crews can be compared to foster learning about productive methods.

There are problem areas in performance measurement which need to be considered. Simplest is the fact that in many cases there are no standards for performance, for example, there is probably no such thing as an acceptable rate of crime, and so such measures as are developed reflect value judgements of some section of the community (Hara, 1976). In many cases, however, this problem is theoretical – what administrators and the public are concerned with is relative rates of change – rising crime and not any absolute level. Of more importance is the point that increasing the efficiency of an ineffective service may well be counter-productive, and the fact that most of these measures are not about goals or effectiveness must always be kept in mind. Related to this is the fact that most workload or cost productivity measures do not reflect ultimate goals. Street cleansing might become highly efficient but if the amount of street litter increases, the streets may well be dirtier than ever. Another problem is that such measures should serve to motivate workers positively but the opposite is always a danger. An emphasis on tons of refuse picked up from the street might encourage workers to favour stones over paper litter. The answer to these dilemmas is to choose appropriate combinations of measures for each service. Street cleansing tonnage and employee hours figures, for example, would be complemented by studies of actual street cleanliness measured by one of the available formulae, and by occasional citizen evaluation.

In collective bargaining agreements there are additional problems. The most common is the failure to recognise that increasing output per employee hour is not necessarily desirable if unit cost increases, caused by higher salaries or reduced working hours, are of such a magnitude as to more than offset productivity gains. This can often be the case in the public sector, especially given the recently increased levels of militancy of public sector unions in the UK and the US. Horton (1976, p. 408) points out, for example, that 'productivity gains may be counter-productive if they are accompanied by or result from too rapid increases in the price of inputs'. This is, of course, the efficiency perspective and unit cost increases in the public sector may be desirable for other reasons. It is important, however, that the relationship between unit labour costs and productivity levels be understood.

Finally, as far as the implementation of performance measurement schemes go, the UK and the US experience suggest very similar guide-lines. The most important prerequisite for a successful scheme is that it is acceptable to management and staff. This requires that as many people as possible have a hand in the design of the measures, the data collection procedures, and the implementation of the scheme. The performance measurement process, as much as possible, must be presented in a positive, constructive, and diplomatic manner so as to appear unthreatening. As with any evaluation this may be the most difficult task of all but the co-operative development of the schemes may alleviate this problem somewhat. In any event, individ-uals must only be held accountable for those aspects of performance which are within their control. As for the measures themselves they should be simple to use to avoid error and distortion, and as cost effective as possible. The data produced should be flexible in as much as it might be used by different departments but in the main it will have to be tailored to the specific needs of each separate operating unit. Attention should be given to the reporting frequency which may be at short or long intervals depending on the needs of management and the data source. There should be a range of measures to give a balanced perspective on any particular service delivery and to avoid the distortion and perverse effects that concentration on a single measure might introduce. Finally, measurement activities should be institutionalised, perhaps by incorporating them into cyclical budget or policy review procedures.

Issues in Evaluation

A recurring theme in any discussion of evaluation research is the potential opposition to, or non-utilisation of, the evaluation by management and staff alike. Sometimes resistance is based on the alienating effect of incomprehensible jargon on the part of evaluation and information systems. These difficulties are relatively straight-forward and the answers are obvious. Many times though the situation is more complex. For elected representatives evaluation stirs up waters better left calm and may provide material useful to opponents at the ever near next election. Administrators are reasonably concerned with such things as keeping their jobs, getting promoted, increasing agency size, power and budget, and minimising organisational conflict, and may not see evaluation as serving any of these ends. If inter-jurisdictional comparisons are intended, for example, among district councils in the UK, the fear is generated that evaluation may be simply to provide 'a league table for the general public' or for central government 'to monitor the spending of individual local authorites' (Capps, 1977, p. 109). There is no easy resolution of these dilemmas. Obviously involving as many of the actors concerned in the design of an evaluation is important, and educating all and sundry as to the value of evaluation is equally important. Evaluations can easily be written in understandable terminology, and the development of an organisational structure where evaluation is a positive activity rather than a threatening prospect is of great value. The literature is rightly packed with exhortations to these ends.

Given that organisations are multi-functional units with tasks other than goal attainment (e.g. maintenance, growth, and conflict resolution), another fruitful approach may be for evaluators to integrate the 'goal-attainment model' of rational evaluation with one that identifies the dynamics within the organisation which contributes to task co-operation, goal attainment, and may foster willingness to participate in an evaluation. Such a behavioural model concentrates on observable patterns of organisational interaction, the motives of individual participants, and the collective purpose of the programme as manifested through organisational activity (Goldstein et al., 1978, p. 24). This is the emphasis of the proponents of implementation research who argue that 'how things get done' should be studied in a framework of an organisational context where problems of the real world have to be matched to relatively fixed channels of action (Lewis and Flynn, 1979). The tools of such research include participant observation, interviewing, issue analysis, and the use of such techniques as the 'repertory grid' for studying the values, perceptions, and beliefs of actors in government. Such an approach does require additional resource expenditure and a considerable knowledge about the purposes, operating routines, and personality interactions of the organisation and will no doubt emerge as an evaluative speciality in its own right. The combination of the goals-achievement model and the behavioural model may eventually help to resolve the dilemma of resistance to evaluation and certainly moves evaluation research towards a more complete perspective on organisational systems.

Even within the rational model the measurement of output presents a methodologically difficult task. Jones and Borgatta (1972) suggest that objectives should be stated in terms of measurable change in intended directions, and if reasonably identifiable criterion variables are not available, evaluative research may not be feasible. The isolation of one or more dependent variables is difficult in the social service field where a variety of services contribute to well-being and client satisfaction. Even where such isolation is possible, the outcome measures may be so abstract as to provide little evaluative information to day-to-day programme operators, and sometimes important positive and negative side effects are ignored in an attempt to isolate variables (Cain and Hollister, 1972). In any case, it is essential that theoretical models of the chains of causation that account for goal achievement be constructed and tested – as argued elsewhere in this book, no methodological improvement can take place without such rigorous model building. Finally, the involvement of the relevant parties to the evaluation in its design and development may help to ensure that all are fully aware of the methodological strengths and weaknesses of evaluative measurement.

Notes on further reading

Olson (1973) with the subsequent commentary by Schultze and Grove provides a good theoretical introduction to the concept of evaluating government services. Rossi, Wright and Freeman (1979) is the most comprehensive guide to evaluation research itself. Alkin, Daillak and White (1979) discuss five US case studies in education in which evaluation played some positive or negative role. Abt (1977), Rutman (1977), and Guttentag and Struening (1976) are all useful collections of articles with varying opinions and perspectives.

Rivlin (1971) and Riecken and Boruch (1974) are both concerned with social experimentation and Haveman and Weisbrod (1976) draw conclusions on the value of experimentation in the light of practical attempts.

The Evaluation Studies Review Annual, now in its fourth volume, is an excellent compendium of articles which draws on recent efforts in this field (Glass, 1976, Guttentag and Saar, 1977, Cook, 1978). Other good articles are Phillips (1977) on objectivity in evaluation and Weiss (1977) on the role of evaluation in policy making.

On productivity measurement Hatry et al. (1977) is by far and away the best guide to the possibilities and pitfalls of such attempts. Horton (1976) is a good article on productivity bargaining and the September 1978 issue of *Social Policy* was devoted entirely to productivity. The *Public Administration Review* (1979, No. 1) contains a number of interesting articles on evaluation and performance measurement in local government.

The third edition of Lyden and Miller (1978) is a useful volume on various aspects of public budgeting including PPBS, productivity and the role of rationality in budgeting procedures.

References

Abt, Clark C. (ed.), 1977. *The Evaluation of Social Programmes*. Beverly Hills and London: Sage Publications.

Alkin, Marvin C., Daillak, Richard and White, Peter, 1979. *Using Evaluations: Does Evaluation Make a Difference?* Beverly Hills and London: Sage Library of Social Research.

Cain, G. and Hollister, R., 1972. 'The Methodology of Evaluating Social Action Programmes' In Rossi and Williams (eds.).

Capps, B., 1977. 'Performance Measurement: a Cautious Welcome' In *Municipal and Public Services Journal*, Vol. 85, pp. 1009–10.

Cook, Thomas D. (ed.), 1978. *Evaluation Studies Review Annual*, Vol. 3. Beverly Hills and London: Sage Publications.

Elkin, Robert and Vorwaller, Darrel J., 1975. 'Evaluating the Effectiveness of Social Services' In *Social Accounting: Theories, Issues and Cases*. Seidler, L. J. and Seidler, L. L. (eds.). Los Angeles: Melville Publishing.

Else, P. K. and Marshall, G. P., 1979. *The Management of Public Expenditure*. London: Policy Studies Institute.

Epping Forest District Council, 1977. *Performance Measurement in Local Government*.

Freeman, Howard E. and Bernstein, I. N., 1975. 'Evaluation Research and Public Policies' In Nagel, Stuart S. (ed.).

Garret, J., 1972. *The Management of Government*. Harmondsworth: Penguin.

Glass, G. V. (ed.), 1976. *Evaluation Studies Review Annual*, Vol. 1. Beverly Hills and London: Sage Publications.

Goldstein, Michael S., Marcus, Alfred C. and Rausch, N. P., 1978. 'The Nonutilisation of Evaluation Research' In *Pacific Sociological Review*, Vol. 21, pp. 21–44.

Guttentag, Marcia and Struening, Elmer, 1976. *The Handbook of Evaluation Research*. Beverly Hills and London: Sage Library of Social Research.

Guttentag, Marcia and Saar, Shalom (eds.), 1977. *Evaluation Studies Review Annual*, Vol. 2. Beverly Hills and London: Sage Publications.

Hara, L. F., 1976. 'Performance Auditing: Where do we Begin?' In *Governmental Finance*, Vol. 5, pp. 6–10.

Hatry, Harry P., 1972. 'Issues in Productivity Measurement for Local Government' In *Public Administration Review*, Vol. 32, pp. 776–84.

Hatry, Harry P. et al., 1977. *How Effective are your Community Services? Procedures for Monitoring the Effectiveness of Municipal Services*. Washington: The Urban Institute.

Haveman, R. H. and Watts, H. W., 1976. 'Social Experimentation as Policy Research: A Review of Negative Income Tax Experiments' In *Evaluation Studies Review Annual*, Vol. 1. Glass, G.V. (ed.). London: Sage Publications.

Heiss, F. William, 1978. 'The Politics of Local Government Policy Evaluation: Some Observations' In *Urban Analysis*, Vol. 5, pp. 37–45.

Horton, Raymond D., 1976. 'Productivity and Productivity Bargaining in Government: A Critical Analysis' In *Public Administration Review*, Vol. 36, pp. 407–14.

Jones, W. C. and Borgatta, E. F., 1972. 'Methodology of Evaluation' In *Evaluation of Social Intervention*, Mullen, E.J. and Dumpson, J.R. (eds.). London: Jossey Bass.

Kahalas, Harvey, 1978. 'A Look at Major Planning Methods, Development, Implementation, Strengths and Limitations' In *Long Range Planning*, Vol. 11, pp. 84–90.

Lewis, Janet and Flynn, Rob, 1979. 'The Implementation of Urban and Regional Planning Policies' In *Policy and Politics*, Vol. 7, pp. 123–42.

Lyden, Fremont J. and Miller, Ernest G. (eds.), 1978. *Public Budgeting: Program Planning and Evaluation* (Third edition). Chicago: Rand McNally College Publishing.

Merewitz, Leonard and Soswick, Stephen H., 1971. *The Budget's New Clothes*. Chicago: Rand McNally College Publishing.

Millar, Annie, Hatry, Harry and Koss, Margo, 1977. *Monitoring the Outcomes of Social Services Volume 1: Preliminary Suggestions. Volume 2: A Review of Past Research and Test Activities*. Washington: The Urban Institute.

Mullen, E. J. and Borgatta, E., 1972. *Evaluation of Social Intervention*. San Francisco: Jossey Bass.

Nagel, Stuart S. (ed.), 1972. *Policy Studies and the Social Sciences*. Lexington, Massachusetts: D. C. Heath and Co.

Olson, Mancur, 1973. 'Evaluating Performance in the Public Sector' In Milton, Moss (ed.), *The Measurement of Economic and Social Performance*. New York: Columbia University Press.

Patton, Michael Q., 1978. 'With God on Your Side: When not to Worry about Productivity' In *Social Policy*, Sept/Oct, pp. 7–14.

Phillips, D. C., 1977. 'When Evaluators Disagree: Perplexities and Perspectives' In *Policy Sciences*, Vol. 8, pp. 147–59.

Poland, O. F., 1974. 'Program Administration and Administrative Theory' In *Public Administration Review*, Vol. 34, pp. 333–8.

Pyhrr, Peter A., 1978. 'The Zero-Base Approach to Government Budgeting' In Lyden and Miller (eds.).

Rich, Robert F. and Zaltman, Gerald, 1978. 'Toward a Theory of Planned Social Change: Alternative Perspectives and Ideas' *Evaluation* Special issue, pp. 41–7.

Ridoutt, Tim, 1977. 'Input or Output? Let's get it Clear' In *Municipal and Public Services Journal*, 21 October, pp. 1052–3.

Riecken, H. W. and Boruch, R. F., 1974. *Social Experimentation*. New York: Academic Press.

Rivlin, Alice M., 1971. *Systematic Thinking for Social Action*. Washington: Brookings Institute.

Rivlin, Alice M., 1973. 'Social Experiments: The Promise and the Problems' In *Evaluation*, Vol. 1, pp. 77–8.

Roos, Leslie, L., 1975. 'Quasi-Experiments and Environmental Policy' In *Policy Sciences*, Vol. 6, pp. 249–65.

Roos, Noralou, P., 1974. 'Proposed Guidelines for Evaluation Research' In *Policy Studies Journal*, Vol. 3, pp. 107–11.

Rossi, Peter and Williams, Walter, 1972. *Evaluating Social Programs*. New York: Seminar Press.

Rossi, Peter, Wright, Sonia and Freeman, Howard, 1979. *Evaluation: A Systematic Approach*. London and Beverly Hills: Sage Library of Social Research.

Rutman, Leonard S. (ed.), 1977. *Evaluation Research Methods A Basic Guide*. Beverly Hills and London: Sage Library of Social Research.

Scott, Douglas, 1976. 'Measures of Citizen Evaluation of Local Government Services' In *Policy and Politics*, Vol. 4, pp. 111–28.

Sprigg, John, 1977. 'Lessons to be learnt from checking on performance' In *Municipal and Public Services Journal*, 7 October, pp. 979–82.

Thomas, Paul, 1978. 'Corporate Planning and PPB: Relevant in Party Political Situations?' In *Environmental Health*, Vol. 86, pp. 255–7.

Weiss, Carol H., 1972. *Evaluation Research: Methods for Assessing Programme Effectiveness*. Englewood Cliffs: Prentice Hall.

Weiss, Carol H., 1977. 'Research for Policy's Sake: The Enlightenment Function of Social Research' In *Policy Analysis*, Vol. 3, pp. 531–46.

Woodie, P. R., 1976. 'From PPBS to Program Strategies' In *Governmental Finance*, Vol. 5, pp. 50–7.

Woodward, M. J., 1976. 'Scientific Approaches to Performance Measurement in the Audit Process' In *Governmental Finance*, Vol. 5, pp. 30–7.

11 Social Indicator Research

In the mid-1960s a growing dissatisfaction with existing social statistics spawned what came to be known as the 'social indicators movement'. Initially, this was a reaction against what was seen to be an over-emphasis on measures of economic performance as indicators of social well-being. By the 1970s, the term social indicators came to encompass a wide variety of diverse attempts to specify indicators of socio-economic well-being, from the most specific indicators such as crime rates to broad integrated 'quality of life' measures based on subjective social indicators.

Although the phrase 'social indicators' as opposed to economic indicators was not coined until the 1960s, there is general agreement that the historical basis for this activity goes back to the work of the British economist, Pigou, described in Chapter 7. This ties social indicator research to the same sources of welfare economics that spawned cost-benefit analysis and its offspring and additionally points out why it quickly became almost impossible to draw a fine distinction between economic and social indicators of well-being.

A second early source also presages recent social indicator activity. This was the establishment in 1929 of a US Presidential Committee to survey changes in American life as measured by social statistics. The committee was directed by the sociologist William F. Ogburn, whose broad interest was promoting the role of social research in government decision making. Ogburn was attempting to establish a 'statistical series that would improve the methods of extrapolation and correlation as a means of predicting the future' (Bell, 1969, p. 75). The result was the publication in 1933 of *Recent Social Trends* which investigated such topics as changing social attitudes and interests, the family, recreation and leisure time activities, crime and punishment, population, and health. Ogburn was especially interested in the hitherto unexplored inter-relationships among these rather disjointed topics, the study of which he hoped would give a more holistic view of American society. The depression and the subsequent war put an end to Ogburn's hopes for an annual publication of this sort but his influence is now reflected in the spate of annual national compendiums of social statistics, for example, the British namesake, *Social Trends.*

Social indicators are, therefore, at the minimum and in every type of rational analysis, statistics. Beyond this there is little agreement as to the definition of a social indicator *per se.* The Conference of European Statisticians (Fanchette, 1974) suggests a hierarchical classification of statistical series which may or may not be termed social indicators:

(1) Raw statistical series.
(2) Key series – commonsense attempts to pick out interesting series of statistics.
(3) Comprehensive schemes of statistics.
(4) Composite indices derived from combining individual series.
(5) Synthetic representative series derived by multivariate techniques.
(6) Predictive series which fit explicitly into formal social models.

This classification is of special interest because each of the categories 2–6 have been termed social indicators at some point in time. Some researchers make use of all types 2–6 as social indicators (Fitzsimmons and Lavey, 1976). Other researchers argue that only 4–6 are social indicators in that they involve summation or aggregation, as distinguished from 1–3, which are termed social statistics (United Nations, 1976). Still others argue cogently that the term social indicators should be confined to category 6 – fitting explicitly into a social model (Bunge, 1975). For our purposes we will consider any usage from 2–6 under the term 'social indicator' – not because we will argue that particular case but because we are attempting to make order of what is common usage in policy analysis.

One of the best policy-oriented classifications of types of indicators remains that of Carlisle (1972, p. 26) who distinguishes:

(1) Informative indicators which are intended to describe the social system and the changes taking place within it. These are social statistics subject to regular production as a time series and which can be disaggregated by relevant variables.
(2) Problem-oriented indicators which point towards policy situations and action on specific problems.
(3) Programe-evaluation indicators which are operationalised policy goals to monitor the progress and effectiveness of policy.

To this Edwards (1975, p. 280) rightly adds a fourth type termed 'decision making indicators' which he defines as variables describing demographic, environmental, pathological or service provision characteristics which are useful for identifying geographical areas or population sub-groups towards which policy is directed. These decision making indicators are often used to allocate resources among these competing geographical areas or sub-groups. If the above two classification systems, one based on a hierarchy of statistical sophistication, the other describing the policy use of indicators, were put together in a 4×6 matrix the cells would certainly describe most attempts at social indicator research.

During the past six years the direction of much of this research has been towards the development of organised groups, or systems, of social indicators. The term 'indicator system' can generally be taken to mean a group of social indicators organised around component parts of the social system. The term is used in differing ways but usually implies an attempt at comprehensiveness in considering the diverse parts, or domains, that make up individual or societal well-being. Less than comprehensive groups of indicators can be termed social indicator sets. The move away from the use of just a few indicators towards groups or sets of indicators stemmed from research indicating a lack of correlation between various posited indicators at any given time. This implied that different variables were measuring different characterestics, and it could not be assumed that any one would act as a good surrogate for another. Also the difficult problems of aggregation, which we have seen again and again in rational analysis, ensured that attempts at highly composite indicators would fail to produce a reasonable measure. Research efforts tended, therefore, to avoid reliance on too few indicators and moved towards multi-indicator systems or sets.

With regard to the construction of these groups, or systems, of social indicators Zapf (1975) suggests four problem areas that must be dealt with to some degree in every case: the definition of some notion of welfare, the determination of system structure on theoretical or practical grounds, the selection and operationalisation of indicators, and the actual process of measurement. Each of these four criteria is not addressed equally in recent research, some avoid one or more component entirely. All social indicator sets and systems, however, have a determined structure, and it is this structure which suggests a classification for examining a variety of attempts at social indicator research.

It can be proposed that this structuring of indicators leads to a breakdown into four types of social indicator systems:

(1) Those organised programmatically.
(2) Those systems developed from social goal areas.
(3) Those systems developed around an individual's interactions and achievements over the course of a life-cycle.
(4) Those systems with a theoretical basis.

These categories are not mutually exclusive, the last especially will tend to combine with the others as research progresses. Perhaps a trend towards the disappearance of theoretically-based systems as a separate category and the blurring of the distinctions among the other three will be a mark of future progress in social indicator development. At present, these categories are good reflections of the state of the art. In subsequent sections we examine in detail these various types of social indicator systems and examine recent research efforts in light of these structural categories, and in terms of the problem areas of indicator system development.

Programmatic Development
Many social indicator sets are developed programmatically, that is, they are organised by means of the convenient breakdown provided by the institutional arrangements of society, such as housing, health services, religion, the law, transportation, education, etc. Certainly it makes sense that indicators would be called on to answer the information needs of various agencies, especially in government, and therefore be structured by organisational divisions among these agencies and by available data bases. It is common for indicator sets to be confined to a particular agency or programme type, for example, education, housing, or employment. More recently systems of indicators organised programmatically have been developed, most commonly by government. These efforts are often termed social reports and generally make use of key statistical series, using the term social statistics and social indicators variously. The latter are generally national in scope, the former may be national, regional, or local. A number of programmatic indicator sets are specifically local in character, and often used to classify neighbourhoods.

National Social Reports
The developing concern of government with the need to supplement data on the national economy with more socially oriented information has resulted in the issuance of social reports in no less than twenty-nine countries (Park and Seidman, 1978). These generally consist of social indicator systems organised programmatically and reflect the percep-

tion that social information is as important in policy making as economic data. Such social reports are compendiums of statistics and contain a wide variety of basic objective data divided into categories reflecting administrative practice and presented in chart or graph form. Some include attitudinal data, others written commentary on the statistics. The Central Statistical Office in the UK, for example, has now issued the ninth volume of *Social Trends* which is designed to 'bring together statistics which would facilitate judgements about social change' in a descriptive, rather than prescriptive manner (Thompson, 1978b, p. 53). The Department of Commerce in the USA has recently issued a second volume of a similar triennial publication entitled *Social Indicators 1976* which is described as 'a comprehensive graphic collection of statistical data selected and organised to describe current social conditions and trends in the United States' (Johnston, 1977, p. XXIII). This volume, too, stresses that the statistics it contains are strictly descriptive and the report does not attempt to provide any explanations of why or how the conditions that are described came about. A list of the social reports of twenty-eight other countries is contained in the introduction to the American volume. At least ten of these specifically use the term 'social indicators' in their title – whether they do contain social indicators is a matter of some contention and most social reports might be described as containing key series or comprehensive schemes of statistics. In terms of Zapf's criteria, social reports generally have no explicit notion of welfare, the system structure is practical, with complete operationalisation of the indicators selected. Quality of measurement generally reflects the quality available in the parent governmental statistical service itself.

Such broad attempts at national social reports are open to criticism from every side. The 'social indicator or not' argument is partly one of definition. The US volume reflects the all-inclusive definition which considers anything non-economic as a social indicator to the extent that even the most basic demographic information on gross population changes are considered 'social indicators of a special kind'. At the other extreme are many social scientists, beginning with Land in 1971, who argue that by very *definition* social indication must be concerned with cause and effect relationships. Bulmer (1979), for example, argues that while *Social Trends* is an intelligent synthesis of available social statistics, it does not really contain any social indicators.

The resolution of this semantic struggle may lie in a definition which differentiates levels of social indication. These definitional arguments stem in part, however, from deeper questions about the relationship of fact to theory. The editors of social reports may feel they are presenting 'facts' for others to interpret but the very selection of some data to the exclusion of other data is of course a normative act based on some implicit theory as to the nature and the important components or domains of human welfare. As such the selection process should be subject to the same scrutiny as any other value judgements in policy analysis.

It must also be made clear that social reports are collections of social statistics and not explanatory measures which represent inferences drawn from the analysis of relationships among specified variables. The use of such models of the process of social change and of hypothesis testing in developing social indicators is essential in the long term. It is too much, however, to expect that current efforts at social reporting be based on such models, given that such a modelling process is only in its infancy in the social sciences generally. Nor can such published social reports be expected to contain time series data extensive enough for anything like a regression analysis. They merely summarise trends for individual consideration.

Programmatic indicator systems are often criticised for their selection of categories within which to organise the statistics. With regard to *Social Indicators 1976*, for example, 'the categories are those a government finds comfortable and familiar, and as the federal government is often criticised for a lack of co-ordination across agencies, so there is a lack of co-ordination across chapters' (Seidman, 1978, p. 718). However, as with many aspects of social indication, to criticise is easy, to construct very difficult. Seidman points out, such a programmatic structure is convenient to users and reflects the necessity to be cost-effective which means that data is bound to reflect the organisation of those bureaucratic agencies responsible for much of the collection of the data (Johnston, 1978a, p. 723). In addition, much of this data will have been collected primarily for other purposes and inclusion in a social report is simply an indirect benefit. Finally, programmatic social reports are criticised for not reflecting social goals and priorities but such goals, of course, are hardly clear-cut and their development, where possible, is difficult, limited in value, and resource consuming. We return to this last point.

Indicators for Local Area Analysis

A variety of programmatic indicator systems and sets have been developed, especially in the UK, out of a concern for identifying or remedying multiple deprivation or social malaise in older inner city neighbourhoods. These schemes either seek to make an *informative* classification of neighbourhood types or to aid positive discrimination programmes by aiding *normative*, or prescriptive, judgements as to where and to whom additional resources should be allocated These latter efforts are sometimes termed priority area policies and are based on the assumption that the multiple deprived can be identified by social indicators as suffering from a complex condition, greater than the sum of its parts, which would benefit from special treatment over and above that normally provided (Smith, 1978).

The best known neighbourhood classification approach is that of the Planning Research Applications Group (PRAG) of the UK's Centre for Environmental Studies. The basic aim of the PRAG scheme is to summarise as precisely as possible the diversity of residential conditions in Britain by developing a series of types of residential neighbourhoods which are as homogeneous as possible in terms of their scores on a variety of specified indicators (Webber, 1977). This classification provides three basic sets of information: first, a conceptual definition of different area types, second, a location in physical space for classified neighbourhoods and thirdly, a means of comparing such areas across a variety of variables.

The PRAG scheme has made use of 40 variables from special UK census data known as Small Area Statistics (SAS) to develop a typology of 36 neighbourhood types out of a set of 999 areal units (wards and parishes). This was done by using a computerised technique known as cluster analysis, which aggregates towards residential types on the basis of their similarity measured by reference to the 40 census variables. A simple example of 10 units is displayed in Figure 11.1. In this case, the cluster analysis would link the two units which

Figure 11.1   Cluster Analysis

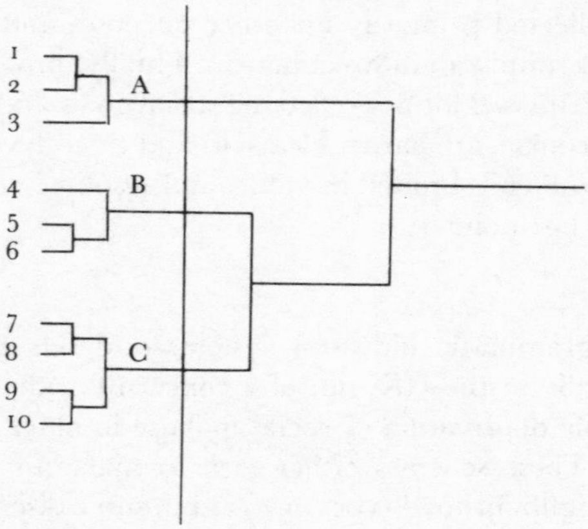

were closest in this 10 dimensional space based on variable scores, and reduce these to a single dimension. The process can be repeated until all the units are linked. At any stage in the process a group of neighbourhoods is identified, and the PRAG analysis was halted at 36 (or three in our example) as the least number of classifications which adequately differentiated neighbourhoods.

The PRAG scheme is seen as having four potential policy applications (Webber, 1977, p. 2). The first is as a sampling frame for other surveys and the second is as a framework for organising non-census data, for example, subjective social indicator data. The third application might be to assist in choosing the relevant social indicators which could be used in defining priority areas. The fourth and related application would be to select priority areas either in terms of particular localities, or for particular types of areas (say older row housing) to which national policies might be directed. In addition, the effect of shifting national policies towards particular types of residential neighbourhoods can be better gauged in a PRAG type framework. In these last two options the PRAG scheme moves towards normative application of social indicator data. In so far as the PRAG scheme remains basically descriptive an important area of contention is whether it actually serves as a good vehicle for classifying Britain's residential neighbourhoods, that is, are the groupings suitable for different cities and regions? The evidence so far is contradictory and more research needs to be done to validate the scheme.

This normative use of indicators as embodied in the third and fourth application of PRAG is most closely identified with many of the British government's positive discrimination programmes, or what in the US is often termed 'affirmative action'. The first of these was the designation of Educational Priority Areas in which schools, in neighbourhoods identified as deprived by certain social indicators, received extra resources. Other programmes included the Community Development Projects (CDP) and Housing Action Areas (HAA), all of which depended on some sort of social indicator for delineating areas and client groups.

These priority area approaches have received considerable criticism of three sorts. The first relates directly to the ability of the indicators to demonstrate that deprivation of a certain magnitude exists within some defined areal unit, and might be called the delineation criticism. For example, one recent study of the designation of an HAA (which gives local authorities certain powers related to housing improvements) casts doubt on the ability of a set of nationally determined indicators to describe a particular neighbourhood's reality (Dennis,

1978). This raises questions as to the policy usefulness of such an approach. The second criticism is the statistical argument which points out that however one uses indicators to define socially deprived areas, unless one half of Britain is so designated, more poor will be outside the areas than in them. Further, within a priority area there is a great likelihood that the majority will not be deprived and thus resources may be misdirected (Holtermann, 1975). Finally, there have been a number of criticisms on structural grounds. This argument is based on the belief that social pathologies are basically linked to national or international factors, most notably inequalities in economic and political systems, and that no areal approach can have any substantial effect. Some final reports of the CDP projects, for example, took the stance that the diversity of deprived situations identified by the use of social indicators provides a case not for isolated local initiatives but for broad policies to deal with the processes of urban and industrial change (Townsend, 1976).

As with so many of the rational techniques the use of social indicators for local area analysis is not therefore simply a matter of application of technical instruments but one of political contention. Value judgements enter into problem definition, indicator choice, and locality or client group selection. There is obviously no single approach or system of indicators which will tell us in some objective fashion to what locales and to whom resources should be directed and, indeed, the concept of priority areas itself is the product of a particular value set.

Social Economic Accounts System

An extensive programmatic system of indicators, developed in the US by Fitzsimmons and Lavey (1976), is the 'Social Economic Accounts System' (SEAS) which presents 477 community level indicators organised into 15 programmatic categories. SEAS is designed to enable public policy officials, programme developers, and social scientists to understand more fully the effects of various types of public investment upon the quality of life of individuals and the relative social position of groups of people in the community.

The indicators within each of the programmatic areas or sectors (e.g. education, health, welfare, etc.) are organised into state variables which describe peoples' lives at one point in time, system variables which describe the institutional arrangements affecting peoples' lives, and relevant condition variables which are state and system variables from other sectors affecting the sector in question. Within the state and system variables some are attitudinal (subjective–ordinal) variables obtained by resident survey. Within the health sector for example, a state variable is 'number of deaths per 1,000 live births', a sector variable is 'mean age of population' and within the state variables an attitudinal variable is personal satisfaction of residents with health services. SEAS is within the recent North American emphasis on determining the social impact and environmental impact of public and private investment decisions.

In terms of Zapf's criteria SEAS contains no explicit notion of welfare. The indicators are comprehensively selected and operationalised, and considerable attention has been paid to measurement. The indicators are organised pragmatically, not theoretically, and SEAS can be described as a comprehensive scheme of statistics and social indicators. Although the lack of models of human behaviour is recognised as a problem with SEAS the authors feel it is beyond the state of the art to expect a policy oriented social indicator system to present a complete causal model of change at this time. Because SEAS falls within the pragmatic sphere of indicator research (i.e., investment decision evaluation) the emphasis on a comprehensive measuring system rather than a causal model is not surprising and the indicators themselves are plausible and relevant to many community level resource decisions. Nevertheless, the amount of implicit social theory embodied in such a comprehensive indicator system is large.

This problem with SEAS was recognised in later work of the authors who took a step closer to the integration of their indicator system into a causal model (Fitzsimmons and Lavey, 1977). They present a paradigm for the analysis of communities which conceptualises the community as a systematic, interactive and dynamic entity. The purpose of this paradigm is to provide the theoretician or researcher with a common framework for using the community, with its sub-systems, as a unit of analysis. An operational definition is proposed in which linkages are established between the 15 programmatic indicator categories, 5 'concept' categories (e.g., interaction, change, etc.) and 8 potential research objectives (e.g., to identify types of inter-action). In this manner, it is suggested that a common framework is provided whereby various research activities relating to a specific community, or the concept of community, can be integrated to improve the theoretical and practical (investment decision) under-standing of community.

Development by Social Goal Area

A second method of structuring a social indicator system is to work from the general to the specific, that is, to identify social goals, refine them to generate sub-goals or objectives, and eventually to arrive at some indicator, or indicators, of the achievement of that goal. The resultant indicator system may appear similar to a programmatically structured system but the important difference is the explicit internal logical consistency of the process of indicator development. This logical structure means that any particular indicator can be related back to some goal or objective specified by some member(s) of society. And although this process is no doubt implicit somewhere in many programmatic approaches the making of it explicit is valuable for two reasons. Firstly, it facilitates the construction of causal models between goal or sub-goal and any specified indicator. Secondly, and perhaps more importantly, it causes the value judgements of the specific member(s) of society structuring the system to be exposed for critical examination. The disadvantage of this goal to indicator approach is that it can be difficult and time-consuming, as in the OECD example below. A further problem is that politicians and administrators may simply resist attempts to measure their achievement in specific areas, just as is the case in evaluation research. Conversely, the values reflected in the indicator system may be more those of the re-searchers themselves and less those of other segments of society, as occurs to some extent in our second example. A brief third example, based on law and public statement, seem to overcome these difficulties.

The OECD Programme

This social goal area approach is the method chosen by the Organisa-tion for Economic Cooperation and Development (OECD, 1973, 1976a, 1976b, 1977, 1979) in its programme to achieve standardised definitions of the social goal areas for which systematic indicators and assessments are most needed by their member governments. The OECD is developing central concepts which guide these member governments in the preparation of such indicators of achieved social well-being of individuals, not indicators of structural or institutional states or achievements. This distinction was made in recognition of the uncertainties in the relationship between changes in structures and institutions and changes in individual well-being, in other words, the lack of causal theories of social behaviour. The programme avoided any attempt to provide explanatory or predictive indicators even though it was recognised that policy evaluation and goal setting endeavours are in great need of information bases which linked cause with effect (Christian, 1974). The reasoning of the OECD is that social theory has not yet evolved sufficiently to provide a conceptual framework for such indicators and that the political needs of the 24 member governments are best served by reaching consensus on a series of basic standards of individual well-being. As developments in theory take place, the system will be improved to take advances in partial or 'middle range' social theory into account.

The diplomatic consensus process, a factor of prime importance to the OECD, required that agreement on the most general level of social goals take place first – these were labelled social concerns and based solely on the judgement of political officers of the member nations. This method was chosen as the one most amenable to consensus. The OECD specifically rejected the derivation of indicators from existing statistics (i.e., programmatic development) because the impetus for their social indicator programme was related to deficiencies in existing data bases. A programmatic approach ran the risk of perpetuating these deficiencies by not generating new indicators or not causing existing statistical sources to be refined to the benefit of member countries. A basic starting point of the effort was to differentiate between the identification of issues related to well-being and the evaluation of those issues. The former activity was seen as amenable to the consensus process in that the components of social well-being are similar across national boundaries and over time, even if the different evaluations leading to policy must be dissimilar to reflect geographic and temporal differences.

The determination of 24 fundamental social concerns grouped into 8 goal areas was followed by the identification of a series of sub-concerns, also by consensus. An example of a social concern under the goal area 'health' is 'the probability of a healthy life through all stages of the life cycle' and two sub-concerns under this area are 'length of life' and 'healthiness of life'. As a result of the continuation of this process and the utilising of the appropriate technical expertise, provisional social indicators have emerged. Under the length of life sub-concern, for example, there are indicators of life expectancy and perinatal mortality. The indicators are ranked as to whether they correspond to all, or part of, a concern or sub-concern, or whether they are the best available approximation of a direct measure. They are expected to reveal the level of well-being for each social concern, and changes in that level over time. Measurement will rely on existing data sources where available, and on extensions to data sources and innovation where necessary.

The OECD programme, in terms of Zapf's criteria, has a defined notion of welfare, i.e., that of individual social well-being. The indicator system is structured by goal area determination by negotiation among nations. The programme recognises that it has two broad objectives: enlightening policy appraisal in the short-run, and contributing to progress in modelling social interaction in the long-run. It is dealing with the first objective immediately and will address the second as it becomes politically and theoretically feasible. The indicators specified to date include key statistical series and synthetic representative series. At present, the programme is focusing on areas of interest to member countries for the purpose of working out precise statistical definitions of indicators, examining different data collection mechanisms, and collecting actual data on a pilot basis. In addition, special reports are issued on relevant topics as they are needed (Jazairi, 1976; Johnston, 1976).

Urban Quality of Life in the USA

A second indicator system developed from social goal areas is that described by Liu (1976) in the report *Quality of Life Indicators in the US Metropolitan Areas*. This was a static study of the 'quality of life' in 1970 in 243 US urban census areas (Standard Metropolitan Statistical Areas). The study was based on a production function model which hypothesised that the quality of life, or satisfaction of wants, is an output which is the function of two factor inputs, the physical and the psychological. It is argued that the physical and psychological inputs can, to a certain extent, substitute for each other and vary in proportion to produce a given level of quality of life, but that at some point over-emphasis on one factor input can degrade the quality of life. This function is set out in a series of capability curves which represent varying degrees of the capability of society to satisfy wants.

The statistical analysis was done by way of approximately 150 indicators drawn from five goal areas: economic, political, environmental, health and education, and social. The researchers chose these goal areas and indicators, which they felt represented the major concerns of most people, with the objective of developing a concept of well-being with as much common ground as possible. However, only physical inputs were included as indicators, the psychological (i.e., attitudinal) inputs were not included because they were considered unavailable or unquantifiable. Certain environmental inputs were substituted in their place. The indicators were all, in fact, objective cardinal data. This lack of any data on one of the two factor inputs to the model equation constitutes a serious problem with this research.

The indicators developed range from the usual 'income per capita' (economic) or 'number of hospital beds' (health) to the somewhat more value-laden 'per cent of occupied housing units with television available' (social) and the decidedly odd 'number of days with thunderstorms occurring' (environmental). The researchers assigned an arbitrary positive or negative factor effect and a weight to each indicator (e.g., thunderstorms – negative, – 0.05) and then went on to tabulate and rank the scores for the census areas for each goal area. No actual testing of the hypothesis embodied in the production function occurred.

In this study the notion of welfare was well-defined, and extensive selection and operationalisation of indicators occurred. Although a theoretical model based on a production function was proposed, the indicators themselves were selected, and weighted as to direction and magnitude, according to the researchers' value judgements on the components of well-being. The individual indicators were combined to give a composite indicator of life quality. The proposed model was not tested, and the research consisted of a tabulation and aggregation of the indicators resulting in a ranking of US cities as to an overall quality of life measure. There exists a wide conceptual gap in this research between the production function model and the actual tabulation of very detailed (to the point of ranking cities) 'quality of life' analysis, which is aggregation to the point of absurdity and of no policy usefulness.

The SPES System

Lastly, another goal-to-indicator system, modelled in fact on the OECD approach, is the German SPES (Sozialpolitisches Entscheidungs) social indicator system (Zapf, 1977). This is similar to the OECD system except that rather than rely on a consensus process among negotiators, the SPES based its 'goal-dimensions' and 'goal-values' on extant German laws, regulations, and programmatic statements of government, major parties, trade unions and employers' associations. In this sense SPES combined the explicitness of the social goal approach with some of the practical ease of the programmatic, which, as suggested, contains implicit social goals of at least some segments of society. This is perhaps easier in Germany where social intentions are specifically stated within the law, but might be more difficult in other countries.

By system, SPES means a systematic catalogue of goal-dimensions and indicators. Some of the goal-dimensions correspond to specific programmatic breakdowns, mostly bureaucratic agencies. Others however are specifically designed to cut across administrative structures, and relate directly to the ascertained social goals. The indicators themselves are developed in a similar manner to the OECD indicators, and are based on a list of hypothetical 'ideal' indicators, subject to real-world cost and data constraints.

From a policy point of view, the SPES is interesting for three reasons. First, each indicator was also seen as 'a theoretical hypothesis about the relationship of indicator and reality which on principle can be proved wrong or insufficient' (Zapf, 1977, p. 5). That is, the indicators are constructed so as to be amenable for testing. Secondly, the authors of SPES anticipated a problem of 'information overload' with 196 disaggregated time series indicators which filled 66 pages. The solution was an additional abridged version which compressed the data into four pages with summary evaluations. The authors of SPES admitted that in compressing data they risked 'unsatisfactory compromises'; nevertheless they were right to offer a full version and an 'executive summary' as alternative packages given that the disaggregated information overload dilemma is hardly amenable to clear cut resolution. Finally, SPES was seen from the start 'as a contribution to political discourse' (Zapf, 1977, p. 5), which is of course what such systems should be.

Development by Life Cycle

A third method of structuring indicator systems is to utilise the life cycle, or stages from birth to death, of an individual as the basis for organisation. The indicators themselves arise from an individual's interactions with institutions during this life cycle and his achievements in terms of societal norms and personal growth. These indicators cut across programmatic divisions.

System of Social and Demographic Statistics

The most well known of the life cycle indicator systems is the System of Social and Demographic Statistics (SSDS) developed for the Statistical Office of the United Nations (1971, 1975). Much of the original concept and development of SSDS is the work of the British economist, Richard Stone (1973). The SSDS system is based on the premise that indicator sets structured programmatically cannot be indicator systems because insufficient provision is made for various kinds of connection between the different parts. SSDS proposes that these linkages can be examined by taking as a frame of reference the life cycle of the individual and examining the relationship of various phases (e.g. the learning phase) to other phases (e.g. the earning phase) and to the institutions involved (schools, employers, etc.). This is done by way of studying the 'stocks and flows' of individuals or groups of individuals where a stock is the state of an individual or group at one point in time, and a flow is changes in these states. In this way, it is seen to be feasible to portray clearly the manner in which changes in the structure and states of welfare of the population occur. These stocks and flows for varying 'life sequences' can be displayed in matrix form and broken down into sub-systems. These sub-systems may well follow in the main broadly separate institutional lines, like health or education, but they do not arise from any particular institutional division.

Within these sub-systems social indicators will be developed. A social indicator is defined as a construct, based on observations and usually quantitative, that tells something about an aspect of social life of interest, or about changes taking place in that aspect of social life. This is a broad definition and social indicators are distinguished from other statistics only by relating to some area of social concern and satisfying purposes of curiosity, understanding or action related to policy. Indicators are to be developed from factor analysis methods, index-numbered formula referring to a base year, utility or optimising functions, demographic life expectancy figures based on actuarial calculating, and subjective indicators arising from public opinion surveys.

The objective of SSDS is to develop a comprehensive social statistics accounting system for world-wide use. In this system demographic data based on life cycle can be linked to institutional areas of government expenditure. A universal standardised form of data collection, classification, and display is encouraged to assist in policy formulation at the international and national levels and to provide a firm basis for research which is needed to enlarge understanding of the social processes. Additionally, some technical benefits in the data handling and processing fields are suggested. There will be a wide variety of indicators including comprehensive statistical series, composite indices and synthetic representative series. In terms of Zapf's problem areas the SSDS system has no defined notion of welfare, and selection of indicators is incomplete as yet. It can be argued that SSDS indicators are being organised on theoretical grounds and Stone has put forward some model-building concepts, especially with regard to education. The framework for social data collection is of prime importance however, and it will be some time before any theoretical testing can take place as a result of SSDS. SSDS is at present a highly complex, comprehensive, organised system for collection and display of social data and demands highly sophisticated data collection procedures.

Development from a Theoretical Base

Some individual social indicators and indicator sets are being explored from a theoretical basis, that is, in the context of causal social models which inter-relate variables and thus explain some of them by others. This structuring by theory relates sequences of social events with data and by quantitative methods, usually systems of equations, estimates relationships between the theoretically specified variables. Social indicators purporting to relate in some discernible fashion to social phenomena can be tested as to their ability to estimate and thus their selection over some other indicators may be justified. A very few social indicator systems are also beginning to be developed based on this explicit intention to advance the state of social theory.

One important source of this theoretical development is the work of the sociologist Kenneth Land and his various associates, who are modelling some of the inter-relationships among aspects of society as represented in time series social statistics (Land and Spillerman, 1975; Land, 1975; Land and Felson, 1976). These dynamic models are to be capable of accounting for changes in various social indicators, including trends and cyclic fluctuations, and they are to be useful for social forecasting. The models are dynamic in that they are concerned with relationships over time rather than with the comparison of cross-section samples. Land argues that systems of structural equations provide the most appropriate framework for the development of these models.

One recent research effort is, in Land's words, 'an integrated 21 equation model of how marriage, family, and population conditions, as indexed by macro social indicators, affect each other and are affected by other social, demographic, and economic forces' (Land and Felson, 1977, p. 328). In this case a *macro* model is one based on summary counts, averages, or rates defined on particular populations, as opposed to a *micro* model which is based on individual level data. This particular model is based on US annual national data for the years 1947–72. It is used to forecast values of some endogenous variables for 1973 and 1974, which it did with less than two per cent error. Land stresses that even a complex 21 equation model like this requires considerable simplification from reality. Some variables are taken as exogenous for convenience, for example economic variables, but are obviously not exogenous to the socio-economic system in general. These variables can be 'endogenised' by integrating this model with other social and econometric models and Land suggests that his model should be integrated into a larger societal model in order to estimate some of the effects of changes in demographic phenomena on other social conditions (Land and Felson, 1977, pp. 1 and 352).

Perhaps the most complete attempt at a theoretically-based system of social indicators to date is the work of Fox (1974), in collaboration with Van Moeseke. This research begins by noting that most activity in social indicator research has concentrated on the establishment of data systems and that theory has been for the most part implicit. Fox then recounts a number of concepts from various social sciences, especially sociology, psychology, and economics, which might be integrated into a social indicator system model. The most important among these are Parsons' 'media of social interchange' and Barker's 'behaviour settings' concept. In very simple terms, Parsons provides a series of 'things' which change hands between individuals, such as influence, money, power, value commitments, ideology, reputation, etc., and Barker puts forward an elaborate classification system for identifying, describing, and measuring the environments in which human behaviour takes place. Fox integrates these and other concepts into a model of 'total income' which postulates that all of an individual's time can be organised as occurring in behaviour settings and that a person will allocate his time, his possible roles, and his 'media' among behaviour settings to maximise his total utility. All such allocations and rewards would be put into monetary values by way of determining opportunity costs of non-participation in the various behaviour settings. Fox puts this in the form of a mathematical programming model which includes methodology for converting media of interchange into monetary units. He further postulates that total income in this form is a more reliable measure of quality of life than economic income and that an aggregation of total income could measure changes in life quality for families, communities, regions, etc. Fox argues that the total income concept can provide a boundary within which the relationships of various social indicators to social sub-systems can be tested, and it can be used as one of a number of criteria for choosing between alternative socio-economic programmes. Fox also suggests that if total income is a valid concept it must be able continually to incorporate tested concepts and models from the social sciences, psychiatry, and social philosophy.

This total income model has a definite notion of welfare, it is structured theoretically, and puts forward an accounting framework for selecting and operationalising indicators which relate to the social model of the concept. It might be argued that such a comprehensive attempt at social theory is premature and that attention is better directed towards establishing causal links between individual indicators and social phenomena. This model, however, provides a rigorous framework for that kind of lower level activity and as such has considerable value. It is, in short, a necessary innovation in social indicator research – a field given more to data measurement and organisation and not generally to attempts at theoretical propositions.

Conclusion

There is little doubt that the social indicator movement will continue to expand and mature – until perhaps one day it will no longer be 'a movement' but rather an accepted facet of a number of academic disciplines and a valuable methodological adjunct to all rational policy analysis techniques. Part of this growth will be in the continued development of the social indicator systems outlined here. As with any rational technique methodological refinement, like improved modelling, must be part and parcel of a more thorough understanding of the limitations of the approach. Social indicator research, for example, is a prime candidate for the aggregation problems discussed in Chapter 6. Value judgements are present in any delineation of indicator sets which may be selected so as to conform to perceptions and commitments of particular parties in the policy process. These value judgements may hide behind a facade of statistical neutrality and policy analysts should endeavour to demolish those facades.

The programmatic structuring of indicator sets and systems will continue to be the favoured approach of many local, regional and national level governments. In spite of a number of theoretical limitations, this approach to indicators is relatively simple and cost effective, and generates data directly relevant to short-term social policy decisions. The chief danger is that the sometimes tenuous cause and effect relationships implicit in the indicators might go unnoticed by administrators who may overvalue the explanatory power of the indicators. Conversely, if the theoretical limitations are presented in an unbalanced perspective the indicators may be dismissed as useless and worse, misleading. These situations can often arise where indicators are presented in an overly complex manner, so as to be unfathomable to all but a knowledgeable few. It can be argued, however, that all decisions are based on imperfect data and, provided the indicators are presented in a simple and meaningful fashion, the programmatic approach to indicators is a practical one for governments faced with day to day resource allocation decisions and limited resources.

Logically, the social goal approach is almost an ideal of sorts. For non-governmental researchers, however, it remains an academic exercise to the extent that the selection of indicators reflects the researchers' own value judgements on the components of well-being. The OECD approach, on the other hand, has evolved indicators in a political fashion in so far as each country's appointees to the OECD are representatives of the populace of their country, as assumption which does not necessarily hold. Further, the process requires considerable resources if a consensus is to appear, and as it is difficult and complex it is unlikely to be undertaken in most pluralistic national contexts. It can be argued that some societal goals are implicit in existing programmatic divisions and in this sense, the German SPES programme is perhaps a reasonable, practical compromise which combines the goal area and programmatic approaches.

SSDS has potential, not only as a systematic means of collecting and displaying social statistics, but also as a theoretical framework for relating elements in society to effects of individual well-being. At the present time, however, SSDS is complex and the statistical requirements of the system are beyond the capabilities of most countries that produce social statistics or indicators, much less those that do not. Obviously the fruition of SSDS as a working system is many years off.

The continued development of causal models based on postulated social theory holds the key to the long range future of most rational analysis. This is being increasingly recognised among researchers and those who make use of social indicators. Although work on complex social models of the scale of macroeconomic models may not be without value, progress will mainly be made by concentration of attention on explanatory models which are at a low level of generalisation and thus close enough to reality to allow empirical testing to take place. In this way all types of social indicator research will move away from simple description to explanatory models useful for social prediction. Eventually the aggregation of these low level models may lead to more general social models and the social indicator movement will have fulfilled some of its earliest objectives. The results of these theoretical endeavours will enhance and change all other approaches to social indicator systems, most rational techniques, and ultimately the policy process itself.

Notes on further reading

Bunge (1975) takes up important definitional aspects of social indication. Wingo and Evans (1977) consider various types of 'quantity of life'. Rossi and Gilmartin (1979) give an overview of the field of social indicator research.

Models of objective social indicators are described in Land and Spilerman (1975) – the chapter by Land is most noteworthy. Subjective social indicators are the emphasis of Andrews and Withy's book (1976).

Other worthwhile references are Brand (1975), de Neufville (1975), and Hope (1978) on public policy and indicators. Land (1975) and Carley (1979b) consider some theoretical aspects and de Neufville (1979) discusses the task of validating social indicators. Zapf (1975a) describes systems of indicators.

Edwards (1975) and Holtermann (1978) look at positive discrimination based on social indicators. The progress towards some kind of national social reports is documented in Brusegard (1977). Excellent dialogues on social reporting can be found in *Contemporary Sociology* (Vol. 7, 1978) and the Annals of the *American Academy of Political and Social Sciences* (Vol. 435, 1978).

A review of the journal *Social Indicators Research* is essential to an understanding of the breadth of the field.

References

Andrews, Frank M. and Withey, Stephen B., 1976. *Social Indicators of Well-Being.* New York: Plenum Press.

Anderson, James G., 1973. 'Causal Models and Social Indicators: Towards the Development of Social Systems Models' In *American Sociological Review*, Vol. 38, pp. 285–301.

Bell, Daniel, 1969. 'The Idea of a Social Report' In *The Public Interest*, No. 15.

Brand, Jack, 1975. 'The Politics of Social Indicators' In *British Journal of Sociology*, Vol. 26, pp. 78–90.

Brusegard, David, 1977. *National Social Reporting: The Elements and the Activity.* Paris: OECD.

Brusegard, David A., 1978. 'Social Indicators 1976 and Perspective Canada II: Elixirs of Reason or of Sleep?' In *The Annals of the American Academy of Political and Social Science*, Vol. 435, pp. 268–76.

Bulmer, Martin, 1979. 'Review of Social Trends No. 9' In *Journal of Social Policy*, Vol. 8, pp. 543–5.

Bunge, Mario, 1975. 'What is a Quality of Life Indicator?' In *Social Indicators Research*, Vol. 2, pp. 65–79.

Carley, Michael, 1979a. 'Recent Development in Social Indicator Systems' In *European Research*, Vol. 7, pp. 2–9.

Carley, Michael, 1979b. 'Social Theory and Models in Social Indicator Research' In *International Journal of Social Economics*, Vol. 6, pp. 33–44.

Carlisle, Elaine, 1972. 'The Conceptual Structure of Social Indicators' In *Social*

Indicators and Social Policy, Schonfield, S. and Shaw, S. (eds.). London: Heinemann Educational Books Ltd.

Christian, David E., 1974. 'International Social Indicators: The OECD Experience' In *Social Indicators Research*, Vol. 1, pp. 169–180.

Coates, B. E., Johnston, R. J. and Knox, P. L., 1977. *Geography and Inequality*. Oxford University Press.

de Neufville, Judith Innes, 1975. *Social Indicators and Public Policy*. Amsterdam: Elsevier Publishing Co.

de Neufville, Judith Innes, 1979. 'Validating Policy Indicators' In *Policy Sciences*, Vol. 10, pp. 171–88.

Dennis, Norman, 1978. 'Housing Policy Areas: Criteria and Indicators in Principle and Practice' In *Institute of British Geographers Transactions New Series*, Vol. 3, pp. 2–22.

Edwards, John, 1975. 'Social Indicators, Urban Deprivation and Positive Discrimination' In *Journal of Social Policy*, Vol. 4, pp. 275–87.

Fanchette, Serge, 1974. 'Social Indicators: Problems of Methodology and Selection' In *Social Indicators: Problems of Definition and Selection*. Paris: UNESCO Press.

Fitzsimmons, S. J. and Lavey, W. G., 1976. 'Social Economic Accounts System (SEAS) Toward Comprehensive Community-Level Assessment Procedure' In *Social Indicators Research*, Vol. 2, pp. 389–452.

Fitzsimmons, S. J. and Lavey, Warren G., 1977. 'Community: Toward an Integration of Research, Theory, Evaluation and Public Policy Considerations' In *Social Indicator Research*, Vol. 4, pp. 25–66.

Fox, K. A., 1974. *Social Indicators Theory: Elements of an Operational System*. New York: John Wiley & Sons.

Gambling, Trevour, 1974. *Societal Accounting*. London: George Allen and Unwin.

Grojer, Jan-Erik, and Stark, Agneta, 1979. *Social Accounting*. Stockholm: Business and Social Research Accounting Institute.

Holtermann, Sally, 1975. 'Areas of Urban Deprivation in Great Britain: an Analysis of 1971 Census Data' In *Social Trends*, No. 6, pp. 33–47. London: Her Majesty's Stationery Office.

Holtermann, Sally, 1978. 'The Welfare Economics of Priority Area Policies' In *Journal of Social Policy*, Vol. 7, pp. 23–40.

Hope, Keith, 1978. 'Indicators of the State of Society' In *Social Policy Research*. Martin Bulmer, (ed.). London: Macmillan.

Jazairi, N. T., 1976. *Approaches to the Development of Health Indicators*. Paris: Organisation for Economic Cooperation and Development.

Johnston, Denis F., 1976. *Basic Disaggregations of Main Social Indicators*. Paris: Organisation for Economic Cooperation and Development.

Johnston, Denis F., 1977. *Social Indicators 1976*. Washington: US Department of Commerce.

Johnston, Denis F., 1978a. 'Social Indicators 1976 – A Reply to the Critics' In *Contemporary Sociology*, Vol. 7, pp. 722–4.

Johnston, Denis F., 1978b. 'Postlude: Past, Present and Future' In *Annals of the American Academy of Political and Social Science*, Vol. 435, pp. 286–94.

Knox, Paul L., 1976. 'Social Well-Being and North Sea Oil: An Application of Subjective Social Indicators' In *Regional Studies*, Vol. 10, pp. 423–32.

Knox, Paul L., 1978. 'Territorial Social Indicators and Area Profiles' In *Town Planning Review*, Vol. 49, January, pp. 423–32.

Kuz, Tony J., 1978. 'Quality of Life, on Objective and Subjective Variable Analysis' In *Regional Studies*, Vol. 12, pp. 409–17.

Land, Kenneth C., 1971. 'On the Definition of Social Indicators' In *The American Sociologist*, Vol. 6, pp. 322–325.

Land, Kenneth C., 1975. 'Theories, Models and Indicators of Social Change' in *International Social Science Journal*, Vol. 27, pp. 7–37.

Land, Kenneth C. and Spilerman, Seymour, 1975. *Social Indicator Models*. New York: Russel Sage Foundation.

Land, Kenneth C. and Felson, Marcus, 1976. 'A Dynamic Macro Social Indicator Model of Changes in Marriage, Family and Population in the United States, 1947–1974' In *Social Science Research*, Vol. 6, pp. 328–62.

Land, Kenneth C. and Felson, Marcus, 1977. 'General Framework for Building Dynamic Social Indicator Models: including an Analysis of Changes in Crime Rates and Police Expenditures' In *American Journal of Sociology*, Vol. 82, pp. 565–604.

Lineberry, R., Mandel, A. and Shoemaker, P., 1974. *Community Indicators: Improving Communities Management*. Austin: University of Texas.

Liew, Ben-Chieh, 1976. *Quality of Life Indicators in US Metropolitan Areas. A Statistical Analysis*. New York: Praegar.

Maslove, Allan M., 1975. *Urban Social Indicators*. Ottawa: Discussion Paper No. 35. Economic Council of Canada.

Michalos, Alex C., 1978. 'Social Indicator Research' In *Policy Studies Journal*, Vol. 6, pp. 393–404.

Organisation for Economic Cooperation and Development, 1974. *Subjective Elements of Well-Being*. Paris.

Organisation for Economic Cooperation and Development, 1976a. *Measuring Social Well-Being: A Progress Report on the Development of Social Indicators*. Paris.

Organisation for Economic Cooperation and Development, 1976b. *Urban Environmental Indicators*. Paris.

Organisation for Economic Cooperation and Development, 1977. *1976 Progress Report on Phase II*. Paris.

Organisation for Economic Cooperation and Development, 1979. *Inventory of Data Sources for Social Indicators*. Paris: Manpower and Social Affairs Committee.

Park, Robert and Seidman, David, 1978. 'Social Indicators and Social Reporting' In *Annals of the American Academy of Political and Social Sciences*, Vol. 435, pp. 1–22.

Presidents Research Committee on Social Trends, 1933. *Report of the Presidents Research Committee on Social Trends*. New York: McGraw-Hill.

Rossi, R. J. and Gilmartin, K. J., 1979. *Handbook of Social Indicators*. New York and London: Garland Publishing.

Seidman, David, 1978. 'Picturing the Nation' In *Contemporary Sociology*, Vol. 7, pp. 717–19.

Smith, David L., 1978. 'Policy Making for Urban Deprivation' In *Public Administration*, Vol. 56, pp. 193–202.

Smith, David Marshall, 1973. *The Geography of Social Well-Being in the United States: An Introduction to Territorial Social Indicators*. New York: McGraw-Hill.

Stone, Richard, 1973. 'A System of Social Matrices' In *The Review of Income and Wealth*, Series 19, pp. 43–66.

Strumpel, Burkhard, 1976. *Economic Means for Human Needs Social Indicators of Well-Being and Discontent*. Ann Arbor: University of Michigan, Institute for Social Research.

Thompson, Eric J., 1978a. *Social Trends No. 9*. London: Her Majesty's Stationery Office.

Thompson, Eric J., 1978b. 'Social Trends: The Development of an Annual Report for the United Kingdom' In *International Social Science Journal*, Vol, 30, pp. 653–9.

Townsend, Peter, 1976. 'Area Deprivation Policies' In *New Statesman*, 6 August. pp. 168–71.

United Nations, 1971. *A System of Demographic Manpower, and Social Statistics Series, Classifications and Social Indicators.* New York: UN Secretariat ST/STAT 49.

United Nations, 1975. *Towards a System of Social and Demographic Statistics (SSDS).* New York: UN Secretariat, ST/ESA/SER.F./18.

United Nations, 1976. *National Social Reports: Contents, Methods and Aims.* Geneva: Division of Social Affairs, SOA/SEM/WP.5.

Webber, R. J., 1977. *The National Classification of Residential Neighbourhoods: An Introduction to the Classification of Wards and Parishes.* London: PRAG Technical papers TP 23. Centre for Environmental Studies.

Wingo, Lowden and Evans, Alan, 1977. *Public Economics and the Quality of Life.* Baltimore and London: The Johns Hopkins University Press.

Zapf, Wolfgang, 1975a. 'Systems of Social Indicators: Current Approaches and Problems' In *International Social Science Journal*, Vol. 27, pp. 479–98.

Zapf, Wolfgang, 1975b. 'The Polity as a Monitor of the Quality of Life' In *The Politics of Environmental Policy.* Millbrath, Lester W. and Inscho, Frederick P. (eds.). London: Sage Publications.

Zapf, Wolfgang, 1977. *Applied Social Reporting: A Social Indicators System for West German Society.* Mannheim: SPES Working Paper No. 70.

12   Postscript

The aim of this book has been to promote a balanced perspective on the partial, but valuable, role of rational techniques in policy analysis. During the course of this 'promotion' I have argued that:

(1) A role for analytic rationality in policy making is not precluded either by problems of comprehensiveness or those surrounding social welfare functions.

(2) The policy making process consists of three elements, namely, the value-conflictive, the bureaucratic, and the rational analytic; the value-conflictive is usually the most important.

(3) A 'balanced perspective' concluded that rational techniques could not substitute for good decision making in resource allocation in the public sector, but did offer a valuable means for systematic and explicit consideration of information important to decisions.

(4) Policy analysis could be defined by the types of problems it addressed, and by the range of activities falling under the title.

(5) The policy analyst's role might be informative, methodological, or value-enlightening, but most profitably all three.

(6) Most rational techniques in policy analysis share an underlying common process and a heritage in welfare economics and systems analysis.

(7) This common process and heritage results in a variety of problems in common, which suggests the importance of integrative, cross-disciplinary approach to policy analysis.

Although many problems and issues in the application of these techniques have been examined we have not had the opportunity to make these case-specific. This has been in no way, however, to argue some idealised model of policy analysis but simply a matter of the need to limit our topic. Glennerster (1975) makes the important point that the ultimate value of such techniques must vary with the political and economic climate existing in the decision environment. He argues, as we do, that in any situation a maximum feasible diffusion of information on the impact of policies is healthy for, and required in, a pluralist society. This may be helped by the application of different perspectives, in the form of differing techniques, to each policy problem.

While there are few policy problems that would not benefit from rational analysis, some are more amenable to different approaches. *Ex post* analysis obviously dictates a form of evaluation research, and in some cases the traditional cost-benefit analysis. Where benefits are intangible, cost-effectiveness analysis is very practical. For *ex ante* analysis cost-benefit is most useful where costs and benefits are readily quantified and monetarised. Where distributional effects are important and quantifiable a variation of the planning balance sheet can be developed. Some form of social impact assessment is valuable for problems where many effects are unpriceable or immeasurable, or where it is important that the public be involved early in the policy making process. Where the biophysical environment is likely to be affected in any potentially significant manner, an environmental impact assessment is obviously worthwhile. Futures techniques are more general and more long-term for considering major policies and for meta-policy making. Finally, social indicators of one sort or another are used in all the techniques. On their own, however, they are especially useful at the problem definition stage for providing background information, in prediction for examining causal effects, and for monitoring over the course of policy implementation.

Beyond this, what technique, or mix of techniques, is applicable to a particular policy problem is best decided in light of that problem, and by the policy maker and his generalist policy analyst. Where feasible, and depending on resources, two or more techniques may be brought to bear on the problem. We have seen how this is common in large projects. For example, a good policy analysis might well consist of objective data gathered and processed by a number of techniques. This data would in the main be disaggregated, but not to the extent that it became too complex to be of use. Where moderate aggregation took place the disaggregated back-up data would always be available. Where possible a sensitivity analysis would reveal how changes in variables would affect the decision criteria and the various recommendations. The objective data would in most cases be complemented by a separate report of preference rankings and other subjective data gathered by involvement in a public participation exercise, and the use of expert opinion where suitable.

Both components of the analysis would be carried out and presented in such a manner as to aid in public debate, often at the expense of any determinate solution. And to further that debate, the results of the analysis would be presented in clear terminology, and with a format understandable to all concerned, with a hierarchical structure of information leading from a general synopsis to detailed data and methodology, and technical jargon confined to detailed appendices. Included in the general synopsis would be a discussion of the limitations and the likely endogenous value judgements to be expected in such an analysis, and the detailed sections of the report should contain a discussion of the methodological limitations of the particular technique being used. In this way the value and limitations of rational analysis will be apparent.

When the results of analysis are in, the decision maker and his advisers will do well to examine each report in light of the following questions, some of which are from Williams (1974):

(1) What precisely are the questions the study is trying to answer?
(2) What questions did it answer?
(3) What are the assumed objectives of the activity studied?
(4) By what measures are these presented?
(5) What assumptions are inherent in the study? Are they made explicit?
(6) What range of options was considered?
(7) What other options might there have been? Would their inclusion have changed the results?
(8) Were they rejected, or not considered, for good reasons?
(9) Is the data aggregated? To what level? Is it clear what might be obscured by this level of aggregation?
(10) How is the value weighting done?
(11) Is anyone likely to be affected who has not been considered in the analysis?
(12) If so, why are they excluded?
(13) Is it apparent what the inherent values and limitations of this technique are, vis-a-vis others that might be applicable?
(14) Where there is uncertainty, or there are known margins of error, is it made clear how sensitive the outcomes or recommendations are to these elements?
(15) Are the results, on balance, good enough for the job in hand?

When these questions are answered positively the decision maker may still face the problem of integrating a variety of studies towards a decision, especially if the policy problem is complex. This may require the understanding of social, economic and environmental impacts and the relative weighting of their respective values in the selection of a preferred alternative. In the end of course this *is* decision making and it is done just as the relative values of political, bureaucratic, and rational elements are integrated.

This fact, however, does not let policy analysts and policy scientists off the hook. Probably the most important, and difficult, task for policy analysis now is to foster integration by a cross-disciplinary perspective, theoretically, methodologically, and in the field. This can only be done by what Jenkins (1978) calls a *linkage of levels* between practical experience and theoretical development. For the practical case study level is only of value if it fits into the broader picture, and the policy scientific approach, which can generalise on the policy making system, must in turn be linked to reality by practical case study. For the policy analyst this means structuring each analysis clearly, consistently, and causally if possible. This might be done, for example, in light of the conceptual framework of Chapter 4, to make it possible to link with other studies and more general models. For the policy scientist the task is not only to develop causal policy models useful for evaluation and prediction but to undertake *ex post* methodological studies of the application of the rational techniques themselves. Finally, policy analysts and scientists must encourage communication at all levels and across disciplines. The problems for a cross-disciplinary approach are only matched by the potential for better policy decisions.

References

Glennerster, Howard, 1975. *Social Service Budgets and Social Policy*. London: George Allen and Unwin.

Jenkins, W. I., 1978. *Policy Analysis*. London: Martin Robertson.

Williams, Alan, 1974. 'The Cost-Benefit Approach' In *British Medical Bulletin*, Vol. 30, pp. 252–6.

Index

DATE DUE   JUL 2 4 2007